30 GREAT MYTHS ABOUT CHAUCER

30 GREAT MYTHS ABOUT CHAUCER

Thomas A. Prendergast and
Stephanie Trigg

WILEY Blackwell

This edition first published 2020
© 2020 John Wiley & Sons, Inc.

The right of Thomas A. Prendergast and Stephanie Trigg to be identified as the authors of this work has been asserted in accordance with law.

Registered Office
John Wiley & Sons, Inc., 111 River Street, Hoboken, NJ 07030, USA

Editorial Office
The Atrium, Southern Gate, Chichester, West Sussex, PO19 8SQ, UK

For details of our global editorial offices, customer services, and more information about Wiley products visit us at www.wiley.com.

Wiley also publishes its books in a variety of electronic formats and by print-on-demand. Some content that appears in standard print versions of this book may not be available in other formats.

Library of Congress Cataloging-in-Publication Data
Names: Prendergast, Thomas A. (Thomas Augustine), author. | Trigg,
    Stephanie, author.
Title: 30 great myths about Chaucer / Thomas A. Prendergast and Stephanie Trigg.
Other titles: Thirty great myths about Chaucer
Description: Hoboken, NJ : Wiley, 2020. | Includes bibliographical
    references and index.
Identifiers: LCCN 2019051841 (print) | LCCN 2019051842 (ebook) | ISBN
    9781119194057 (paperback) | ISBN 9781119194064 (adobe pdf) | ISBN
    9781119194071 (epub)
Subjects: LCSH: Chaucer, Geoffrey, -1400. | Chaucer, Geoffrey,
    -1400–Criticism and interpretation.
Classification: LCC PR1905 .P68 2020 (print) | LCC PR1905 (ebook) | DDC
    821/.1–dc23
LC record available at https://lccn.loc.gov/2019051841
LC ebook record available at https://lccn.loc.gov/2019051842

Cover Design: Wiley
Cover Image: Harl 4866 f.88 Portrait of Chaucer, from the poem 'Regement of Princes' by Thomas Hoccleve (c.1368-1426) (vellum), English School, (15th century)/British Library, London, UK/Bridgeman Images

Set in 10/12pt Sabon by SPi Global, Pondicherry, India
Printed and bound in Singapore by Markono Print Media Pte Ltd

10 9 8 7 6 5 4 3 2 1

CONTENTS

ACKNOWLEDGMENTS

We would like to express our gratitude to Helen Hickey and Anne McKendry, who have provided their customary efficient and thoughtful assistance with the research that sits behind this book, and who helped us with careful formatting and sub-editing. Thanks, too, to our editor at Wiley-Blackwell, Richard Samson, to Pilar Wyman who prepared the index, and to the anonymous readers who helped us shape the book's structure.

Most of all, of course, we would like to thank each other.

INTRODUCTION: MYTHICAL CHAUCER

A roly-poly, slightly chubby poet gets up early in the morning to go and pick daisies, or falls asleep while reading a book and dreams about gardens, forests, birds and beautiful women. He makes a pilgrimage to Canterbury with a bunch of rogues and sinners he describes in affectionate and loving terms. He narrates and translates other people's stories, but he is a wildly original poet, and more or less single-handedly invents the English language. He is knowing and cynical about human failure, but also childishly enthusiastic about all forms of human endeavor. His poetry is outrageously bawdy and full of fart jokes and he is a profoundly pious religious thinker, while also being guilty of anti-Semitism. His poetry is utterly imbued with medieval culture, but he is also way ahead of his time in his anticipation of our own concerns. His poetry is some of the greatest in the English language, but is also too difficult to read. Chaucer himself is wise and cynical, but his achievement was limited by medieval ignorance and superstition, just as his sympathetic respect for women was restricted by patriarchal ideologies. He is praised as a genius in his own time and has variously been celebrated as a satirist, a reformer, a lyricist, a pre-Shakespearean lover of bawdy, a sentimentalist, a religious apologist, a humanist, a feminist, a post-modernist and a queer theorist.

And so it goes. Chaucer's long reception history is a contradictory mess of changing opinions and ideas about the character of the medieval poet, the nature of his poetic achievement and the interpretation of his poetry. These aspects of his history are so interwoven it can be quite difficult to untangle critical readings of his works from ideas about the medieval poet himself. And nor are these debates confined to the past alone.

All the volumes in this series bring literary history, reception and cultural studies into conversation. They acknowledge that we necessarily approach the writing of well-known authors with expectations heavily mediated by earlier readers and shaped by a range of expectations that may be based only loosely on historical fact. These expectations shape our choice of which poems to read, how we edit and teach them and, in the case of Chaucer, what we think about the Middle Ages and the meaning of that past for contemporary culture.

In the case of our *30 Great Myths About Chaucer*, we are also contending with the extremely complex phenomenon of medievalism. That is, in addition to the myths about Chaucer that emanate mostly from the world of literature, there are many associated "myths" about the Middle Ages that color and inflect the reception of Chaucer. Many of these myths implicitly posit the idea that medieval people and culture were somehow discontinuous with the modern present; as if they inhabited a different world from the social and cultural forms that produced the realist novel, for example, or the poetry of the romantic movement. The medieval past has been profoundly shaped – in both the scholarly and the popular imagination – as an era substantially different from modernity in areas of religious, artistic and political practice and knowledge, to say nothing of social forms, health sciences, costume, dress and the like. A separate volume, entitled something like "30 Great Myths about the Middle Ages," would be easy to write. No, medieval people did not think the earth was flat; no, women did not wear chastity belts; and no, medieval intellectual life was not stifled by superstition or religious repression.[1]

One of the dominant features of much study in the field of medievalism is the pleasant pastime of "correcting" these and other mistakes, or anachronisms in the popular representation of the Middle Ages in fiction and film. We have written elsewhere about the nature of this pleasure, and its implications for both the professional and the amateur study of the medieval past.[2] In the case of literary history, however, and the reception of a poet like Chaucer, the situation is a little more complex. We can certainly appeal to the "facts," as we know them from the surviving, albeit partial, records of his life and employment, but we are often talking about the interpretation of literary works where of course, we are on much more shaky ground.

We will find with many of these "myths" that they arise from tiny suggestions in the poems or in the life-records, hints that have generated beliefs and assumptions that have then shaped the traditions of critical interpretation. It is a pattern that is very familiar from the archives of medievalism.

As with other books in this series, "myth" here does not mean (as it often does) a widely shared, structurally enabling fiction that subtends every aspect of modern life. Rather, it conveys a more localized conception (or misconception) about an author or group of authors. Some of these myths are more deeply held familiar ideas about Chaucer and his works than others; and some have larger grains of truth to them than others. Nearly all, however, are the products of the long history of reading Chaucer's works for over six hundred years and the intertwined history of biography, criticism and popular culture. Many of our chapters consider the relationship between what we know about Chaucer from external records and what he appears to tell us in his fictions. These stories embrace a range of genres and styles, and in the *Canterbury Tales* at least, they are voiced by a range of distinctive narrators such as the Pardoner, the Wife of Bath and the Prioress. Such is Chaucer's mastery of the middle style, in the fearful, lovelorn narrators of *The Book of the Duchess* and *The Parlement of Foules*, or the nostalgic romantic with an interest in philosophy in *Troilus and Criseyde* and the more personal poems addressed to his friends, that it is hard not to compile a relatively coherent composite picture of Chaucerian voice and attitudes. But the external "life-records" tell us a different story again: these are records of payments, permissions to travel, notices of court cases, grants of clothing and annuities to himself and his family. We need to emphasize that there is no written, textual or documentary allusion to Chaucer as a poet, outside his own writings, from his own lifetime. The witnesses to his life and influence as a writer are entirely posthumous.

This poses a distinctive problem for any biographer of Chaucer. They must all negotiate this gap between the lively personalities and narrative voices that populate Chaucer's fictions and the "real" or "concrete" evidence found in the surviving documents. Many of our "myths" find their origins in these gaps, and the desire to make satisfying imaginative links between Chaucer's fictions and what we can piece together of his life. For example, in a number of Chaucer's early poems, the narrator constructs the persona of a young man who is unlucky or unsuccessful in the art of love, or who is suffering an unrequited love. Fueled by the desire to fill in the historical gaps and to tie this narrative voice to the biographical record, early historical critics went to work to discover the identity of Chaucer's early love, though without ever resolving the issue (see Myth 3).

The biographical tradition of Chaucer studies dates back to the sixteenth-century editions of his works, many of which included biographical speculation and narrative along with genealogical and heraldic tables affirming Chaucer's place in the history of medieval English culture. John Urry also included a biography in his edition of 1721, but the first biography to appear independently of an edition of Chaucer's poetry was that of William Godwin in 1804. In the twentieth century, John Gardner, Donald Howard and Derek Pearsall all wrote scholarly biographies, and in the early twenty-first century, Richard West and Peter Ackroyd's biographies reached a more popular audience. There has also been a recent flurry of biographical activity. In 2014, Paul Strohm published a focused account of one important year in Chaucer's life: *Chaucer's Tale: 1386 and the Road to Canterbury* (2014); and just before this book went to press, Marion Turner's *Chaucer: A European Life* appeared to great acclaim. Another study, from Ardis Butterfield, provisionally titled *Chaucer: A London Life*, is forthcoming. In this book we draw on this biographical tradition, but we also go back to many of the primary source materials, as well as attempting to keep track of some of the recent developments in a range of discursive fields.

Contemporary Chaucerian studies continues to scrutinize the past reception of the medieval poet, and is particularly interested in the way the scribes of his manuscripts and the editors of the early printed texts mediate his works for us in influential ways. Equally, modern criticism is keen to re-examine the political, social, linguistic and literary contexts in which Chaucer lived and worked; as well as bringing insights and critiques from other fields such as gender studies, queer studies, environmental studies, animal studies and cognitive literary studies. In this book we also engage with some of the striking or influential representations of Chaucer and his characters in the fictions of medievalism, as this has become one of the most popular sites in which people encounter Chaucer today.

Many lovers and teachers of Chaucer are currently grappling with sterner voices and critiques that challenge his central and foundational position in the canons and syllabi of literary criticism. These voices are sometimes raised in defense of less familiar, marginalized writers; but are also sometimes raised in more direct critique of Chaucer's poetry and the ideas and ideologies it appears to promote. Increasingly, Chaucer has come to stand for a celebration of "canonical" literature that for many is outdated. These traditions are no longer universally admired or taught; and some commentators feel that writers such as Chaucer dominate the field at the expense of other voices and other perspectives. Ideological and political critiques of his texts abound as critics and lovers of Chaucer struggle with the apparent anti-Semitism of the *Prioress's Tale* (see Myth 15), for example, or read about Cecily Champaigne's abandonment of "raptus" charges against him in the context of the apparent "revenge rape" of the Miller's wife and daughter in the *Reeve's Tale* (see Myth 11).

We acknowledge that, in the contemporary moment, Chaucer is not always a beloved poet, not even among medievalists. But it is fascinating to see how quickly this "lack of universal love" has given rise to what might be the thirty-first great myth: "Chaucer is no longer relevant." For some, it is easy to dismiss him as a relic, an antiquated vestige of a bygone era whose mores are as outdated as his language. Nevertheless, we would like to affirm, despite these challenges to Chaucer's centrality and privileged position as a representative voice, that we have taken great pleasure in this opportunity for re-reading and re-visiting his works: for us, they continue to produce a potent cocktail of pleasure, danger and difficulty that provokes powerful questions about literature, its uses and its pleasures. The history of myths about Chaucer is in many ways the history of our long-standing collective love affair with this most engaging and seductive medieval poet. It is a continuous, unbroken history and its importance is signaled both by the multitude of manuscripts and printed editions containing the poet's works as well as by six hundred years of popular interest. We hope you enjoy working through these long traditions with us.

Notes

1 See, for example, the reflective analysis on the myth of the chastity belt by Albrecht Classen, *The Medieval Chastity Belt: A Myth-Making Process* (New York: Palgrave, 2007); and the many angry responses by medievalists to Stephen Greenblatt's critique of medieval culture in *The Swerve: How the World Became Modern* (New York: W.W. Norton, 2011); for example, Jim Hinch, "Why Stephen Greenblatt Is Wrong—And Why It Matters," *Los Angeles Review of Books,* 1 December 2012, https://lareviewofbooks.org/article/why-stephen-greenblatt-is-wrong-and-why-it-matters/#!, accessed 22 December 2018.

2 Thomas A. Prendergast and Stephanie Trigg, *Affective Medievalism: Love, Abjection and Discontent* (Manchester: Manchester University Press, 2018).

Myth

1 CHAUCER IS THE FATHER OF ENGLISH LITERATURE

Chaucer is regularly named as the father of English poetry, the father of English literature, the father of English literary history,[1] the father of the English language, even the father of England itself.[2] This first "myth," with all these associations, is probably the most foundational one for this book, as it sits behind many of the conceptions and emotional investments readers have in the familiar figure of Geoffrey Chaucer. It is also the myth that exemplifies the ways in which this concept in literary history is both instructive and yet also potentially confusing. The idea of fatherhood over a literary tradition is a powerful metaphor that is intimately tied up with ideas of nationalism, masculinity and poetic influence, but we can fruitfully unpack its significance and its history. We may also observe that this kind of praise can be a mixed blessing in the changing fashions of literary study.

It was Chaucer's immediate successor Thomas Hoccleve who first wrote about Chaucer as a father figure. In several stanzas of his *Regiment of Princes*, written in 1412, just twelve years after Chaucer's death, Hoccleve laments the death of his "maister deere and fadir reverent."[3] He praises Chaucer as "universel fadir in science" ("science" is best glossed as knowledge, or wisdom),[4] and twice calls him his "worthy maistir,"[5] suggesting a close link between fatherhood and authority. Hoccleve also describes Chaucer as "The firste fyndere of our faire langage."[6] This is a tricky phrase to analyze, as "fyndere" in Middle English can mean "poet" as much as "discoverer" and "first" can mean "pre-eminent" as well as "first." But the praise is unequivocal: Hoccleve compares Chaucer to Aristotle in philosophy, to Cicero in rhetoric and to Virgil in poetry.

30 Great Myths About Chaucer, First Edition. Thomas A. Prendergast and Stephanie Trigg.
© 2020 John Wiley & Sons, Inc. Published 2020 by John Wiley & Sons, Inc.

Other writers who did not know Chaucer personally were quick to take up this description of Chaucer as father and laureate poet, moving on from the elegiac mode that dominated Chaucerian reception in the first decades after his death in 1400. Indeed, during the fifteenth century, much writing in English was "Chaucerian" in style and voice, leading to considerable uncertainty – or perhaps we should say fluidity – about the authorship of many texts that appear in the early printed "Works" collected under the name of Geoffrey Chaucer. For many of these editions, the commercial incentive of adding works "never before printed" was an invitation to include poems by Lydgate, Usk and other writers under the "Chaucerian" banner.

By the late sixteenth century, however, Chaucer was already being seen as a figure from a distant or "antique" past. For example, in his *Faerie Queene* (1596), Edmund Spenser addressed him in old-fashioned terms as "Dan Chaucer, well of English undefyled" – that is, as the source of pure English – and worthy of being listed on "Fame's eternall beadroll."[7] In his *Shepheardes Calendar* (1579) and the *Faerie Queene*, Spenser combined neo-classical genres (eclogues and epic) with medievalist diction to pay homage to Chaucer. At the same time, Thomas Speght was presenting Chaucer in his editions as an "ancient and learned poet" whose work needed the full apparatus of scholarly introduction, commentary and glosses to be intelligible to modern readers.

It is important to recognize, too, that Chaucer was not always singled out as the *only* father figure from the medieval period. For example, Richard Baker wrote, in 1643, "The next place after these, is justly due to *Geoffry Chaucer*, and *John Gower*, two famous Poets in this time, and the Fathers of *English* Poets in all the times after."[8]

By far the most influential naming of Chaucer as a father, however, appears in John Dryden's *Preface to Fables Ancient and Modern* (1700). This was a collection of Dryden's own translations of Chaucer, Boccaccio, Homer, Virgil, Ovid and others, prefaced with a long essay in which he describes Chaucer as "the Father of English Poetry." Yet Dryden acknowledges the imperfections of Chaucer's poetry: "Chaucer, I confess, is a rough diamond, and must be polished ere he shine."[9] Dryden also pairs this statement about Chaucer's paternity with the admission that he lived "in the Infancy of our Poetry" and that "We must be Children before we grow Men."[10] We will return to Dryden's *Preface* several times in this book: it is one of the single most influential texts in the making of several myths about Chaucer.

Veneration of the medieval past is often paired with this sense that modernity offers a vast improvement on these faltering first steps towards sophistication. Nevertheless, it is an important aspect of a powerful literary tradition to name its origins and forebears, and Chaucer's paternity looms large over most standard histories of English literature. If canons of authors and literary histories are structured around the names of individual authors, there is an obvious reason why this might be so: Chaucer is simply the most famous name to pre-date Shakespeare. But Chaucer's status as father is significantly bolstered by ideological structures and the particularities of English literary history, especially in the fifteenth century.

Seth Lerer takes a lead from Michel Foucault's theories of authorship to argue that the ideological and genealogical structures of Chaucer's authorship are firmly grounded in the dominant conditions shaping literary production in the early fifteenth century:

> Like the originary authors Marx and Freud, who would produce a discourse and a form of writing for a culture, Chaucer produces in his own work the "rules of formation for other texts." The genres of the dream vision, pilgrimage narrative, and ballad, and the distinctive idioms of dedication, patronage, and correction that fill those works, were taken up by fifteenth-century poets, not simply out of imitative fealty to Chaucer but instead largely because they were the rules of formation for poetry.[11]

Lerer also suggests that the desire to find an influential and authoritative father figure in Chaucer, in a world where poets and writers actively sought patronage from powerful court figures, is also informed by "the great social anxieties of fifteenth-century dynastic politics."[12] It is a curious historical accident that the year of Chaucer's death, 1400, was the same year in which Henry Bolingbroke, having deposed Richard II in 1399, inaugurated the Lancastrian dynasty, which would be subjected to many challenges and result in violent civil warfare, especially in the second half of the fifteenth century. But even the first decades after Chaucer's death were shadowed by political instability and anxiety about Henry's succession; and in literary circles, this anxiety seems to have been felt more deeply through the lack of an obvious successor to Chaucer's poetic authority.

The scholarly narratives of literary history thrive on such coincidences (Chaucer's death, the end of the century and the last of the Plantagenet kings); but even more significantly, this pattern suggests that the original idea of Chaucer's fatherhood is intimately connected with the shadows of mortality and melancholy, as much as with the glory of origins. That is, the metaphorical language of many myths is itself quite telling, and indicative of deeper structures and assumptions about the way we read literature.

For example, the historical context of deep transition from one cultural authority to later imitators finds a methodological echo in the darker, Freudian aspect of literary paternity famously proposed by Harold Bloom in the 1970s.[13] His concept of "the anxiety of influence" explains literary history and literary tradition as a dynamic, creative struggle fueled by anxiety and defensiveness: to find his own voice, a poet must displace the poet who is his greatest influence, by absorbing but somehow diverging from that voice. (In his first formulations, Bloom wrote only of male poets.) Poetic influence is seen as an agonistic, even Oedipal, struggle for the "strong" poet to displace the poetic father figure by misreading him, and re-appropriating the imaginative space he occupies, as the best strategy for negotiating the inevitable influence of an admired predecessor.[14] While Bloom was not initially concerned with pre-Romantic poetry, A.C. Spearing offers a powerful reading of John Lydgate's *The Siege of Thebes*, written between 1420 and 1422 (and including the story of Oedipus), as Lydgate's own Oedipal response to Chaucer: "It is tempting to suppose that in the early part of the *Siege* Lydgate was unconsciously dramatizing precisely the innocent destructiveness he had to engage in himself in order to survive a father as powerful yet benevolent as Chaucer."[15]

Much of the discussion around Chaucer's fatherhood is necessarily somewhat circular. He is *perceived* as a father for a number of reasons: because there is no earlier named candidate for the role in English tradition; because his poetry strikes us as so original and inventive; because his poetic presence and authorial personality seem so benevolent; and, of course, because we often approach him with the expectations of authority and originality that the metaphor of "father" implies. And as many critics point out, his successors sometimes felt infantilized by his greatness. But of course, to name this early influential figure in this gendered language sets up a powerful dominant image of what constitutes poetic authority.

We discuss in Myth 2 the question of whether Chaucer was the first writer of poetry in English; a question that is much easier to resolve at a factual level. There were certainly other poets writing in Middle English before Chaucer (let alone the substantial body of poetry in Old English), and contemporaneously with him. Yet as with Chaucer's fatherhood, his early followers heavily promoted the idea that English poetry had all begun with him. So, for example, the anonymous author of *The Book of Courtesy* (1477) wrote:

O fader and founder of ornate eloquence,
Than enlumened hast alle our Bretayne,
To soone we loste thy laureate scyence.
O lusty lyquour of that fulsome fontayne![16]

Like Spenser's "well of English undefyled," this imagery draws on the classical tradition of Mount Parnassus, the mythic source of poetry and learning.

Similarly, in the 1532 edition of Chaucer's works, Sir Brian Tuke also marvels how, during the medieval period, "when doubtless all good letters were laid asleep throughout the world," nonetheless "suche an excellente poete in our tonge, shulde as it were (nature repugnyge) sprynge and aryse."[17]

Ironies abound even here, though. The idea of a poet "illuminating" a land itself comes from Chaucer, whose Clerk introduces his translation of Petrarch's tale of Griselda (itself a translation from Boccaccio) with praise of Petrarch's "rethorike sweete" that has "Enlumyned al Ytaille of poetrie" (IV.33–34).[18] Many of the metaphors and myths of origin we discuss in this book have at least two temporal dimensions: sometimes, as here, we look back through the past to see the shape of each myth as it has developed; in others we also try to examine the conditions that give rise to each idea about Chaucer. We consider here the myth of Chaucer's "fatherhood" as it has been perceived and expressed by his literary "children" who claim him as forebear; in Myth 2, we will consider the reception of Chaucer in contrast to other, earlier English poets.

Was Chaucer the father of English literature? Perhaps perversely, we suggest that indeed he was, if only because so many writers have thought and written about him in this way. A literary tradition constitutes itself by choosing its own forebears, and by very selective processes of ideological and national interest. Chaucer has held this position in the scholarly and popular imaginary for so long that his position is no longer disputed, though this is not to say that the idea of literary paternity has not come under severe critique from a number of quarters. Many literary scholars over the last forty or so years have worked hard to destabilize such self-affirming genealogies, critiquing the exclusions and ideological assumptions about the *kind* of poetic voice and attitudes that are normalized through precisely this sort of self-selecting tradition. Like other white, male writers, Chaucer is subject to critiques of the canon he seems to inaugurate. If Chaucer is the father of English literature, then he should be the first place we go to in order to re-think the kinds of literature we want to study. This book is another step in that project, as we turn to examine the origins and implications of many of our ideas about the poet that some have named "Father."

Notes

1 A.C. Spearing, *Medieval to Renaissance in English Poetry* (Cambridge: Cambridge University Press, 1985), 34, 59.

2 "Shakespeare and Milton were the greatest sons of their country; but Chaucer was the Father of his Country, rather in the style of George Washington." G.K. Chesterton, *Chaucer* (London: Faber and Faber, 1932), 15.

3 Thomas Hoccleve, *The Regiment of Princes*, ed. Charles R. Blyth (Kalamazoo, MI: Medieval Institute Publications, 1999), l.1961.

4 Ibid., l.1964.

5 Ibid., ll.2080, 4983.

6 Ibid., l.4978.

7 Edmund Spenser, *The Faerie Queene*, ed. Thomas P. Roche, Jr. (London: Penguin, 1978), IV.ii.32.

8 Richard Baker, *A Chronicle of the Kings of England* (London: Printed for Daniel Frere, 1643), 45.

9 John Dryden, *The Poems of John Dryden*, vol. IV, ed. James Kinsley (Oxford: Clarendon Press, 1958), 1457.

10 Ibid., 1452–3.

11 Seth Lerer, *Chaucer and His Readers: Imagining the Author in Late-Medieval England* (Princeton, NJ: Princeton University Press, 1993), 11.

12 Ibid., 16.

13 Harold Bloom, *The Anxiety of Influence: A Theory of Poetry*, 1973, 2nd edn. (Oxford: Oxford University Press, 1997).

14 Spearing, *Medieval to Renaissance*, 108–9.

15 Ibid., 109.

16 J.A. Burrow, ed., *Geoffrey Chaucer: A Critical Anthology* (Harmondsworth: Penguin, 1969), 44.

17 *The Workes of Geffray Chaucer newly imprinted*, ed. William Thynne (London, 1532), A2v.

18 All quotations from Chaucer's works, unless otherwise specified, are taken from *The Riverside Chaucer*, gen. ed. Larry D. Benson (Boston, MA: Houghton Mifflin, 1987), and are cited by fragment or book and line numbers.

Myth

2

CHAUCER WAS THE FIRST ENGLISH POET

Of all the "myths" in this book, of old or of more recent standing, this is one of the easiest to dispel. It is the other side of the coin, as it were, to Myth 1, "Chaucer is the father of English literature." As we saw there, for better or worse, Chaucer is consistently thought of as the oldest poet to exert a benevolent but deep influence on later poetic tradition in England and by extension, on all Anglophone writing.

But was he the first poet to write in English? This is a very different question. There is one linguistic issue to clear up first, and that is what we mean by "English." Chaucer's language is known as "Middle English," the language written and spoken in England between around 1100 and 1500. The phrase makes a careful distinction from "Old English," the language spoken by the Germanic tribes who settled in England around the mid-fifth century after the Romans had withdrawn. Most of the surviving manuscripts in Old English were written in the ninth, tenth and eleventh centuries. Many of these texts contain a mixture of Christian and pagan Germanic ideas as a result of the Christian missionary program starting in the sixth century, which had a profound influence on both religious and scribal culture.

Old English is the language of *Beowulf*, as well as a mixed corpus of heroic narratives, saints' lives, sermons, letters, translations, personal lyrics and other writings. For our purposes, one of the earliest and most important fragments of poetry is preserved in a Latin text, *Historia ecclesiastica gentis Anglorum*, translated into modern English as *The Ecclesiastical History of the English People*, written by the monk Bede in 731 CE. Here Bede recounts the story of Caedmon, a cowherd, who would routinely leave gatherings when it was his turn to sing because he had no musical ability. But inspired by God in a dream, he produces a

30 Great Myths About Chaucer, First Edition. Thomas A. Prendergast and Stephanie Trigg.
© 2020 John Wiley & Sons, Inc. Published 2020 by John Wiley & Sons, Inc.

short poem in Old English, using words and expressions he has never spoken before, honoring the Creation:

> Nu sculon herigean / heofonrices Weard
> [Now must we praise / heaven-kingdom's Guardian,]
> Meotodes meahte / and his modgeþanc
> [the Measurer's might / and his mind-plans,]
> weorc Wuldor-Fæder / swa he wundra gehwæs
> [the work of the Glory-Father, / when he of wonders of every one,]
> ece Drihten / or onstealde
> [eternal Lord, / the beginning established.]
> He ærest sceop / ielda bearnum
> [He first created / for men's sons]
> heofon to hrofe / halig Scyppend
> [heaven as a roof, / holy Creator;
> ða middangeard / moncynnes Weard
> [then middle-earth / mankind's Guardian,]
> ece Drihten / æfter teode
> [eternal Lord / afterwards made—]
> firum foldan / Frea ælmihtig.
> [for men earth, / Master almighty.][1]

The language of Caedmon's poem is substantially different from Chaucer's Middle English, and we quote the text in its entirety, partly to give a sense of what English poetry looks like without French and Latin vocabulary, and also to show the patterns of non-rhyming alliterating poetry, with the first stress after the mid-line caesura often acting as the foundational alliterating syllable. The literal translation also shows the flexible word order possible when a language is more heavily inflected (for example, when variable suffixes do the work of prepositions), and when the verse form proceeds by paratactic phrases in apposition, rather than sentences structured around a controlling principal verb, as most of Chaucer's sentences are, even in the syntax of his more complex stanzaic forms, like the seven-line "rhyme royal" stanza. Bede's narrative similarly draws attention to the strong oral component in Old English poetry, and again, this is closely related to its appositional form.

Old English is classified as a Germanic language, as are Middle English and Modern English, too. Nevertheless, after 1066 and the defeat of the Anglo-Saxon King Harold Godwinson by William of Normandy, the language changed gradually but substantially, developing in increasingly fluid exchange with Anglo-Norman, the French spoken in England after William's victory. It is difficult to underestimate the enormity of this cultural change, though the greatest linguistic effect was felt first among the nobility, as many Anglo-Saxon lords were dispossessed after this defeat.

So what was poetic writing like between the eleventh century and the 1360s, when Chaucer began to write? A fair amount of poetry in English has survived, though possibly more has been lost. Lyric poems and songs were not always written down or preserved in manuscripts, and while romances were popular in the thirteenth century, few survive from this period. However, romances such as *King Horn* and *Havelok the Dane* offer energetic and enthusiastic accounts of complex dynastic and cross-cultural plots, determined young heroes, resourceful maidens and the popularity of values such as courage, loyalty and determination.[2] Some of the more improbably complicated plotlines of these and later romances such as *Bevis of Hampton* give us some idea of the tradition Chaucer was confidently parodying in his *Tale of Sir Thopas*. Verse forms varied, too, from the rhyming couplets and tail-rhyme stanzas of the romances and other poems such as the querulous debate poem, *The Owl and the Nightingale* (late twelfth or early thirteenth century), to the uneven history of unrhymed alliterative verse form that seems to have undergone a kind of "revival" in the mid-fourteenth century, and the separate history of prose writing in chronicles and various forms of devotional literature. These writings were not always isolated, either. A significant cluster of writing in English, from a range of styles and genres (romances, chronicles, devotional poems, saints' lives), had been anthologized in the Auchinleck Manuscript (now in the National Library of Scotland, Advocates MS.19.2.1), written in London in the 1340s, and it may be that Chaucer saw and read parts of this manuscript.

Chaucer, then, was very far from the first poet to write in English. Conversely, it seems likely that when he began to write poetry his chosen language would have been French, which was still the dominant language for literary works in England in the fourteenth century, and the language of his first workplaces, the households associated with the royal court. For example, many scholars believe, on circumstantial evidence, that a number of the anonymous French lyrics preserved in the "Ch" manuscript (University of Pennsylvania MS French 15), dated around the 1360s, were written by Chaucer.[3]

Chaucer was also the first English poet to translate extensively from Italian, though we should always remind ourselves of the great achievement of John Gower, Chaucer's contemporary, who wrote substantial works in each of English, French and Latin. In many ways, Gower is the more typical example of fourteenth-century court culture.

In Myth 1, we discussed briefly the question of Chaucer's use of English, and the common view, repeated throughout the fifteenth century, that he revitalized the English language and made it worthy of poetry in the high style. As Marion Turner writes of Chaucer's early poem,

The Book of the Duchess, "no one had written this *style* of poem in English before, and it is extraordinarily interesting that Chaucer now made his intervention into the world of stylized courtly letters in a language that had not previously been a language of literature at the English court."[4] Turner stresses Chaucer's relationship with writers in both France and Hainault (now part of Belgium, and the birthplace of Edward III's queen Philippa), and argues against the idea that Chaucer might be inaugurating some kind of competitive defense of English to rival the dominance of French. This "could only have seemed ludicrous to a multilingual man such as Chaucer, whose deep and engaged reading of his French and Hainuyer contemporaries is evident in almost every line of the *Book of the Duchess*."[5]

Turner follows Ardis Butterfield here, who shows that "there was nothing isolated or autonomous about fourteenth-century written English." For Butterfield, to use English in this kind of courtly setting was to be "profoundly aware" of other languages and the relations between languages.[6] She argues that in its subtle re-voicings of poems by Guillaume de Machaut and Jean Froissart, this early Chaucerian poem is "brilliantly ambiguous" in its dramatization of poetic subjectivity across cultures and languages: Chaucer is participating in international developments, not striking out for nationalism. As Turner points out, however, after writing *The Book of the Duchess* Chaucer drew increasingly on the work of Italian writers, especially the poetry of Boccaccio: "Poetically, Chaucer's consumption of Italian verse was exceptionally productive, generative, and liberating: it energized him and gave him tools and models for innovative literary play."[7]

The misleading myth of Chaucer inaugurating poetry in English can be read as a symptom of proud nationalist (or English-speaking) ideology that wants to conflate literary greatness with linguistic inventiveness, and that feeds the idea that English poetry and the English language developed more or less in splendid insular isolation. It also falls prey to the desire to attribute the effects of wide-ranging social and cultural change to one influential genius, and is part of a self-perpetuating circle: Chaucer is the oldest poet who regularly finds a place on the English curriculum; and so it therefore appears as if he is the first.

By the late sixteenth century, however, Chaucer's language was regarded as either intriguingly archaic or hopelessly obsolete, requiring a growing panoply of glossing and commentary to render it legible to all but antiquarians. Larger cultural forces will always be more influential than the work of one writer.

Chaucer's primacy is bolstered by the fact that his language still seems at least recognizable to modern readers, though this familiarity is a result of the happy accident that the Southeast Midlands dialect spoken by Chaucer was the same language as that of the court's administration. The stability of London as the capital city meant that modern English has most in common with this dialect of Middle English, rendering Chaucer's language relatively familiar. The language of the *Gawain* poet, by contrast, seems far more alien, with different dialectal inflectional forms and a far more specialized and regional vocabulary. Chaucer's own consciousness of dialect variation (in the *Reeve's Tale*) and differences in regional poetic styles (in the *Parson's Prologue*) play no small part in this sense that his language represents a kind of "norm" for English.

Nevertheless, Simon Horobin advises us not to make too many assumptions about the similarities and continuities between Chaucer's language and our own: in syntax, semantics and vocabulary there are still many important structural differences.[8] On the question of whether Chaucer invented poetic language in English, he did introduce a number of new words (according to J.D. Burnley, Chaucer's vocabulary was approximately twice as large as Gower's),[9] though Horobin advises caution here, too: "it is important that we do not treat all French words used by Chaucer as of equivalent status."[10] For example, one of Chaucer's linguistic traits involved moving words from legal or political discourse into other contexts, so while the word may not be "new," it appears so in this unfamiliar setting. This is particularly the case in what is termed Chaucer's "high style," which is characterized by words that stand out stylistically and draw attention to themselves.[11]

This is one of the areas in which Chaucer's poetic language was more distinctive, and indeed when his successors praised his innovations, it was often in terms of this more elevated, "laureate" and adorned style, though now we would prefer to praise the subtle and fluid movements between different styles in his work.

Recent work on the linguistic context of fourteenth-century England also emphasizes its multicultural nature, and many of these words would still have been experienced as borrowings. For Butterfield, for example, there were *two* vernacular languages in late medieval England: English and French. She also reminds us of the distinction between continental French and Anglo-French,[12] which was still the dominant language of the English court in the fourteenth century. There is only limited evidence to suggest that the Ricardian court embraced this new English poetic tradition; and indeed, Christopher Cannon suggests that in Chaucer's time, "the use of English in literature remained rebellious, even if not politically charged," through its associations with the Wycliffite movement promoting English religious literacy, and the use of English in some political and legal contexts.[13] Moreover, it has been suggested that poetry in

English was really taken up in even a semi-official way only by the Lancastrians under Henry IV, and more particularly by Henry V, well after the death of Chaucer in 1400.[14]

We can confidently "bust" this myth, then. Chaucer was far from the first English poet, and while his own poetic followers were quick to applaud and praise his originality, his apparent primacy in this regard is the effect of much larger historical forces and critical desires.

Notes

1 Bede, *An Ecclesiastical History of the English People*, in *The Norton Anthology of English Literature, Volume A: The Middle Ages*, ed. James Simpson and Alfred David, 9th edn. (New York: W.W. Norton, 2012), 30–31.

2 Christopher Cannon, *Middle English Literature: A Cultural History* (Cambridge: Polity Press, 2008), 39.

3 James Wimsatt, *Chaucer and the Poems of "Ch"* (Kalamazoo, MI: Medieval Institute Publications, 2009), 12–14.

4 Marion Turner, *Chaucer: A European Life* (Princeton, NJ: Princeton University Press, 2019), 128.

5 Ibid., 129.

6 Ardis Butterfield, *The Familiar Enemy: Chaucer, Language, and Nation in The Hundred Years War* (Oxford: Oxford University Press, 2009), 11.

7 Turner, *Chaucer: A European Life*, 330.

8 Simon Horobin, *Chaucer's Language*, 2nd edn. (Houndmills: Palgrave Macmillan, 2013), 2.

9 David Burnley, *A Guide to Chaucer's Language* (Houndmills: Macmillan, 1983), 133.

10 Horobin, *Chaucer's Language*, 83.

11 Ibid., 128.

12 Butterfield, *The Familiar Enemy*, 11.

13 Cannon, *Middle English Literature*, 70.

14 John H. Fisher, "A Language Policy for Lancastrian England," *PMLA* 107, no. 5 (1992), 1168–80.

Myth 3

CHAUCER SUFFERED AN UNREQUITED LOVE

The idea that youthful poets should be inspired by love, and preferably the unrequited love of a beautiful, unavailable noblewoman, is of very long standing in the West. It is a tradition that goes back to Catullus and it features in the poetry of Dante, and the sonnet cycles of Philip Sidney and William Shakespeare. Chaucer certainly presents himself as unlucky or unhappy in love, especially early in his career, in dream-vision poems such as *The Book of the Duchess* and *The Parlement of Foules*.[1] In the mid-career *Troilus and Criseyde*, the fiction of personal unhappiness has been displaced by a general sense of his "unlikynesse" in love (I. 16). If he is an unsuitable candidate for love, he argues, he may nevertheless serve love's devotees by writing their stories and providing a vocabulary and narratives for love. In this poem, Chaucer passes the role of slightly comical unrequited lover on to Criseyde's uncle Pandarus, whose own desire seems to be displaced onto the sexual union of the younger lovers.

These poems about love voiced through the misery and self-deprecating humor of the unhappy, unrequited lover give psychological depth and dramatic tension to the idea of desire in the psychoanalytic sense: desire that desires nothing more than to perpetuate its own state. As Chaucer writes mockingly in the poem "To Rosamounde," "I brenne ay in an amorous pleasance" (l.22). The continuation of such pleasant desire comes to constitute an argument for the amorous and erotic power of love poetry, especially for noble readers who are interpellated in this way as more worthy of, or ennobled by, such suffering than incompetent bourgeois or clerkly poets. The reading and circulation of such poetry perpetuate the myth of the deeper aristocratic capacity for suffering that is also ennobling.

30 Great Myths About Chaucer, First Edition. Thomas A. Prendergast and Stephanie Trigg.
© 2020 John Wiley & Sons, Inc. Published 2020 by John Wiley & Sons, Inc.

By the time of writing the *Canterbury Tales*, Chaucer's narrative persona has been modified once more, as the Host describes him as a childlike, cuddly darling: "This were a popet in an arm t'enbrace / For any womman, smal and fair of face" (VII.701–2; see Myth 24).

Early Chaucer criticism often sought to identify an autobiographical motivation in his writing, and the opening lines of his early dream-vision poem *The Book of the Duchess* have been much discussed in this light. The poem features a leisurely introduction in which the poet complains that he has been unable to sleep for a long time:

> I holde it be a sicknesse
> That I have suffred this eight yeer;
> And yet my boote is never the ner,
> For there is phisicien but oon
> That may me hele;
>
> (ll.36–40)

The idea that one might suffer the sickness of unrequited love for such a long time is a familiar trope in medieval poetry, and in modern criticism this passage is often "explained away" as a simple imitation of a European convention of courtly poetry: the poet establishes his credentials for writing about love by invoking the depth of his own feeling.

Yet in older biographical and critical traditions, this passage generated some heated debate about whether Chaucer was paying a compliment, either heartfelt or performative, to a lady of the court. This tradition goes back at least to William Godwin's biography of 1804, which suggested Chaucer was the "unsuccessful lover of the lady to whom he professes himself attached."[2]

Godwin based his claim on the passage from *The Book of the Duchess*, a reading of *The Parliament of Foules* and a third work known as *Chaucer's Dream*. In this poem, the narrator dreams that his beloved consents to his suit but awakens to find it is a delusion: "Lo, here my blisse! lo, here my paine! / Which to my ladie I complaine, / And grace and mercy her requere, / ... / That of my dremé [*sic*] the substaunce / Might turnen once to cognisaunce."[3] If we believe that the narrator is actually referencing his personal experience and that the narrator is Chaucer, then it would seem that the poem confirms Godwin's notion that Chaucer suffered from unrequited love. The poem was first included in Thomas Speght's 1598 edition of Chaucer and was accepted by Thomas Tyrwhitt as genuine, so Godwin had good reason to believe that the poem was by Chaucer. By the late nineteenth century, however, scholars had begun to question the Chaucerian attribution, and by 1878 it had been relegated to the ever-growing Chaucerian apocrypha (it was ultimately renamed *The Isle of Ladies*).

Despite this setback, some critics continued to insist that the passage from *The Book of the Duchess* (even in the absence of the evidence from *Chaucer's Dream*) was a direct reference to an unsuccessful love suit to some high-placed member of the court. The most frequently named contender was Joan of Kent, the mother of Richard II.[4] Margaret Galway argues that Chaucer would have traveled to Aquitaine with Gaunt in 1370, and would have read his "important new poem at the English court in Angoulême" with Joan (the "Fair Maid") of Kent presiding.[5] The poem would thus have been a courtly compliment to his hostess and her son. Galway goes even further to suggest that Joan "was evidently the subject of all [Chaucer's] extant serious love-poems," especially identifying her with Alceste in *The Legend of Good Women*.[6] Galway argues that Chaucer would have known Joan before her marriage to the Prince of Wales: "it is *a priori* not improbable that the young court poet paid Joan the compliment of posing as one of her disappointed admirers and vowing that he would always remain her faithful servant."[7] (Nevertheless, others suggest that the reference to Alceste in the *Legend* is a compliment to Anne of Bohemia, Richard II's first wife.[8])

Interestingly, in this essay from 1945 Galway makes no claims about the poet's "real" feeling, but her identification of Joan of Kent as the subject of these lines has been interestingly misread as if Galway were making a biographical statement about Chaucer's state of mind. Galway had first proposed this identification in 1938, and it was the subject of much debate in the 1940s. Most scholars argued against Galway, suggesting that the idea of a long lovesickness was a conventional feature of the French love poetry of the period – especially the poems by Guillaume de Machaut which were the sources for *The Book of the Duchess* – and so there was no need to argue for a particular candidate. In 1971, though, Edward Condren revived the idea and suggested that in *The Book of the Duchess* Chaucer is describing his own "profound emotional reaction to the death of Blanche of Lancaster."[9]

The argument that a motif, an image, an allusion or a metaphor is "conventional" and therefore less interesting or less worthy than an idea that might come from the poet's own heart or mind has a long and interesting history in English poetry, and the history of Chaucer criticism plays an important role here. For many decades in the twentieth century it was a truism that Chaucer began his poetic career as a more or less slavish imitator of French poetry, and as a devoted servant of rhetorical models and manuals such as Geoffrey of Vinsauf's *Poetria Nova*. He then looked to Italy and the writings of Dante, Petrarch and Boccaccio as narrative models, before finally developing his own distinctively English poetic style and inaugurating the traditions of English poetry. In an influential essay for the British Academy, J.M. Manly laid out this trajectory of Chaucer moving away from the "thin prettinesses" of the French tradition to a more robust and native poetic line.[10] Through articles such as this, the idea of "convention" was devalued, but also strengthened as an explanation for much of Chaucer's poetry, and there was, we suggest, an insistent masculinization of Chaucer in the critical practice that dismissed biographical equivalents and lovesickness in favor of a learned familiarity with poetic traditions and conventions. As we will see on many occasions in this book, the critical "myths" about Chaucer are deeply imbricated in the politics of changing critical styles.

Derek Pearsall takes a different, more meta view and argues that the lines in *The Book of the Duchess* are a deliberately opaque allusion that invites exactly this kind of speculation or gossip about the identity of this early love: "At the beginning, the poet pictures himself as sorrowful and unable to sleep, because of some eight-year sickness that he mysteriously refuses to specify: Chaucer put this in as a talking-point, and it has certainly provoked a great deal of talk."[11]

Indeed, the phenomenon of courtly gossip is important here, and there are a number of myths surrounding the identity and actions of Joan of Kent, who was apparently famous for her beauty as well as her fashion sense.[12] In some accounts of the founding of the Order of the Garter by Edward III in 1346, she is identified with the "Countess of Salisbury" (with whom the King was apparently enamored), whose garter embarrassingly fell to the ground (itself an important "myth of origins"[13]). Joan was first Lady Holland, then Countess of Salisbury, before becoming the Princess of Wales after marrying Edward III's eldest son, the Black Prince. But as Leo Carruthers points out, there is considerable doubt as to who might have been the Countess of Salisbury at the time of the Order's founding.[14]

Even though the critical tradition is at best equivocal about the possibility of diagnosing "genuine" as opposed to a performative, complimentary unrequited love, the idea of Chaucer's own loves has a second life in the biographical and fictional traditions of medievalism and medievalist historical fiction.

One of the most influential texts here is Anya Seton's extremely popular fictionalized biography of Katherine Swynford, Chaucer's sister-in-law.[15] Katherine, the younger sister of Chaucer's wife Philippa, was governess to John of Gaunt's children from his first wife, Blanche of Lancaster, including the eldest, who would become Henry IV. She then became his mistress, and the mother of four children with Gaunt, before becoming his third wife in 1396. In Seton's novel, Katherine comes to court when Philippa is engaged to Chaucer, and he becomes her confidant, explaining the gossip and the ways of the court to her. From the very beginning it is made clear that

Chaucer adores Blanche, not as a publicly performed compliment to the Duchess or to Gaunt, his patron, but with a deeply felt, serious and hopeless love, which will never be expressed in public. The contrast is made clear: "His heart was laid at the feet of the lovely white Duchess and his practical future lay with Philippa, who suited him well enough."[16] When Blanche dies of plague in September 1368, Chaucer is devastated and writes *The Book of the Duchess* in her honor as his own heartfelt expression of love. He sends the poem to Gaunt, who is appropriately amazed to read the depths of poetic feeling Chaucer has produced out of English forms. In contrast to the rumors about Philippa and Gaunt sharing a bed (see Myth 5), there is no hint in this work of any unseemly relationship between Philippa and Gaunt. Indeed, Katherine's passionate sensuality is drawn in stark contrast to Philippa's proper and practical character.

This idea that Chaucer suffered some kind of "unrequited love" for Blanche occurs in a number of other, later fictions that feature Chaucer,[17] though it plays no part in any recent biographical or critical study, such have the fashions in this area changed. We give the last word here to Derek Pearsall, who summed up the issue in his usual pithy style in his biography, dismissing the gossip about Chaucer's relationship with Gaunt: "The desire to turn their association into a long-running soap opera, which has inspired two biographers of Chaucer to prove how every one of Chaucer's writings turns upon some event in his supposed patron's exciting life, must be regarded as wishful thinking."[18]

Notes

1 In this sense, Chaucer's career fits the model outlined by Richard Helgerson for Renaissance poets, in *Self-Crowned Laureates: Spenser, Jonson, Milton, and the Literary System* (Berkeley, CA: University of California Press, 1983), 80–82, where it fits a model first exemplified by Virgil. L. Lipking, *The Life of the Poet: Beginning and Ending Poetic Careers* (Chicago, IL: University of Chicago Press, 1981), xi, 76–80.

2 William Godwin, *The Life of Geoffrey Chaucer, the Early English Poet including Memoirs of his near friend and kinsman, John of Gaunt, Duke of Lancaster: with sketches of the Manners, Opinions, Arts and Literature of England in the Fourteenth Century,* 4 vols., 2nd edn. (London: Printed by T. Davison for R. Phillips, 1804), II:372.

3 Qtd. in Godwin, II:369–70.

4 Margaret Galway, "Chaucer's Hopeless Love," *MLN* 60, no. 7 (1945), 431–9.

5 Froissart refers to her as "cette jeune damoiselle de Kent," but she does not seem to be called the "Fair Maid of Kent" in any contemporary authority. *Les chroniques de Sire Jean Froissart,* vol. II (Paris: Wattelier, 1867), 243.

6 Galway, "Chaucer's Hopeless Love," 433.

7 Margaret Galway, "Chaucer's Sovereign Lady: A Study of the Prologue to the 'Legend' and Related Poems," *MLR* 33, no. 2 (1938), 145–99, here 176.

8 Thomas Tyrwhitt was first to identify Alceste with Queen Anne; Paul Strohm, *Hochon's Arrow* (Princeton, NJ: Princeton University Press, 2014), 116–19, concurs with this view. For the less common association with Queen Philippa's damoiselle, Alice Cestre, see Frederick Tupper, "Chaucer's Lady of the Daisies," *Journal of English and Germanic Philology* 21, no. 2 (1922), 293–317.

9 Edward Condren, "The Historical Context of the *Book of the Duchess*: A New Hypothesis," *Chaucer Review* 5, no. 3 (1971), 195–212, here 208.

10 J.M. Manly, "Chaucer and the Rhetoricians: Warton Lecture on English Poetry, no. 17, read before the British Academy June 2nd, 1926," *Proceedings of the British Academy* 12 (London: Humphrey Milford, 1926), 110. This is often misquoted as "thin prettiness."

11 Derek Pearsall, *The Life of Geoffrey Chaucer: A Critical Biography* (Oxford: Blackwell, 1992), 84.

12 The Chandos Herald described her as "Que bêle fut, plesante et sage" in his life of Edward, Prince of Wales, written some time between 1376 and 1387. See *Le prince noir poème du héraut d'armes Chandos: texte critique suivi de notes par Francisque-michel* (London: J.G. Fotheringham, 1883), 106: "A une dame de grani pris / Qui de s'amour l'avoit espris, / Que bêle fut, plesante et sage" (ll.1586–8). Froissart refers to her "en son temps la plus belle de tout la roiaulme d'Engleterre et la plus amoureuse" (II:243).

13 Stephanie Trigg, *Shame and Honor: A Vulgar History of the Order of the Garter* (Philadelphia, PA: University of Pennsylvania Press, 2012), 27.

14 Ibid., 65; Leo Carruthers, "'Honi soit qui mal y pense': The Countess of Salisbury and the 'Slipt Garter,'" in *Surface et Profondeur: Mélanges offert à Guy Bourquin*, ed. Colette Stévanovitch and René Tixier, Grendel 7 (Nancy: AMAES, 2003), 221–34, here 232.

15 Anya Seton, *Katherine* (1954; London: Hodder and Stoughton, 2006).

16 Ibid., 45.

17 See, for example, Duane Crowley's *Riddle Me a Murder* (Manchaca, TX: Blue Boar Press, 1986), whose plot depends on a brief romance between Chaucer and Blanche that led to the birth of Henry Bolingbroke, the "son" of John of Gaunt who would become Henry IV. See also Myth 27 about Chaucer's deathbed retraction.

18 Pearsall, *Life of Geoffrey Chaucer*, 83, n.37. Pearsall is referring to Godwin's *Life of Geoffrey Chaucer* and George Williams's *A New View of Chaucer* (Durham, NC: Duke University Press, 1965). More specifically, he rejects outright the idea that *The Book of the Duchess* was written uninvited by Gaunt: "The poem could hardly have been written without Gaunt's knowledge, and it is natural to assume that it bespeaks a certain intimacy. A young pipsqueak of an esquire would not have presumed to write on such a subject in such a way had he not been assured of a sympathetic reception" (84).

Myth

4

CHAUCER'S MARRIAGE WAS UNHAPPY

In 1931, England's poet laureate, John Masefield, reported:

> We gather from the poems that Chaucer's own marriage was one of the utmost and liveliest unfortunate horror. The Wife of Bath describes her fifth marriage as being to much such [sic] a Clerk as Chaucer's description of himself. Can it possibly be that the Wife of Bath is a portrait of Mrs. Chaucer?[1]

This is one of the more extreme cases of collapsing the words that Chaucer uses in his public poetic productions with his private life, but it is hardly unique. Towards the end of the nineteenth century, J.W. Hales, quoting a couple of lines from the envoy to the *Clerk's Tale* ("O noble wyves, ful of heigh prudence, / Lat noon humylitee youre tonge naille," IV.1183–4), says, "It seems impossible to put a pleasant construction on these passages. It is incredible that they have no personal significance. The conclusion clearly is that Chaucer was not happy in his matrimonial relations."[2] It is unclear precisely when historical thoughts about Chaucer's marital status and his poetic musings about marriage were collapsed, but the prolific nineteenth-century editor of Chaucer, F.J. Furnivall, was certainly responsible for the currency of the myth. In 1871 he makes one of those offhand comments for which he is so notable:

> Poets are curious cattle about love and marriage. They can have a love or many loves quite independent of their wives: as indeed can and do many other men. If Chaucer's wife was not a bit of a tartar, and most of his chaff of women meant for her, I have read him wrongly.[3]

30 Great Myths About Chaucer, First Edition. Thomas A. Prendergast and Stephanie Trigg.
© 2020 John Wiley & Sons, Inc. Published 2020 by John Wiley & Sons, Inc.

Suspending, for a moment, commentary on the sexist implications of this quotation, it is clear that Furnivall, Hales and Masefield all were engaged in broader reading practices of the nineteenth and early twentieth centuries that understood poetry as biographical. And it is perhaps unremarkable that both Masefield and Hales locate their evidence for Chaucer's unhappy nuptials in the *Canterbury Tales*, in which Chaucer himself is a character.[4] But is there any basis for this belief?

It is first important to understand what drove critics to look almost exclusively to Chaucer's poetry when talking about the poet's marriage. We have very few historical records that deal with Chaucer's marriage to Philippa de Roët. We do not possess any private correspondence between them and we are not even sure when they were married. An enrolment of letters patent tells us that Edward III granted an exchequer annuity to a Philippa Chaucer on 12 September 1366, so Geoffrey and Philippa must have been married either before or by that date (provided her maiden name was not Chaucer).[5] Most critics now believe that she was the sister of Katherine Swynford, John of Gaunt's mistress (see Myth 3). She served in the household of the queen, and then in the household of the Duchess of Lancaster, Constanza (Gaunt's wife), and is described as ascending to *domicella* (the female equivalent of a knighthood). Marion Turner emphasizes the family connections between Chaucer's family and Gaunt's household, remarking that the children of these four couples (John of Gaunt and Blanche; Katherine and Swynford; Gaunt and Katherine; and Philippa and Chaucer) all "seem to have spent a lot of time together as children in various Lancastrian great houses."[6] This is a useful reminder that the medieval "household" was a far more fluid concept than the modern nuclear family; and that the relationship between living and working arrangements might also be more fluid.

It also seems quite likely that Chaucer and Philippa spent long periods living apart, but it is unlikely that they were estranged, as Philippa's annuity through the early 1380s most often designated her husband as the payee.[7] She is last mentioned in the payment of her annuity on 18 June 1387. The absence of her name in the record of a payment to Chaucer of his Michaelmas installments on 7 November 1387 suggests that she had died somewhere in between. The couple had two sons, Thomas and Lewis (though see Myth 5), and probably a daughter, Elizabeth, who was nominated in 1377 by John of Gaunt (acting on behalf of his nephew King Richard, only ten years old at the time) as a novice to the convent of St Helen's Bishopsgate. In the same year, Gaunt also nominated Margaret Swynford, the daughter of Katherine (Chaucer's sister-in-law), to Barking Abbey in Essex.[8] Elizabeth moved to Barking after four years, possibly after the death of her grandmother.

This is the extent of our external historical knowledge of the marriage, though many critics believe that Chaucer makes a reference to Philippa in *The House of Fame*. In Book II, after narrating how he had fallen into a stupor, Chaucer tells us that an enormous eagle caught him up in his claws

> And called me tho by my name,
> And for I shulde the bet abreyde,
> Me mette "Awak," to me he seyde
> Ryght in the same vois and stevene
> That useth oon I koude nevene;
> And with that vois, soth for to seyn,
> My mynde cam to me ageyn,
> For hyt was goodly seyd to me,
> So nas hyt never wont to be.

(lines 558–66)

Is the "vois and stevene" of "oon I koude nevene" an indirect reference to the voice of his wife? It is tempting to think so. Certainly, the distinction between the tone of the Eagle and Philippa's voice has led some to claim that this is evidence of Chaucer's being a "henpecked husband." Further, they claim that Chaucer begins his dream-vision with a direct reference to his harried status as he makes a pilgrimage to "the corseynt Leonard." St. Leonard was the patron saint of prisoners, so critics have traditionally understood this as a reference to marriage as a prison – a reading that seems to be supported by a humorous invocation of St. Leonard that Chaucer might have known from Jean de Meun's *Roman de la Rose*.

Recently, however, it has been demonstrated that the linkage between bad marriages and St. Leonard in Chaucer is probably the invention of an early, prominent editor and critic. In fact, Chaucer was likely invoking Leonard in his traditional role of the patron saint of travelers.[9] But what of the mention of Philippa's supposed hectoring voice in Book II? At best, this reference is highly speculative. It may even be seen to be doubtful if we understand Chaucer's claim that the Eagle spoke to him "in mannes vois" as referring to the gender of the voice (as opposed to a more neutral understanding of the phrase as "in a human voice").[10]

Even if we do not understand *The House of Fame* as referring to marital woes, there is, as we saw earlier, still a good deal of writing that explicitly portrays marriage as a troubled and troubling institution. One might well argue that the Wife of Bath's comments on marriage or the Host's suggestion that his wife is a shrew are colorful inventions reflective of the fictional world of the *Canterbury Tales*, rather than personal expressions by Chaucer about Chaucer. But other works seem to connect these ideas about marriage to Chaucer's personal life. *Lenvoy de Chaucer a Bukton*, a verse letter ending with an envoy to either Robert or Peter Bukton (both had connections with the court), has Chaucer claiming that though he had promised to tell Bukton of "the sorwe and wo that is in marriage," he will not do so – proceeding by a rhetorical figure known as paralipsis (the summary mentioning of a thing while professing to omit it). He characterizes marriage as a prison and invokes the image of Satan gnawing on his chain as an accurate representation of the married man. At the end (in the envoy) he recommends to Bukton, "The Wyf of Bathe I pray yow that ye rede / Of this matere that we have on hond" (ll. 29–30). This connection of personal epistolary advice with the fictional subcreation of the *Canterbury Tales* is undoubtedly meant to be humorous, yet it is worth remembering that in Chaucer's envoy attached to the *Clerk's Tale* (which, as we have seen, made such an impression on J.W. Hales), the *Wife of Bath's Prologue* is similarly referenced. These forms of direct Chaucerian address, mingled with the fictional world of the pilgrimage, suggest a connection between fictional utterances by Chaucer's characters and the discourse of Chaucer himself. It might then seem unsurprising that both the occasional poems of Chaucer, as well as his larger work, were mined by critics for details about the poet's marital status.

Yet simply to collapse poetic production with lived life would suggest that there is no distinction between the two. Chaucer's normally unreliable early nineteenth-century biographer, William Godwin, makes precisely this point about reading the *Envoy*: "It would be unjust, however, from his playfully expressing an aversion to marriage in the character of a satirist, to infer that he had not lived in perfect harmony and happiness with the mother of his children."[11] Nineteenth- and twentieth-century critics were well aware of the distinction between a poetic persona and the person of the poet. Why, then, did they indulge in this treasure hunt for clues about Chaucer's personal life? We might take a hint from the great early twentieth-century critic George Lyman Kittredge. Referencing Chaucer's comments about marriage in the *Envoy*, he says that "probably such utterances were no more seriously meant than the jests which are passed upon an intending bridegroom by his intimates at pre-nuptial 'stag dinners' now-a-days."[12] Chaucer's audience here is male and engages in a casual misogyny that might be in bad taste (as Kittredge also notes), but cannot be taken too seriously – certainly, it should not be read as autobiography.

Yet Kittredge, of course, *is* making biographical claims about Chaucer. He may dismiss the idea that Chaucer's own marriage was troubled, but he presents a portrait of Chaucer as one who replicates misogynistic and misogamic (anti-marital) commonplaces in the service of male comradeship.

As any number of critics have noted, this is the way misogyny works: the discourse of anti-feminism is often the rhetoric of the joke – "not meant to be taken seriously" even while it replicates misogynistic stereotypes. These stereotypes, then, are monolithic representations of all women that are, of course, fictional. Yet, as Chaucer himself often demonstrates, these fictions retain their power because people in some sense believe in them. On one level, we know that the *Envoy to Bukton* is a joke. And we also know that Harry Bailly's complaint about his ironically named wife, Goodelief (Goodlove), is just a bit of funny "business" after a serious tale about a truly "good" wife. And yet, as we have seen, our lack of knowledge about the marriage has led critics (and poets) to assign historical value to claims about "Mrs. Chaucer" that are ultimately no more than conventions and stereotypes. Not incidentally, these readings have often been made by men, who have perpetuated stories about "the woes of marriage" perhaps to consolidate their own relationship with what has historically been a largely masculine audience.

Notes

1 John Masefield, *Chaucer* (Cambridge: Cambridge University Press, 1931), 33.
2 J.W. Hales, *Dictionary of National Biography* (Oxford: Oxford University Press, 1885–1900), 10:158.
3 F.J. Furnivall, *Trial-Forewords to my "Parallel-Text Edition of Chaucer's Minor Poems"* (London: N. Trübner, 1871), 31.
4 And, in Hales's case, the Envoy is identified in the manuscripts as "*Lenvoy de Chaucer*," though what this actually means is a matter of interpretation.
5 Martin M. Crow and Clare C. Olson, eds., *Chaucer Life-Records* (Oxford: Oxford University Press, 1966), 68.
6 Marion Turner, *Chaucer: A European Life* (Princeton, NJ: Princeton University Press, 2019), 125.
7 Derek Pearsall, *The Life of Geoffrey Chaucer: A Critical Biography* (Oxford: Blackwell, 1992), 142.
8 Crow and Olson, *Chaucer Life-Records*, 545–6. For Gaunt's patronage, see Turner, *Chaucer: A European Life*, 205.
9 Scott Lightsey, "Chaucer's Return from Lombardy, the Shrine of St. Leonard at Hythe, and the 'corseynt Leonard' in the *House of Fame*, lines 112–18," *Chaucer Review* 52 (2017), 188–201.
10 David Lawton, *Voice in Later Medieval Literature: Public Interiorities* (Oxford: Oxford University Press, 2016), 40.
11 William Godwin, *Life of Geoffrey Chaucer: The Early English Poet*, 4 vols., 2nd edn. (London: Printed by T. Davison for R. Phillips 1804), 2: 163.
12 George Lyman Kittredge, "Chaucer's *Envoy to Bukton*," *Modern Language Notes* 24, no. 1 (January 1909), 14–15, here 15.

Myth 5

CHAUCER'S SON THOMAS WAS JOHN OF GAUNT'S BASTARD

In the biography attached to Thomas Speght's 1598 version of Chaucer's works there appears this curious, almost throwaway line: "Yet some hold opinion (but I know not vpon what grounds) that Thomas Chaucer was not the sonne of Geffrey Chaucer, but rather some kinsman of his, whome hee brought up."[1] Speght almost immediately distances himself from this "opinion," arguing that "this pedigree [the *Stemma peculiare Gaufredi Chauceri* that appears on the previous page] by the hands of Master Glouer *alias* Somerset, that learned Antiquarie, as also the report of Chronicles shew it to be otherwise."[2] If Speght was interested in offering reassurance about the parentage of Thomas Chaucer, however, his refutation of this discarded opinion had the opposite effect.

In the preface to his magisterial edition of Chaucer in 1775, Thomas Tyrwhitt lamented that we did not know the date of Chaucer's marriage because if we did, "we should know better what to think of the relation of Thomas Chaucer to our author. Mr. Speght informs us 'that some hold opinion that Thomas C. was not the sonne of Geffrey' and there are certainly many circumstances that incline us to that opinion."[3] There is no further reference to Thomas Chaucer's doubtful parentage until 1872, when F.J. Furnivall announced in the pages of *Notes and Queries* that "there is not one scrap of direct or indirect evidence that the wealthy Thomas Chaucer was the son, or any relative, of the poet."[4] Ten years later, Mary Elizabeth Haweis cites a letter from Henry Beaufort that confirms Thomas Chaucer was cousin to the children of John of Gaunt and Katherine Swynford. This *seems* to confirm his status as the son of Geoffrey and Philippa Chaucer, since she was sister to the Duchess of

30 Great Myths About Chaucer, First Edition. Thomas A. Prendergast and Stephanie Trigg.
© 2020 John Wiley & Sons, Inc. Published 2020 by John Wiley & Sons, Inc.

Lancaster, Katherine Swynford. Yet, strangely, Haweis says, "such hypotheses rather increase the cloud which still enshrouds Thomas Chaucer's birth."[5] Whether or not Speght's refutation of the "opinion" and Tyrwhitt's and Furnivall's speculative notes constitute a "cloud" might be debated, but in Haweis's eyes the suspicion about Thomas's parentage could lead in only one direction.[6] Using language that Mary Flowers Braswell has termed "purposefully ambiguous," she implied that Thomas Chaucer was not some kinsman of Chaucer's but John of Gaunt's son.[7]

Haweis's speculation led several medievalists to weigh in on the potential legitimacy or illegitimacy of Thomas Chaucer, but it was Russell Krauss who wrote the most detailed defense of the position in 1932.[8] Krauss rehearsed earlier arguments and added some of his own, including Gaunt's "life-long interest in Philippa and Thomas" (as against his ignorance of Geoffrey later in his life), the coats of arms on Thomas Chaucer's tomb, John Lydgate's failure to mention that Thomas was Geoffrey's son and the comment by Speght that started the debate about Thomas Chaucer's paternity.[9]

It is true that Gaunt favored both Philippa (sister to his wife) and Thomas. Philippa received a number of annuities from the Duke, and she was given New Year's gifts several times through the 1370s and 1380s.[10] Thomas had a long career in the employ of the Duke and was well compensated throughout the 1390s.[11] Moreover, "John of Gaunt also interested himself in the affairs of Elizabeth Chaucer [Philippa's daughter], since it was he who paid for her admission to the Black Nuns, a payment that has led some Chaucerian biographers to fear the worst."[12] Geoffrey also received annuities, but these were given in part because of his wife's services to John of Gaunt's mother (Edward III's queen, Philippa) and his wife (Constance).[13] It is possible that these annuities stopped after Philippa's death, but the records of payments are imperfect and so it is difficult to draw any conclusions about Gaunt's disinterest in Chaucer as opposed to his wife or son. We do know that Gaunt's son, Henry of Derby, gave gifts to Geoffrey in the 1390s, while John of Gaunt was still alive, and once he reached the throne confirmed an annuity for Chaucer (even if that confirmation was delayed; see Myth 26) that may have taken the place of Chaucer's annuity that had been given by John of Gaunt.[14] There is thus little indication that Gaunt or his house showed sufficient disinclination towards Geoffrey Chaucer or a sufficiently unusual inclination towards Philippa or Thomas to indicate a suspicious connection.

Krauss and others also maintain that it is telling that Geoffrey Chaucer's arms do not appear on Thomas Chaucer's tomb. Of the twenty shields on the tomb at Ewelme in Oxfordshire, the only male ones are those of the sons of John of Gaunt by Katherine Swynford, Philippa Chaucer's sister.

The arms of Philippa de Roët (the maiden name of Philippa Chaucer) are quartered with those of Thomas Chaucer's wife, Maud Burghesh. The suggestion would seem to be that Thomas was the son of Philippa but not Geoffrey. Yet it was not abnormal for men to put their mother's arms on their tombs if those noble connections surpassed their father's. And, as it was Thomas's daughter Alice, the wife of the Earl of Sussex, who raised the tomb, it is not unusual that she would wish to stress the Chaucers' connections with nobility.[15]

Finally, Krauss et al. argue that the omission of any mention of Thomas Chaucer's relationship with his father in a poem by John Lydgate that was addressed to Thomas "has always been one of the worst stumbling blocks in the way of the view that Thomas was Geoffrey's son."[16] The logic is that Lydgate, who made something of a career out of encomia to Chaucer, certainly would have mentioned Thomas's connection to "Father Chaucer" had Chaucer really been Thomas's father. Of course, it is always risky to argue from negative evidence. There might be any number of reasons that Lydgate did not include genealogical information in his poem. But in any case, the work is an occasional poem that marked the departure of Thomas for France. It is also very much a work that celebrates "not literary but social and political associations. It accurately depicts Thomas Chaucer's actual and symbolic role at Ewelme and its locality rather than his place in literary history."[17]

What we are left with, then, is Speght's disavowal of what can only be called early modern gossip about the lineage of Thomas Chaucer. Krauss attempts to deal with Speght's own dismissal of this opinion by claiming that Speght's dependence on Glover's pedigree is faulty, because it can only be based on heraldic information that we already possess, and so his interpretation is no more valid than Krauss's own. His reasoning is that Speght and Glover were almost two hundred years removed from the poet and so they could not claim any special knowledge about the paternity of Thomas. But really this is very much what Speght says regarding the opinion about Thomas itself – he does not know of any grounds for the belief. Without grounds for the belief, all we really know is that the belief existed. And there are good reasons to think that the belief was mistaken.

First, it is not only Speght and Glover who claimed that Thomas was Geoffrey's son. An action to recover debt was brought against Thomas Chaucer in 1396, and it explicitly names Thomas as Geoffrey Chaucer's son.[18] And Thomas Gascoigne, early fifteenth-century theologian and sometime Chancellor of Oxford, when writing about Chaucer's supposed deathbed repentance (see Myth 27), also wrote "this same Chaucer was the father of Thomas Chaucer, Knight, which Thomas is buried in Ewelme near Oxford."[19] Thomas Chaucer and Gascoigne both lived in Oxford at the same time (for sixteen years), so there is reason to believe that Gascoigne would have at least known who he was given Thomas's social standing. Those who wish to make the case for Thomas's illegitimacy have argued that Gascoigne is not reporting anything of which he has personal knowledge, but is merely making assumptions based on the fact that Thomas was raised by Geoffrey and Philippa Chaucer. One might well argue that such an assumption would be warranted (especially in the absence of any other compelling counter evidence), but there is another reason that we should believe Gascoigne. He was no friend of John of Gaunt and by extension was no friend of the Chaucers. He most likely concocted the slander that Geoffrey Chaucer attempted too late to repent his sins (comparing him to Judas; see Myth 27) and reported that John of Gaunt had been a "magnus fornicator" and had died of putrefaction of the genitals. Had there been any contemporary gossip about the legitimacy of Thomas, one would think that Gascoigne would have included it.[20] Finally, had Gaunt cuckolded Chaucer, "he [Gaunt] would not have been allowed to marry Chaucer's wife's sister because of the undispensable degree of incest involved."[21] In addition, he would have been in a state of mortal sin and automatically excommunicated. As H.A. Kelly has said, "it is impossible to believe that he would have taken such a risk."[22]

Yet, despite the slender evidence supporting the idea and its sheer improbability, the belief has remained remarkably enduring.[23] There seem to be a few reasons for this. First, there is the delicious irony that the father of English literature (see Myth 1) might not have fathered his own child. Second, Geoffrey Chaucer's poetic autonomy is reinforced. Any patronage flowing to Chaucer from Gaunt or his sons becomes a matter of reparation for a decidedly non-literary injury. The poet's art remains (seemingly) pure and unsullied by the ministrations of Mammon. Finally, it fits into a romantic notion of the suffering poet. Poor Geoffrey is betrayed by Gaunt, abandoned by Philippa and in old age, in serious debt (Myth 26), unable even to get his annuity from his "son's" brother.

Notes

1 Thomas Speght, ed., *The Workes of our Antient and Learned English Poet, Geffrey Chaucer, newly Printed* (London, 1598), b5r.
2 Ibid., b5r.
3 Thomas Tyrwhitt, ed., *The Canterbury tales of Chaucer: to which are added, an essay on his language and versification; an introductory discourse; and notes* (London, 1775–78), 1:xxxiii.

4 F.J. Furnivall, "Thomas Chaucer, Not the Poet Geoffrey's Son," *Notes and Queries*, 4th Series 9 (1872), 381–3, here 381.

5 Mary Elizabeth Haweis, "More News of Chaucer, Part I," *Belgravia: A London Magazine* 48 (1882), 34–46, here 43.

6 Especially as she references the Glover pedigree contained in Speght's edition.

7 Mary Flowers Braswell, *The Forgotten Chaucer Scholarship of Mary Eliza Haweis* (New York: Routledge, 2016), 17.

8 Russell Krauss, Haldeen Braddy and C. Robert Kase, *Three Chaucer Studies* (New York: Oxford University Press, 1932).

9 Ibid., 169.

10 Martin M. Crow and Clair C. Olson, eds., *Chaucer Life-Records* (Oxford: Oxford University Press, 1966), 80, 85, 88–91.

11 Martin B. Ruud, *Thomas Chaucer* (Minneapolis, MN: University of Minnesota Press, 1926), 4–67; Krauss, Braddy and Kase, *Three Chaucer Studies*, 161.

12 Peter Ackroyd, *Chaucer, Brief Lives* (London: Chatto & Windus, 2004), 28.

13 Crow and Olson, *Chaucer Life-Records*, 272.

14 Ibid., 273.

15 Alison Weir, *Mistress of the Monarchy: The Life of Katherine Swynford, Duchess of Lancaster* (New York: Ballantine Books, 2009), 94, 332.

16 Krauss, Braddy and Kase, *Three Chaucer Studies*, 143. Furnivall goes even further, claiming that the scribe who copied the poem (John Shirley) would have been sure to mention Thomas's connection to Geoffrey if there had been one ("Thomas Chaucer," 381).

17 Jacquelyn Fernholz and Jenni Nuttall, "Lydgate's Poem to Thomas Chaucer: A Reassessment of Its Diplomatic and Literary Contexts," in *Identity and Insurgency in the Late Middle Ages*, ed. Linda Clark, The Fifteenth Century 6 (Woodbridge: Boydell Press, 2006), 123–44, here 132.

18 Crow and Olson, *Chaucer Life-Records*, 341.

19 Quoted in Míceál Vaughan, "Personal Politics and Thomas Gascoigne's Account of Chaucer's Death," *Medium Aevum* 75 (2006), 103–22, here 115. See Myth 27.

20 Ibid., 109.

21 H. Ansgar Kelly, "Shades of Incest and Cuckoldry: Pandarus and John of Gaunt," *Studies in the Age of Chaucer* 13 (1991), 121–40, here 137.

22 Ibid, 137.

23 See, for instance, Sheila Delany, *Writing Woman: Women Writers and Women in Literature Medieval to Modern* (New York: Schoken Books, 1983), 58; John H. Fisher, *The Importance of Chaucer* (Carbondale, IL: Southern Illinois Press, 1992), 19–23; R. Allen Shoaf, *Chaucer's Body: The Anxiety of Circulation in the* Canterbury Tales (Gainesville, FL: University of Florida Press, 2001), 100–1; and its persistence as a recurring theme in contemporary historical fiction featuring Chaucer, for example Garry O'Connor, *Chaucer's Triumph* (Lancaster: Petrak Press, 2007).

Myth
6
CHAUCER'S LANGUAGE IS TOO DIFFICULT FOR MODERN READERS

Evidence that Chaucer's language was perceived as difficult appears quite early. Thomas Speght's 1598 edition of Chaucer, for instance, contains a glossary entitled "the old and obscure words of Chaucer explaned." At least two translations of Chaucer's works into modern English were attempted in the early seventeenth century (though only in manuscript), and in 1668 the poet/politician Edmund Waller claimed about the poet that the "years have defac'd his matchless strain."[1] Things had gotten so bad some twenty-five years later that the poet and essayist Joseph Addison maintained: "But age has rusted what the poet writ, / Worn out his language, and obscur'd his wit; / In vain he jests in his unpolish'd strain / And tries to make his readers laugh in vain."[2] It was perhaps to be expected that admirers of Chaucer would attempt to remedy this situation by publishing versions of the poet's work that would be accessible to the larger reading public.

Most famously, the poet John Dryden undertook to translate three of Chaucer's tales (and another work that he thought was by the poet) in his *Fables, Ancient and Modern*. Dryden acknowledges that some readers prefer to read Chaucer in the original and that to translate the poet is to sully his poetry. His response to these naysayers encapsulates the ongoing argument for translation: "Yet I think I have just Occasion to complain of them [those who can read Chaucer in the original], who because they understand Chaucer, would deprive the greater part of their Countrymen of the same Advantage, and hoord him up, as Misers do their Grandam Gold, only to look on it themselves, and hinder others from making use

30 Great Myths About Chaucer, First Edition. Thomas A. Prendergast and Stephanie Trigg.
© 2020 John Wiley & Sons, Inc. Published 2020 by John Wiley & Sons, Inc.

of it."[3] Chaucer's poetry, so Dryden argues, should not be the province of the learned few, but belonged to all those who made England their home.

The central question about translation – whether it is possible to capture the effect of the original – really depends on another question that Dryden elides: Is Chaucer's Middle English readable in the present moment? One might think that if Dryden thought it had to be translated in 1700, then it must be illegible in the twenty-first century. Even though we are a lot closer to the English of Dryden than Dryden was to the English of Chaucer, as in the eighteenth century, there is a widespread perception that Chaucer's language is too difficult to read without specialist training. And of course – as we show many times in this book – such myths are often self-perpetuating. The more Chaucer is perceived as needing expertise and training to make sense of his language, the more reluctant will non-specialists be to teach Chaucer; while the less he is taught, the more unfamiliar he becomes, and the more obscure become the skills needed to read him. None of this linguistic uncertainty has any bearing on the generally held idea that Chaucer is an important literary figure, but it does affect whether, and how, Chaucer is, or should be, taught in secondary schools, colleges and universities.

Chaucer scholars participate in a further form of contradiction in relation to Chaucer's perceived difficulty. When they want to argue that Chaucer's poetry should be included in every mainstream English syllabus they minimize the linguistic difficulties of reading Middle English, but once they are in the classroom they work hard to correct students' pronunciation, teach vocabulary and medieval syntax, and draw attention to other Middle English dialects.

There are certainly some learnable and teachable skills that can make the experience of reading Chaucer easier and more enjoyable for students familiar with the conventions of English poetry. Teaching Chaucer to students for whom English is a second language, or for whom "standard English" bears little relation to their own dialect or spoken English, is a different challenge altogether. When we ask about Chaucer's "readability" we should also consider the wide range of contexts in which Chaucer might or might not be taught, from secondary schools through to a broad variety of college and university settings, whether in the UK, or in postcolonial contexts, or in countries where English is increasingly unlikely to be a student's first language.

Leaving aside for a moment the question of the "real" linguistic differences between Middle and modern English, let us pause to consider some of the cultural and ideological patterns that construct Chaucer as "difficult." For one thing, poetry itself is increasingly not taught in some school contexts, so students might equally struggle with the highly metaphorical structures of Shakespeare's language, and the effects of rhyming and stanzaic patterns on everyday syntax. And second, the Middle Ages are conventionally presented through the cultural and ideological lenses of the deep alterity that renders all of the period's works both culturally alien and difficult to read. Again and again, we read the phrases "medieval" and "Middle Ages" as code for contexts and languages that are irrelevant, outmoded or archaic.

Some aspects of popular culture tell a different story, however. Even though Chaucer is associated with the structures and practices of cultural elites that might render him unapproachable to many potential readers, he is a regular and familiar feature in many works of the contemporary medievalist imagination that have a broader cultural reach. He appears as a character in numerous historical fictions, especially in medievalist detective fiction; and in cinematic and television adaptations of the *Tales* or fictions about the Middle Ages. Equally, there is also a growing number of translations or adaptations of his works (especially the *Canterbury Tales*) into rap poetry or modern creole dialects: part of a growing global movement of adaptations and translations. These adaptations have the effect of bringing Chaucer into a closer relationship with contemporary culture, helping to ease the path of modern students to read and follow his language, though of course there are various linguistic and cultural differences that must be negotiated, while some tales and poems are more readily assimilated into contemporary social contexts.

A final contradiction runs through our best efforts to teach Chaucer. Nearly every critical or teaching edition of his works features a phonetic chart or list that indicates the etymological history and pronunciation of his vowel sounds. Another regular feature of such editions is a typically confusing message about the inconsistency and irregularity of Chaucerian orthography. Equally inhibiting to students who may have little or no experience studying grammar or with inflected languages will be a complicated account of the grammatical forms and structures of Middle English. Yet in spite of all this technical information, it is a common feature of many introductory guides or editions designed for classroom use to say something like, "the best way to learn Chaucer's language is to find a good teacher and learn from them."[4] Even the Harvard website, under its "Teach Yourself to Read Chaucer's Middle English," concedes, "The best way to learn to read Chaucer's Middle English is to enroll in a course with a good and enthusiastic teacher (as most teachers of Chaucer are)."[5] This is an instruction that sends typically mixed signals to contemporary readers. While we embrace the performative and oral delivery of Chaucer, such advice strains against the growing importance of auto-didacticism in medieval studies, in a context where the general expectation is that nearly everything can be learned online.

Nevertheless, once readers have accustomed themselves to a few principles – pronounce all the consonants; remember that long "i" and long "a" are pronounced differently; and be aware that the decision of whether or not to pronounce the final -e will be contextual and at best uncertain – they can mostly get to the point where they can start to imitate their teacher or the growing number of recordings available online, and perhaps even get a sense of what Middle English might have sounded like. There is also a time-honored tradition of encouraging students to memorize the famous first eighteen lines of the *General Prologue* to the *Canterbury Tales*, as a kind of "rite of passage": a form of induction into the mysteries of medieval studies that their teachers and professors might also have endured and passed through. Sometimes students are encouraged to come and speak in front of the professor; other teachers orchestrate a "read aloud competition."

The *General Prologue* lends itself well to this challenge through its complex syntax and the subordinate clauses leading up to the principal clause. Curiously, this insistence on the efficacy of the spoken word takes us right back to Chaucer's time, and the reminder that much of his poetry would have been read aloud. Insisting that students read out loud and master Chaucerian pronunciation accelerates their comprehension, but also deepens appreciation of the persistent orality of medieval literature. As we know, medieval texts were not read just in private study; they were shared and recited in small or larger gatherings. Baba Brinkman draws a powerful analogy when he compares the story-telling competition in the *Tales* to a competitive rap battle.[6] It reminds us that later medieval poets fought to keep and retain the attention of their audiences by a range of rhetorical means (direct address, exclamations, etc.), as well as the cultivation of strong authorial or narrative personalities.

That said, there are some impediments to the immediate comprehension of Chaucer's poetry, in addition to the questions of pronunciation, orthography and inflections. The vocabulary is one example. Nearly all readers of Chaucer (academics, teachers and students) need glosses for words that are completely unfamiliar, or that are drawn from technical vocabulary of various kinds, or those whose semantic connotations vary according to changing contexts, as well as those that have different meanings (the famous "false friends" that appear deceptively similar to modern words). It would be a mistake to underestimate the linguistic alterity of Chaucer, but while his language may be becoming further distanced from the varieties of modern English, there are more and more resources available online, such as the literal line-by-line translations of many of the *Tales* available on sites such as Harvard's The Geoffrey Chaucer Page. With such aids, the language of Chaucer is no more difficult than the complex metaphorical structures of many passages in Shakespeare, for example. As with so many things, "difficulty" is in the eye of the beholder and can always be trumped by the desire to understand. Nevertheless, in an increasingly global culture, teachers and scholars of Chaucer need to acknowledge that there is no simple, "natural" or even single path to familiarity and ease with Chaucer's language.

Notes

1 John Lane translated the *Squire's Tale* into couplets in 1614 (and continued it). See *John Lane's Continuation of Chaucer's* Squire's Tale, ed. F.J. Furnivall, from the original ms. version of 1616, Douce 170, collated with its ms. revision of 1630, Ashmole 53; with notes "On the magical elements in Chaucer's 'Squire's tale,'" and analogues by W.A. Clouston (London: Kegan Paul, Trench, Trübner & Co, 1888, 1890). In the 1630s, Jonathan Sidnam modernized the first three books of *Troilus and Criseyde*. Edmund Waller, *Poems … upon several Occasions … The third Edition with several Additions …* (London: 1668), 234–5.

2 Joseph Addison, "An Account of the Greatest English Poets, 1694," in *The Works of the Right Honourable Joseph Addison*, notes by Richard Hunt, edited by Henry G. Bohn, Bohn's Standard Library (London: H.G. Bohn 1854–56), 1:23.

3 James Kinsley, ed., *The Poems of John Dryden* (Oxford: Oxford University Press, 1958), 4:1457.

4 See, for example, Robert Boenig and Andrew Taylor, eds., *The Canterbury Tales*, 2nd edn. (Peterborough: Broadview, 2012), 18; and V.A. Kolve and Glending Olson, eds., *Geoffrey Chaucer: The Canterbury Tales*, 2nd edn. (New York: W.W. Norton, 2005), xv.

5 http://sites.fas.harvard.edu/~chaucer/teachslf/less-0.htm, accessed 7 November 2018.

6 https://music.bababrinkman.com/album/the-rap-canterbury-tales, accessed 8 November 2018.

Myth 7

THE CANTERBURY PILGRIMS REPRESENT ALL SOCIAL CLASSES AND CHARACTER TYPES

If Chaucer has a reputation for capacious social insight to rival Shakespeare's, it rests on this myth: in the *General Prologue* to his *Canterbury Tales* he describes representatives of all social classes, from high to low, and all character types, from virtuous to vicious, and all the interesting mixed cases in between. According to this influential myth, Chaucer is both comprehensively alert to his own times, observing all the details of costume, behavior and rank, but equally brimming with insight into the universal human condition.

The origins of these paired myths, which in truth are actually sometimes quite hard to disentangle from each other, go back at least to the sixteenth century. In his "Argument to the Prologues" in his edition of Chaucer's *Works* published in 1598, Thomas Speght writes:

> Vnder the Pilgrimes, being a certaine number, and all of differing trades, he comprehendeth all the people of the land, and the nature and disposition of them in those daies; namely, giuen to deuotion rather of custome then of zeale.[1]

Speght's last clause here evokes the proto-Protestant reformation Chaucer, critiquing the corruption of the church, and the routinized, even casual nature of medieval religious observation (see Myth 14).

---

30 Great Myths About Chaucer, First Edition. Thomas A. Prendergast and Stephanie Trigg.
© 2020 John Wiley & Sons, Inc. Published 2020 by John Wiley & Sons, Inc.

Similar observations are made, even more influentially, a hundred years later by John Dryden in 1700, and by William Blake, a century later again in 1809. Each describes the *General Prologue* in glowing terms for its inclusivity. Dryden, who voices many of our myths in pithy, oft-quoted phrases, attributes this generous vision of humanity to Chaucer's own personality:

> He must have been a man of a most wonderful comprehensive nature, because, as it has been truly observ'd of him, he has taken into the compass of his *Canterbury Tales* the various Manners and Humours (as we now call them) of the whole English nation, in his Age. Not a single Character has escap'd him. All his Pilgrims are severally distinguish'd from each other; and not only in their Inclinations, but in their very phisiognomies and Persons.[2]

Dryden sums up this view in a proverb that is one of the most popular phrases used to describe the pilgrim company, "God's plenty":

> 'Tis sufficient to say according to the Proverb, that here is God's Plenty. We have our Fore-fathers and Great Grand-dames all before us, as they were in Chaucer's Days; their general Characters are still remaining in Mankind, and even in England, though they are call'd by other Names than those of Moncks and Fryars, and Chanons, and Lady Abbesses, and Nuns: for Mankind is ever the same, and nothing lost out of Nature, though every thing is alter'd.[3]

This universalizing view of human nature subtends Dryden's whole project in the *Fables*, translating selected works from Latin, Greek, Italian and English authors the better to compare their achievements. But, as Glenn Burger points out, it also consolidates a sense of sense of "Englishness," delineating different identities even as it subordinates these identities to a sense of sameness.[4] This essentialization of Englishness, however, rests uneasily with Dryden's desire to portray Chaucer as a universal poet who is able to talk about all "Mankind." Individual identity – and by extension English identity – is accidental because it is human nature that is essential. And it is, seemingly, the essential nature of "Mankind" that Chaucer's poetry encompasses.

William Blake explicitly says as much, in his "Advertisement" for his famous engraving of the pilgrims as they set out for Canterbury:

> The characters of Chaucer's Pilgrims are the characters which compose all ages and nations: as one age falls, another rises, different to mortal sight, but to immortals only the same; for we see the same characters repeated

again and again, in animals, vegetables, minerals, and in men; nothing new occurs in identical existence; Accident ever varies, Substance can never suffer change nor decay.

Of Chaucer's characters, as described in his Canterbury Tales, some of the names or titles are altered by time, but the characters themselves for ever remain unaltered, and consequently they are the physiognomies or lineaments of universal human life, beyond which Nature never steps. Names alter, things never alter. ... As Newton numbered the stars, and as Linnaeus numbered the plants, so Chaucer numbered the classes of men.[5]

Blake's project is global rather than national. Like the understanding of Linnaeus or Newton, Chaucer's taxonomic understanding encompasses an entire part of the world. It is not subordinated to incipient nationalism (though we note that two of Blake's taxonomists are English). Blake's appeal to scientific logic here is hard to sustain. Chaucer does draw on the scientific traditions of physiognomy and humoral theory, but hardly does so systematically. By naming his characters by their professions, not individual names, and by starting both the *General Prologue* portraits and the tale competition itself with the Knight, he nevertheless gives a vague impression of surveying a great diversity of people from an ordered perspective.

This false analogy with science, and its occulted attack on English exceptionalism, did not disable claims about Chaucer's ability to represent all social classes and types, but many scholars made more historically localized claims about Chaucer's ability to comprehend human variety. For example, J.R. Hulbert wrote in 1949, "The result therefore is a conspectus of mediaeval English society: it would be possible to use the prologue as basis [sic] for a survey of fourteenth century English life."[6] More recently, Velma Bourgeois Richmond wrote, "the large number of pilgrims is necessary to show a full range of society, and one of Chaucer's concerns is precisely that. His selection of characters, their exclusively English nationality, argues the poet's interest in analysing that social world."[7] The more modest terms "conspectus" and "full range" seem to limit the ambitious assessments of Dryden and Blake, who link Chaucer's abilities to the divine and the immortals.

Nevertheless, as many scholars point out, a quick examination of that social world suggests that the socio-economic range of Chaucer's pilgrims is not comprehensive. The most highly ranked pilgrim, the Knight, belonged to a category that was really at the bottom of the stepladder of nobility, with baron, earl and duke above, while the size of a knight's income and rents could vary widely. And the lowest-ranked pilgrim, the Plowman, especially if he owned his own plow, might have been relatively secure economically, in contrast to less prosperous peasants, even though his work was seasonal.[8] Mark Bailey, indeed, describes plowmen as "elite peasants," commenting that their wages had increased dramatically in the labor shortages that resulted from the various outbreaks of plague.[9] For Bailey, the virtuous Plowman is a model of the new labor relations in place from around the 1380s.[10] The Plowman is not given a tale to tell, and his portrait is one of the shortest and least individuated, so it can hardly be said that Chaucer has fully entered into the imaginative life of the laboring poor at the lowest level of society. For example, we might contrast *Peres the Ploughmans Crede*, whose ploughman labors to work the frozen ground, accompanied by his barefoot wife, and sighing as his baby children wait, crying, at the edge of the field. Such a ploughman is hardly likely to be able to undergo the luxury of a pilgrimage, but like Chaucer's *Prologue*, this text draws on naturalistic detail to flesh out the traditional iconography of estates literature: ploughmen often feature as emblematic or allegorical figures as well as illustrations of lower social classes.

One of the reasons the *General Prologue* continues to fascinate readers is its combination of apparently timeless character traits with its complex sense that traditional expectations of a number of these social roles are in the process of change. Commentators such as Jill Mann and Stephen Knight emphasize the rival schemes that structure the *General Prologue*, as Chaucer imaginatively captures recent and dynamic changes in medieval society. The *General Prologue* combines the traditional eleventh-century three estates scheme (those who fight to defend the community; those who care for its spiritual welfare; and those who till the soil) with a more modern view, structured around the "social actualities" of fourteenth-century life. Mann corrects older, character-driven critical narratives by showing how Chaucer draws on the rich and extensive traditions of estates satire.[11] Knight argues that the *General Prologue* is arranged in "four different socially functional groups": the manorial family (Knight, Squire, Yeoman); the regular religious (Prioress, Monk, Friar); the "professionals (from the Merchant and Clerk through to the Doctor and the Wife of Bath)"; and the "lower classes," those who serve others. Here he makes further distinctions between the Parson and Plowman, who fulfill their roles well, and those who in different ways abuse their professional roles; and then between the Miller, Manciple and Reeve, as secular figures, and the Summoner and Pardoner, as religious ones.[12] Other commentators draw attention to the dominance of figures in the middle: it is the world of the middle-class artisan and professional that most fascinates Chaucer.

When it comes to the articulation and analysis of character types and personalities, Chaucer's discussion in the *General Prologue* is less schematic, though he certainly draws on elements of humoral theory in his description of the Franklin's "sangwyn" complexion (I.333) and the "colerik" Reeve (I.587); or physiognomic features such as the Wife of Bath's gap between her teeth (I.468), or the hairy wart and wide nostrils of the Miller's nose (I.554–7).[13]

For many readers, the analysis of these structures glosses over the difficulty of describing as "representative" a company that includes only three women: the Prioress; the unnamed "Second Nun" who travels with her as her chaplain, and who tells the tale of St. Cecilia; and the Wife of Bath. We might also mention the wives of the five guildsmen, who, although they are not included in the number of "nyne and twenty" pilgrims, are characterized in almost as much detail as their husbands, who remain silent throughout the pilgrimage.

In any case, the women in Chaucer's company are clearly outnumbered. There is thus a strong contrast with Boccaccio's *Decameron*. His company of ten young people is far more homogenous than Chaucer's in that they are drawn from the same social class. Chaucer's assembly of pilgrims is often contrasted favorably as being more diverse, from a greater social range, while his story collection as a whole is praised for developing a far more nuanced set of relationships between teller and tale, between social class, genre and style. This diversity is usually read as an indication of Chaucer's originality, but where Boccaccio's company of ten includes seven female narrators, Chaucer's collection favors male story-tellers.

Chaucer's narrative technique in the *General Prologue* is to juxtapose the schematic and the random in a way that brings these "portraits" alive, and often in a manner that is quite surreal; for example, the curious hat as broad as a shield worn by the Wife, or the Summoner in turn using a loaf of bread as a shield. We do not really learn much about the Cook's personality from the "mormal" – the unhealed ulcer on his leg – but the abject juxtaposition in the next line with his excellent "blankmanger" certainly contributes to this accumulation of rich and individualized detail that gives the impression of infinite human variety. This promise is fully borne out only in the long "autobiographical" prologues of the Wife of Bath and the Pardoner, where these two characters offer more sustained characterizations of their lives in their own words. There are smaller moments of character development, however, when pilgrims interrupt each other, or try, variously, to outdo each other in story-telling or professional rivalry.

The myth of the *Tales*' inclusiveness begins in the *General Prologue* itself, when Chaucer introduces his description of the pilgrims' "condicioun" (I.38), "degree," "and array" (I.40–41); and when he concludes the *General Prologue* by declaring he has covered "Th'estaat, th'array, the nombre, and eek the cause / Why that assembled was this compaignye" (I.716–17). This, then, is a myth that is established firmly by Chaucer himself.

Overall, Chaucer's method of characterization is to suggest by indirection, rather than by classification. It is the way the pilgrims do *not* fit with conventional expectations that seems to bring them to imaginative life: the restless Monk; the socially aspirational Prioress; the scurrilous Summoner; and the ambiguously gendered Pardoner. In this way Chaucer opens up the possibility of tremendous variety between these mostly unnamed individuals and the job they do or the social role they perform. We may even speculate that this disparity sits at the heart of the appeal of this text to modern readers, who might equally not wish to be defined solely by their occupations or professions.

Notes

1 Thomas Speght, "Arguments to euery Tale and Booke," in *The Workes of our Antient and Learned English Poet, Geffrey Chaucer, newly Printed*, ed. Speght (London, 1598), in *Geoffrey Chaucer, The Works, 1532: with supplementary material from the Editions of 1542, 1561, 1598 and 1602* [in facsimile] (Ilkley: Scolar Press, 1976), c4r.
2 John Dryden, *The Poems of John Dryden, Volume IV*, ed. James Kinsley (Oxford: Clarendon Press, 1958), 1455.
3 Ibid., 1455.
4 Glenn Burger, *Chaucer's Queer Nation* (Minneapolis, MN: University of Minnesota Press, 2003), xix.
5 William Blake, *Blake: Complete Writings*, ed. Geoffrey Keynes (Oxford: Oxford University Press, 1969), 567.
6 J.R. Hulbert, "Chaucer's Pilgrims," *PMLA* 64, no. 4 (1949), 823–8, here 823.
7 Velma Bourgeois Richmond, *Geoffrey Chaucer* (New York: Continuum, 1992), 46–7.
8 The Knight embodies the ideals of his class: chivalry, fighting wars (often overseas) and "gentilesse." See Stephen H. Rigby, *"The Knight," in Historians on Chaucer: The "General Prologue" to the* Canterbury Tales, ed. Stephen H. Rigby (Oxford: Oxford University Press, 2014), 42–62. See also Daniel Pigg, "With Hym Ther Was a Plowman, Was His Brother," in *Chaucer's Pilgrims: An Historical Guide to the Pilgrims in* The Canterbury Tales, ed. Laura C. Lambdin and Robert T. Lambdin (Westport, CT: Greenwood Press, 1996), 263–70, here 266–7. Pigg draws here on the work of labor historian R. Hilton.
9 Mark Bailey, "The Ploughman," in *Historians on Chaucer: The "General Prologue" to the* Canterbury Tales, ed. Stephen H. Rigby (Oxford: Oxford University Press, 2014), 353–367, here 366.

10 Ibid., 367.
11 Jill Mann, *Chaucer and Medieval Estates Satire: The Literature of Social Classes and the General Prologue to the* Canterbury Tales (Cambridge: Cambridge University Press, 1973), 6.
12 Stephen Knight, *Geoffrey Chaucer* (Oxford: Blackwell, 1986), 73.
13 See, for example, the discussion of Chaucer's use of physiognomic theory and the Miller's nose in Walter Clyde Curry, *Chaucer and the Mediaeval Sciences*, rev. edn. (New York: Barnes and Noble, 1960), 85–9.

Myth
8 THE CANTERBURY PILGRIMS ARE BASED ON REAL PEOPLE

As we saw in the previous myth, Chaucer's collection of tales told on the pilgrimage to Canterbury is rightly famous as a compelling snapshot of fourteenth-century life that somehow also seems to transcend its historical setting. The pilgrims who gather in Southwark are especially beloved, as an indication of Chaucer's pre-eminence as a student of character. As if he pre-figured Shakespeare's capacious genius in the comprehension of the human condition, Chaucer is often praised for the balance he seems uncannily able to strike between features that are historical and those that are timeless. For example, while terms like "franklin" and "pardoner" have no easy modern equivalents, and while some of the finer details of humoral and physiognomic theory need to be explained to modern readers, we still feel we might be able to understand these pilgrims as well as any other literary characters. Indeed, the idea of Chaucer's genius rests in no small part on the achievement of his *General Prologue*. In 1949, J.R. Hulbert wrote, "In no other part of his writings was Geoffrey Chaucer more original than in the series of sketches of the pilgrims in the prologue to the *Canterbury Tales*."[1]

A persistent myth that seeks to account for this originality is the idea that Chaucer based many of these sketches, or "portraits" as they are commonly known, to a greater or lesser degree on real people, and that this is what gives them their striking verisimilitude. This thesis was developed at greatest length by J.M. Manly in 1926 in his *Some New Light on Chaucer*, and while there is historical evidence to support some of his claims, the critical issues they raise are crucial to the way we read Chaucer and the way we think about the originality of his work.[2]

30 Great Myths About Chaucer, First Edition. Thomas A. Prendergast and Stephanie Trigg.
© 2020 John Wiley & Sons, Inc. Published 2020 by John Wiley & Sons, Inc.

Manly was keen to emphasize Chaucer's pointed and detailed observations of the world around him, in contrast to the "abhorrent doctrine that [Chaucer] built up his matchless pictures of human life entirely by piecing together scraps from old books, horoscopes, astrological and physiological generalizations."[3] In another famous essay, "Chaucer and the Rhetoricians," Manly similarly argued that "Chaucer's greatness arose from his growing recognition that for him at least the right way to amplify a story was not to expand it by rhetorical devices, but to conceive it in terms of the life which he had observed so closely."[4]

Manly rejects the idea that the pilgrims represent all walks of life (see Myth 7), and emphasizes the seemingly random selection of crafts and trades represented in the *General Prologue*: "The basis of choice would seem to be, not a principle of systematic representation, but something else—perhaps Chaucer's personal interests and prejudices."[5] Manly reminds us that the population of London at this time would have been only around 40,000. Chaucer, he says, "was not writing for posterity or even for the whole contemporary population of England, but for a handful of courtiers, gentlemen, churchmen, professional men, officials and city merchants. There was no need to give them a systematic view of fourteenth century life."[6]

Having relieved Chaucer of the burden of comprehensive representation and argued that Chaucer was writing with close reference to a small community, Manly examines the hints provided by proper names and evidential traces in Chaucer's text that might support some historical identifications. It is a very pleasurable form of detective work that others have also taken up. It also shares affinities with the pleasurable research – and creative invention – involved with the writing of historical fictions set in the Middle Ages.

In contrast to the characters who are named in the prologue to Boccaccio's *Decameron*, Chaucer identifies his pilgrims primarily by their profession or vocation. Only two are given proper names in the *General Prologue*: Madame Eglentyne the Prioress (I.24) and Huberd the Friar (I.269). Others are named in the prologues to their own tales: Robin the Miller (I.3129); Osewold the Reve (I.3860); Hogge of Ware, the Cook, addressed by the Host as Roger (I.4336); Alisoun the Wife of Bath (III.804); John the Nun's Priest (named in the prologue to his tale at l.VII.2810), and Harry Bailly the Host (named in the *Cook's Prologue*, I.4358).

Of these, scholars have been able to identify an "Henricus Bailiff, Ostyler" on the Subsidy Roll for Southwark for 1380–81, and there are other contemporary records of this name. Manly makes it clear that one cannot be certain that this Henry Bailly was innkeeper for the Tabard Inn or that all references to Henry Bailly are to the same person. However, he argues that it is highly likely that there was more than one Henry Bailly, so that one may "safely conclude that the host of the Tabard in Chaucer's day actually was named Harry Bailly and consequently that the Host of the *Canterbury Tales* was modeled upon him."[7] Many scholars now accept this identification: it serves to ground the pilgrimage in time and space, if only as a jumping-off point for the rest of Chaucer's imaginative and fictional projection.

Amusingly, Manly speculates that one day he will not be surprised if someone in the future turns up evidence for a cook named Hogge of Ware;[8] and indeed, in 1937 E.D. Lyon found a reference to a "Roger de Ware, Cook" dating from 1373.[9] In this case, Manly's "myth" turned out to be proleptic, a kind of self-fulfilling prophecy. In 1996, Laura and Robert Lambdin published a study of Chaucer's pilgrims and their historical contexts: "Some of the leading figures of the *Canterbury Tales* may be traced with a degree of certainty to well-known contemporaries, as Harry Bailly to Henricus Bailly, host of the Tabard, and Thomas Pinchbek, sergeant-at-law."[10] Similarly, Anthony Musson suggests that "it has been surmised on the basis of the inclusion of 'pinche at' (line 326) that a model for the pilgrim was Thomas Pynchbeck (called to be a sergeant in 1383 and later appointed Chief Baron of the Exchequer (1388–9))."[11]

Even if we could find no real historical correspondences, the other proper names Chaucer distributes so sparingly can be read as little pointers in the direction of realism, encouraging us to imagine a concrete and material world that might sit closely behind the *Tales*. The Shipman's boat is called the Maudlayn; the Reeve's horse is called Scot (though this was a common name for a horse); the Wife of Bath's fifth husband is called Jankyn; and the Host's inn is called the Tabard. At the very least, we may argue that Chaucer is suggesting the possibility of a world in which these characters and names might share in a plausible or material reality of real locations; and certainly, the Tabard was known as an inn in the fourteenth century. This is the fiction embraced by John Dryden, who in 1700 was the first to praise what we might call Chaucer's "naturalism": "I see ... all the Pilgrims in the *Canterbury Tales*, their Humours, their Features, and the very Dress, as distinctly as if I had supp'd with them at the *Tabard* in *Southwark*."[12] As one of us has noted elsewhere, the naturalism of the *General Prologue* is one of the features of the text that seems to invite the modern reader into the congenial company of pilgrims: the invitation that Dryden seems here to accept.[13]

This is one of those myths that tends to go underground in the scholarly tradition but persists in the popular imagination, where it feeds the idea of Chaucer as the native, inspired genius, or a kind of social scientist or anthropologist, who observes the world closely and reports its foibles and weaknesses back to us, implicitly inviting us to recognize these personality types as plausible simulacra of human beings, and to see and feel the material world he conjures, and thus to acknowledge the power of his fictional achievement. At a second-order level, too, this opposition between bookish knowledge and real human science, based on observation of the natural world, is a theme in the *Wife of Bath's Prologue*, where textual authority is displaced in favor of a woman's lived experience.

But perhaps most importantly, it provides us with a possible explanation for why Chaucer chose to characterize the Miller as a drunk or the Wife as a wanton. If we could only identify the original inspirations for these characters from Chaucer's own biography, then we could explain their tendencies and mores. This biographical fallacy is memorably invoked by the 2001 film *A Knight's Tale*, in which "Chaucer" threatens revenge on the two characters (Simon the Summoner and Peter the Pardoner) who have stripped and humiliated him: "I will eviscerate you in fiction. Every pimple, every character flaw. I was naked for a day; you will be naked for eternity."[14] This fantasy, that two of Chaucer's more notorious pilgrims can be rationalized as objects of the poet's animus, is further enabled by Chaucer's ability (as a twenty-first-century audience would know) to carry out his threat. And not incidentally, it also confirms the immense power of poetic representation.

However, critics in the main are skeptical about the value of any specific identifications. Derek Pearsall, for one, is quite unforgiving on this topic. He argues that the question of the "reality" of the *General Prologue*

> has led to some rather sterile arguments concerning the extent to which Chaucer drew on his observation of real historical persons, and similarly unproductive debates concerning the relationship between the "typical" and the "individual." The former has no chance of contributing much to our understanding of what we read, since even when we can identify a Harry Bailly, innkeeper, or a Roger of Ware, Cook, and even if we had a complete dossier on them from an unimpeachably authoritative source, the associations and comparisons that can and might be made are of merely curious interest.[15]

The debate about the realism of the *General Prologue* took a radically different form after the publication in 1973 of Jill Mann's *Chaucer and Medieval Estates Satire*.[16] Mann mounts a convincing argument that Chaucer's *General Prologue* is "an example of a neglected medieval genre—that both its form and its content proclaim it to be part of the literature dealing with the 'estates' of society."[17] Mann takes us through all the descriptions of the pilgrim portraits and demonstrates just how deeply they are indebted to the traditions of estates satire, helping us see the development of character and personhood in the *Tales* in close relation to the pilgrims' occupations and professions. As Chaucer says towards the end of the *General Prologue*, using the vocabulary of "estates": "Now have I toold you soothly, in a clause, / Th'estaat, th'array, the nombre, and eek the cause / Why that assembled was this compaignye ..." (I.715–17)

As Mann herself comments, her approach is not necessarily antithetical to Manly's: "Even if the basis for the Canterbury pilgrims *was* Chaucer's observation of real people, we should still have to discuss and analyse the literary techniques by which he re-created them for his readers."[18] Mann's approach in turn helped generate much later discussion about the professional rivalries among some of the pilgrims (see Myth 9), while of course the tales themselves have also been read as important complements to the analysis of characters. Perhaps it is significant, indeed, that Harry Bailly does *not* tell a tale, and that Roger the Cook barely gets started on his before it breaks off. In spite of the great detective pleasures to be found in trying to identify the "real" people behind these characters, it may indeed be the case that such a historical hook is an impediment, rather than an inspiration for narrative invention.

Notes

1 J.R. Hulbert, "Chaucer's Pilgrims," *PMLA* 64, no. 4 (1949), 823–8, here 823.
2 J.M. Manly, *Some New Light on Chaucer* (Gloucester, MA: Peter Smith, 1959).
3 Ibid., 263.
4 J.M. Manly, "Chaucer and the Rhetoricians: Warton Lecture on English Poetry, no. 17, read before the British Academy June 2nd, 1926," *Proceedings of the British Academy* 12 (London: Humphrey Milford, 1926), 95–113, here 110.
5 Manly, *Some New Light on Chaucer*, 73.
6 Ibid., 76.
7 Ibid., 83.
8 Ibid., 259.
9 E.D. Lyon, "Roger de Ware, Cook," *Modern Language Notes* 52 (1937): 491–4.
10 Laura C. Lambdin and Robert T. Lambdin, eds., *Chaucer's Pilgrims: An Historical Guide to the Pilgrims in* The Canterbury Tales (Westport, CT: Greenwood Press, 1996), xiv.
11 Anthony Musson, "The Sergeant of Law," in *Historians on Chaucer: The "General Prologue" to the* Canterbury Tales, ed. Stephen H. Rigby (Oxford: Oxford University Press, 2014), 206–26, here 222.

12 John Dryden, *The Poems of John Dryden, Volume IV*, ed. James Kinsley (Oxford: Clarendon Press, 1958), 1450–51.

13 Stephanie Trigg, *Congenial Souls: Reading Chaucer from Medieval to Postmodern* (Minneapolis, MN: University of Minnesota Press, 2002), 23–5, 145–52.

14 Brian Helgeland, dir., *A Knight's Tale* (Columbia Pictures and Escape Artists, 2001).

15 Derek Pearsall, *The Canterbury Tales* (London: George Allen and Unwin, 1985), 70–71.

16 Jill Mann, *Chaucer and Medieval Estates Satire* (Cambridge: Cambridge University Press, 1973).

17 Ibid., 1.

18 Ibid., 2.

Myth 9

THE CANTERBURY PILGRIMS FORM A "MERRY COMPANY"

The dominant image of the Canterbury pilgrimage is of a merry company of men and women, exchanging tales, making friendships, and perhaps indulging in some good-humored rivalry and banter along the way. This myth is closely linked to our Myth 7 of Chaucer's pilgrims representing a wide variety of human characters, since the poem is often read as offering a microcosm of the best of humanity: tolerant of difference and taking pleasure in human variety.

Such celebration of difference finds many echoes in Chaucer's works. For example, in the pilgrims' response to the *Miller's Tale*: "Diverse folk diversely they seyde" (I.3857); in the courtiers who debate the marvelous gifts brought to Cambyuskan's court in the *Squire's Tale*: "Diverse folk diversely they demed" (V.202); and in the variety of advice about marriage given to the Merchant by his friends: "Diverse men diversely hym tolde / Of marriage manye ensamples olde" (IV.1469–70).

This myth of convivial diversity is fed by one of the most powerful images of the Canterbury pilgrimage, the illustration to Lydgate's *Prologue* to the *Siege of Thebes* in MS BL Royal 18 DII, f. 148, which appears to show the pilgrims leaving Canterbury to commence their return journey (the moment Lydgate describes when he imitates Chaucer's own opening). This image features on the cover of many editions and studies of Chaucer, where it seems to model convivial community.[1] Almost as popular in such contexts is the image of the pilgrims seated around a communal table from Caxton's second edition of the *Canterbury Tales*: the idea of commensality – eating and drinking together – is never far from the image of the congenial Chaucer society.

30 Great Myths About Chaucer, First Edition. Thomas A. Prendergast and Stephanie Trigg.
© 2020 John Wiley & Sons, Inc. Published 2020 by John Wiley & Sons, Inc.

This model of conviviality and merriment is first enforced by the Host, who is himself described as "right a myrie man" (I.757). His discourse is of "myrthe" (I.759); he has never seen so "myrie" a company (I.764); and he would like to bring further "myrthe" to the company (I.766), if only he knew how. And then in the next line he has devised "a myrthe" (I.767), which turns out to be the tale-telling competition. Thus, in eleven lines, the words "myrie" and "myrthe" are used five times. By the end of his plan, merriment has become practically compulsory: "But ye be myrie, I wol yeve yow myn heed!" (I.782) – "If you don't become merry, you can take off my head!"

After this insistent repetition, the discourse becomes more contractual, as the Host sets out the terms of the narrative competition, but when the Knight begins his tale it is with a "myrie cheere" (I.857). Throughout the *Tales*, too, there is consistent reference to the "solaas" or pleasure of narrative and story-telling, though this is often paired with the ethical imperatives of "sentence" (morality, wisdom); for example, in the Host's competition to find the best "Tales of best sentence and moost solaas" (I.798). As Philippa Maddern shows as well, the word "merry" is also often associated with spiritual and physical wellbeing in this period, not just good-humored entertainment.[2]

In the decades following the composition of the *Canterbury Tales*, pilgrimages to local or European shrines came under increasing attack from church reformers as a frivolous, secular and inappropriately social activity. Even Chaucer's contemporary William Langland wrote of pilgrims' "license to lie" (*leve to lyen*),[3] while his Pardoner exposes the thriving trade in false relics. The idea of pilgrims being "merry" both echoes and anticipates such critiques. However, in increasingly secular centuries, the idea of a jolly company exchanging humorous stories as a model of good behavior has persisted, sustained by the general understanding of Chaucer, but also in many of the popular versions and adaptations of the *Tales*. The carnivalesque associations of pilgrimage with holidays, the pleasure of travel, good company, plentiful food and wine, and the exchange of stories are never far away. Chaucer's pilgrimage begins in a tavern, after all, and several scenes of drunken revelry will appear later; for example, the *Prologue to the Manciple's Tale*, where the Cook has drunk so much that he falls off his horse (but where the sharing of wine is also used to ease the tension between the Cook and the Manciple, XI.95–98); or, more darkly, in the *Pardoner's Tale* about three young revelers who end up murdering each other.

The drinking of wine plays a major part in the Host's agreement with the pilgrims, too. The food served at the Tabard Inn is excellent, and the wine is strong (I.749–50); the proposed prize for the competition is a dinner on their return; and once they all agree to the Host's proposal, more wine is fetched and they drink to celebrate their arrangement. The next morning, as they set out, the Host swears "As ever mote I drynke wyn or ale" (I.832) that if anyone disputes his judgments they must pay for the whole company's expenses. This is a kind of enforced merriment, then, fueled by wine.

Nevertheless, there are many other indications that the pilgrimage is not a uniformly happy occasion. The pilgrims respond to each other's stories with a mixture of emotions, from impatience, rage, envy, anger and outrage to compassion and reflective sobriety. And of course, a number of them are inspired in their decision to go on pilgrimage by religious motives; or they tell stories of morality, philosophy and spirituality, such as Chaucer's own *Tale of Melibee*, the Second Nun's life of St. Cecelia and the *Parson's Tale*. These stories contribute to the work's celebrated diversity, but do not have the same popularity as the more famously bawdy tales told by the Miller or the Merchant, for example.

The other side of this apparently great merriment is the querulous drama of character, and the clash of personalities and professions that generates many of the argumentative sequences and narrative contestations that are structural to a number of "fragments" or groupings of tales. The Friar and Summoner, for example, each tell a tale that rehearses a kind of institutional and professional rivalry between their two offices.

The most celebrated example, though, is found in the first fragment: the sequence of tales that runs from Knight, through to Miller, Reeve and, finally, Cook. The Knight tells an epic romance which is organized around the competitive love of two companions, Palamon and Arcite, for the beautiful Amazon maiden Emily, who is the sister-in-law of Theseus, Duke of Athens. The tale is framed by its epic setting and sustained by two conceptually rich frameworks: an elaborate Boethian philosophy about human happiness; and a divine rivalry between the gods Mars and Venus that is arbitrated by Saturn. The tale of the Miller that follows plays out a comparable rivalry between two lovers Nicholas and Absolon for the favors of Alison, the young wife of John, the old carpenter. But this is a very different tale. There is no supernatural intervention here; the setting is a fourteenth-century town; the characters' desires are decidedly non-spiritual; the comedy is physical and obscene as well as tonal (though see Myth 22); and the rhetorical mode is emphatically of the middle, rather than the high style. The famous dénouement involving a burning hot poker, a naked arse and a desperate call for "Water!" is one of the most decidedly "merry" – that is, humorous – moments in Chaucer's entire oeuvre. But the Reeve, who is both old and a carpenter by trade, takes offense at the Miller's mockery of the foolish old husband. He takes up the Host's invitation to "quite" (repay, outdo) the

Miller's story and tells a tale about two young Oxford scholars who take revenge on a miller for cheating them of some of their wheat and releasing their horses, by raping his wife and daughter. Chaucer does not describe these as rapes; indeed, he says the wife enjoys a "myrie ... fit," while the daughter Malyne rewards young Aleyn by telling him where to find the loaf of bread made with the stolen flour. These encounters are not romanticized, but it is clear that sexual violence against women in this tale is normalized as a form of rivalry between men (and see further our discussion at Myth 11). We can thus read "merriment" through many different perspectives, including as a coded term for sexual violence; this is very far from the inclusive conviviality that is such a celebrated aspect of Chaucer's fame. The fourth tale in this sequence, that of the Cook, barely gets off the ground before the text breaks off. This is not a professional rivalry; the narrative sequence of the fragment takes the form here of bringing sexuality, sexual violence and exploitation increasingly to the fore. The Cook begins a story with an apprentice and a master whose wife "swyved for hir sustenance" (I.4422), and at that low point the fragment comes to an end.

In his important study of 1997, *Chaucerian Polity*, David Wallace emphasizes the originality and novelty of the way Chaucer presents his Canterbury pilgrims coming together and forming a company. Wallace argues that "the voluntary, oath-bound group formed in the *General Prologue*" represents a distinctive form of social organization, one that grows out of the "associational ideology" that found its fullest form in the Florentine republic: "This process of group formation, where the right to exit *as* a group is simply assumed from within rather than conferred from without, represents a singular moment of political confidence that will not be repeated on English territory."[4] Unlike a parish, for example, which is structured on a much more hierarchical institutional frame that could compel compliance, the agreement and oath on which we have seen the Host insist – albeit accompanied by a great deal of wine – are more reminiscent of guild behavior. Wallace writes about this agreement and the formation of the company: "forms of associational behavior learned and practiced in the guilds facilitate its formation and regulation."[5]

By contrast, Marion Turner challenges Wallace's thesis about Chaucer's general "natural amiability,"[6] and the widespread enthusiasm of Chaucer critics for the shared idea that Chaucer's world-view is essentially optimistic. For Turner, "pessimism about social possibility is everywhere apparent in Chaucer's texts: his writings are dependent on a heart of darkness at their very core."[7] For example, she comments that the guild practices of feasting and drinking were "activities often dominated by tension and coercion,"[8] and argues, in reference to the *Tales* and the frequent drama between characters, that "The fact that Harry spends so much time in the link passages attempting to force the fellowship to be harmonious suggests that the group is fundamentally flawed."[9]

Of course, any group of people gathered together will not be perfectly merry and amiable, all the time. This debate between modern scholars about the social forms Chaucer uses as a model for his *Tales* reminds us how complex a work this is: that it can hold both optimism and pessimism together. Similarly, it seems to address both traditional ideologies and newer forms of social organization. It seems to us that while Chaucer does not hold back from exploring dissent, the clash of personalities and the rivalry of professions, he manages to hold these together under the ideology (complex as that may be) of merriment and social inclusiveness. And for whatever complicated reason, the desire to read Chaucer as a poet of merriment has triumphed over the details of the tensions that also render him a poet of diversity. One can always, of course, read against the grain of the text, but maybe it is not necessary to read Chaucer's "merriness" as naturalized or forced, but aspirational – an "attempt to represent for a new social group a cohesive identity" that also acknowledges the contingent nature of that identity.[10]

Notes

1 See the discussion in Stephanie Trigg, *Congenial Souls: Reading Chaucer from Medieval to Postmodern* (Minneapolis, MN: University of Minnesota Press, 2002), xiii–xvii.
2 See Lois Ebin, "Chaucer, Lydgate and the 'Myrie Tale,'" *Chaucer Review* 13, no. 4 (1979), 316–36; and Philippa Maddern, "'It Is Full Merry in Heaven': The Pleasurable Connotations of 'Merriment' in Late Medieval England," in *Pleasure in the Middle Ages*, ed. Naama Cohen-Hanegbi and Piroska Nagy (Turnhout: Brepols, 2018), 21–38.
3 William Langland, *The Vision of Piers Plowman: A Critical Edition of the B-Text based on Trinity College Cambridge MS B.15.17*, ed. A.V.C. Schmidt (London: Dent, 1987), B.Prol.49.
4 David Wallace, *Chaucerian Polity: Absolutist Lineages and Associational Forms in England and Italy* (Stanford, CA: Stanford University Press, 1997), 2.
5 Ibid., 84.
6 Ibid., 10.
7 Marion Turner, *Chaucerian Conflict: Languages of Antagonism in Late Fourteenth-Century London* (Oxford: Clarendon Press, 2007), 7.
8 Ibid., 143.
9 Ibid., 152.
10 The phrase is Glenn Burger's, though in the service of a slightly different argument, *Chaucer's Queer Nation*, xxii.

Myth
10 CHAUCER WAS A FEMINIST

In an anxious and sometimes angry contemporary world, where many of the traditional forms and practices of literary studies are often challenged by decolonizing, feminist and queer perspectives, Chaucer is sometimes dismissed as a figure of privileged white male and heteronormative achievement, no longer deserving of the uncritical adulation – or praise for his inauguration of English poetic traditions – that has so often been his share. As we discuss in our Introduction, and in Myth 30, there are periodic resurgences of a critical movement *against* Chaucer, even in medieval studies. This movement is based equally on a critique of the content of some of Chaucer's poetry, his apparent attitudes and world-view, and the argument that other neglected writers and perspectives might well supplement or displace his centrality in our pedagogical traditions and practices. Nevertheless, we think it is important to set these modern critiques against the much older tradition, dating back to the sixteenth century and still quite dominant in contemporary Chaucer studies, of seeing Chaucer as a writer who was deeply sympathetic to women, even as a proto-feminist.

The first writer to articulate this vision of Chaucer was the Scottish poet Gavin Douglas, who died in 1522, just before completing his translation of Virgil's *Aeneid*. In the prologue to this translation, Douglas takes issue with Chaucer's partisan and sympathetic portrayal of Dido, and his correspondingly dim view of Aeneas as an oath-breaker in his *Legend of Good Women*. Douglas says, however, that he will not press his case against Chaucer:

> For he was euer, God wait, wemenis frend.
> I say na mair, bot gentill redaris hend,
> Lat all my faltis with this offence pas by.[1]

30 Great Myths About Chaucer, First Edition. Thomas A. Prendergast and Stephanie Trigg.
© 2020 John Wiley & Sons, Inc. Published 2020 by John Wiley & Sons, Inc.

This full context is an important part of the picture. Douglas's description of Chaucer as "ever women's friend" is often quoted as a kind of proverbial one-liner, but his remark, like many in the long literary traditions of feminism and anti-feminism, is part of a complex power play between the sexes. Douglas self-consciously refrains from expounding on his remark – "I say na mair" – and appeals to his readers with a plea for their indulgence. He implies that there is more to say, but, out of respect to his gentle, noble company of readers, he asks forgiveness for this "offence" in criticizing Chaucer for taking Dido's part.

Douglas certainly learned this strategy from Chaucer, whose most overt comments about women are often similarly directed to a mixed context of men and women, or voice a mock civility towards women, as if the debate between the sexes were an amusing game he would like to provoke. Think of the Nun's Priest's mock fear that he will give offense if we take Chantecleer's dismissal of Pertelote's advice as reflecting his own view:

> But for I noot to whom it myght displese,
> If I conseil of wommen wolde blame,
> Passe over, for I seyde it in my game.
> Rede auctors, where they trete of swich mateere,
> And what they seyn of wommen ye may heere.
> Thise been the cokkes wordes, and nat myne;
> I kan noon harm of no womman divine.
>
> (VII.3260–66)

The contextual "dramatic" reading here often attributes this retraction to the priest's perception of a disapproving glance from the Prioress, his superior. Thus the priest seems to cede authority towards women and women's feelings, while also invoking the now notorious defenses of the misogynist: "I was just joking"; or "I'm sorry if anyone was offended."

When Chaucer ventures to express general attitudes to women, they are almost invariably associated with contest and conflict of some kind. Sometimes they take the form of this kind of throw-away remark. Sometimes his feminist and anti-feminist statements are hard to read through layers of a kind of habitual tonal awkwardness, as in the uncomfortable closure to the *Clerk's Tale*. After praising the astonishing forbearance and patience of Griselda, the Clerk admits it would be "importable" (intolerable) if all women were to behave like this. Indeed, he begs men not to test their wives in this way, but does seem to invite further debate between men and women when he introduces a song "for the Wyves love of Bathe" (IV.1170), which appears to encourage married women to be less slavishly patient than Griselda. The tone is uncertain, though: as with the many layers of gendered and dramatic impersonation in the *Wife of Bath's Prologue*, Chaucerian voice and attitudes can be extremely difficult to pin down. It would be almost impossible to point to a particular line of poetry as straightforward evidence for or against Chaucer's feminist views.

An early example of this problem of dramatic voice in relation to Chaucer's actual views might be found in R.M. Lumiansky's assessment of Chaucer's portrayal of the Wife of Bath:

> we shall find that the Wife's outstanding traits are aggressiveness and amo-rousness, and that the two combine to produce her militant feminism, which leads her to argue strongly for female sovereignty. Obviously, the tale she tells is aimed at illustrating this tenet; and her tale fits into the context of her antagonism toward antifeminist clerics, such as the Nun's Priest, who has just completed his tale, and towards recalcitrant husbands, such as Harry Bailly. But we shall also see that in the course of her perfor-mance Chaucer causes her to make clear certain unfavorable aspects of her character which she does not intend to reveal; she no doubt would look upon such revelation as a source of embarrassment.[2]

Such separations of author and text were, of course, characteristic of New Critical treatments and would come under a good deal of pressure from later critics, but it is true that a reductive reading of, for instance, Alison does not do justice to the sophistication of Chaucer's text.[3]

At other times, questions of tone are set aside for less ambiguous physi-cal strife, such as the rape that occasions Queen Guenevere's challenge to the young knight – what do women want? – in the *Wife of Bath's Tale*; or the episode of ugly domestic violence that concludes the Wife's *Prologue*. Frustrated by her handsome young husband Jankyn's perpetual reading aloud to her from his collection of anti-feminist stories about wicked wives, Alison snatches the book from his hand, rips out several pages and hits her husband on the cheek, whereupon he jumps up, enraged, and knocks her out (III.788–96), rendering her permanently deaf in one ear.

As an argument over a book, this contest between husband and wife plays out a famous literary struggle that was brewing in France at this time over the reception of *Le Roman de la Rose*. French writers such as Christine de Pizan and Jean Gerson, Chancellor of the University of Paris, defended women against some of the more misogynistic claims made against them by Jean de Meun, while in her *Book of the City of Ladies* (1405), Christine would assemble a whole allegorical city and commu-nity of women from Christian narratives, classical myths and contempo-rary examples. This is a far more programmatically pro-feminist literary work than anything Chaucer ever wrote. Perhaps Arlyn Diamond's assessment of Chaucer's partiality toward women best encapsulates 1970s-era attempts to enlist Chaucer in a feminist cause: "he means to be women's friend, insofar as he can be, and it is this painfully honest effort, this unwillingness to be satisfied with the formulas of his age, which we as feminists can honor in him."[4]

Yet, if we might look at Chaucer's *Legend of Good Women*, which at one level seems comparable to Christine's work, the poet seems a little less friendly to women. The conceit of the poem's elaborate dream-vision preface is that, having told the story of the faithless Criseyde in *Troilus and Criseyde*, Chaucer must now make amends and produce a text that is resolutely pro-woman. The God of Love and Queen Alcestis (the exemplary faithful woman who offered to die in place of her husband Admetus) appear in a dream and commission Chaucer to make recompense by writing the stories of some of the "twenty thousand" woman who were either virtuous or poorly treated by men. Chaucer does not complete this commission, however. His work presents only nine legends, and it is hard not to see the quality of the writing in these radically truncated stories as inferior to that of the *Troilus*. So much so, in fact, that a number of critics have been tempted to read this poem ironically, as if Chaucer were deliberately writing poorly in response to a commission from the queen. Would the point be that writing about virtuous women was boring? Or that writing to a commission (even from a queen) was boring?[5] Chaucer is careful not to say either of these things directly, and it may be that his encyclopedic intentions were indeed genuine, at least initially.

The individual legends are often quite curious in their attitudes. We will consider just one example here: the legend of Philomela. Chaucer uses this tale – and the sad laments of the two sisters turned into birds after Procne's husband Tereus had raped, mutilated and imprisoned Philomela – as an important point of lyrical reference in his *Troilus and Criseyde*. More generally, in European literary tradition the story has frequently been read as a narrative of women's work and sisterly understanding. Chaucer's *Legend* actually focuses more closely on Tereus's point of view, though the narrator roundly condemns the rape: "Lo! Here a dede of men, and that a right!" (F.2326). But soon after the rape, Chaucer is keen to close out the story: "O sely Philomene, wo is thyn herte! / God wreke thee, and sende the thy bone! / Now is it tyme I make an ende sone" (*Legend*, F.2339–41).

Although Tereus tears out Philomela's tongue, she is still able to weave a tapestry telling the story of her rape. She sends this to Procne, who then seeks out her sister in prison. Chaucer draws the story to an end at this point, leaving the two sisters in each other's arms, without telling the grisly tale (one that Gower does not scruple to omit in his *Confessio*

Amantis) of Procne's murder of her own and Tereus's son, served up for her husband's dinner in revenge for her sister's rape, or the Ovidian transformation of the two unhappy sisters into the swallow and the nightingale. Chaucer's narrator is impatient to get on with the next tale: "The remenaunt is no charge for to telle, / For this is al and some," he writes (F.2383–4). Like many of the re-told narratives in Christine's *Book of the City of Ladies*, this version represses the sisters' violent infanticidal revenge, closing with their sad reunion, and dwelling, albeit briefly, on their sorrow.

This sequence of tales about women as victims of men's infidelity and violence is woman centered, but the stories are very plot driven, and, like the *Philomela*, are often preoccupied with establishing the narrative contexts. Many of them also finish abruptly or bluntly in a similar fashion, as if ticking off another example of women's victimhood or virtue. The *Prologue* is far more complex, engaged with questions of representation and method as they concern the poet. It has attracted far more critical attention for what it seems to say about Chaucer's own attitudes to women, his relation to literary history and to patronage. So, while the *Legend of Good Women* is ostensibly a work in praise of women and subjects itself to women's authority, it puts the intellectual and artistic dilemmas of the male poet at its argumentative heart. Women's issues here are a problem for the narrator, so much so that Elaine Hansen acknowledges that either the narrator should be radically separated from "Chaucer" because "so overt are the biases of the narrator that readers are prevented from trusting him," or, perhaps, "the narrator might be much closer to the author ... but the object of the irony is still the antifeminist tradition; the narrator merely dons the mask of the antifeminist to make his satiric point."[6] As might be evident, Hansen's attempts to elicit a feminist Chaucer from his works (especially the *Legend*) reveal the difficulties in recuperating an ideological position from a work of art.

Of course, to many readers the idea developed in the *Legend* that Chaucer's *Troilus* might be an *anti*-feminist text actually comes as something of a surprise. Yes, it tells the story of a woman who "betrays" her lover, and yes, in the last section of the fifth book, from many perspectives we are encouraged to abandon the sympathy for her that the narrator has painstakingly developed. Troilus looks down from the heavens and laughs at the follies of earthly love; Pandarus has been quick to wash his hands of her ("I hate, ywis, Cryseyde," V.1732); and even the narrator starts to find fault with his heroine. In the most famous and most damning reading, D.W. Robertson reduces Criseyde's complex psychology to little more than a figure of "vanity," "fickleness," with a "conception of honor" that is "pitifully inadequate."[7]

Yet one of the first points of attention of the feminist critical tradition in Chaucer studies in the 1970s was to trace Chaucer's sympathetic portrayal of Criseyde: his subtle analysis of her emotional state, the fearfulness with which she faces an uncertain future in Troy without the protection of her father, her love for her homeland and her fear of disrupting the hard-won truce. Early feminist critics honored her community of female friends, who read and sing to each other; and drew attention to Criseyde's own wariness, in that having been married once before, she might not wish to subject herself again to the rule of a husband. Even though she is the subject of careful manipulation by Pandarus in his vicarious seduction on Troilus's behalf, and then becomes a pawn to be disposed of in the interests of the peace treaty proposed in Book IV, Criseyde nevertheless shows a high level of self-knowledge and self-determination, summed up best, perhaps, in her admission to Troilus, when he tries to claim his successful seduction, that she had knowingly and willingly followed the tortuous paths laid down by Pandarus: "Ne hadde I er now, my swete herte deere, / Ben yold, ywis, I were now nought heere" (III.1210–11; "If I had not already yielded, my dear sweet heart, I wouldn't be here now").[8]

As many critics observe, *Troilus and Criseyde* is a poem about predestination and free will. The poem is also particularly alert to the special disempowerment of women in a patriarchal society where women are "exchanged" between men (whether illicitly, in the case of Helen, or as a means of brokering peace, as in the case of Criseyde). Chaucer gives full recognition to the conflicting emotional states this produces, and it is not only Troilus who ponders these questions in his long soliloquy on predestination in Book IV; Criseyde also considers the nature of free will and fortune (III.820–36).

We can get a sense of the prevailing views on women, however, by contrasting the less sympathetic judgments of Criseyde by Chaucer's followers: Wynkyn de Worde, who adds several stanzas to the end of his copy praising "parfyte" Troilus and likening Criseyde to Fortune; or Robert Henryson, whose *Testament of Cresseid* invents a book which portrays Criseyde as abandoned by Diomede, becoming used "in commune" by the Greeks, before she is eventually cursed with leprosy after profaning the god Cupid. Jonathan Sidnam, too, circa 1630, translated the first three books of the poem, but refused to go any further, not wanting to rehearse "the wanton slipps of this deceitfull Dame."[9]

Such responses remind us how quickly debates about attitudes to women slip easily into conventional and stereotypical anti-feminist discourse, and how rapidly the "bad" behavior of a female character can lead to discussions about feminism. As R. Howard Bloch points out, this structural shift from an individual to a gendered collective is one of the structural features of misogyny.[10]

Since the 1980s, the varieties of feminist criticism have offered a number of more subtle accounts of Chaucer's writing, sometimes praising a sensibility that seems attuned to women's lives, sometimes critiquing his complicity with patriarchal norms, sometimes examining the rhetorical forms of address that use women's narratives as a means of appealing to a predominantly male readership, and sometimes analyzing the pro- or anti-feminist ideologies of older criticism.

When we ask whether Chaucer was a feminist, though, we seek in vain for any firm evidence of his philosophical attitudes to women beyond his writings, and the default position has been to extend the general idea of his benevolent humanity to include his attitudes to women.

Our next myth, however, offers an unpleasant challenge to this idea of a benevolent Chaucer.

Notes

1 Gavin Douglas, *The Poetical Works of Gavin Douglas, Bishop of Dunkeld*, Vol. II, with notes and glossary by John Small (Edinburgh: William Paterson; London: H. Sotheran, 1874), 18.

2 R.M. Lumiansky, *Of Sondry Folk: The Dramatic Principle of the Canterbury Tales* (Austin, TX: University of Texas Press, 1955), 119.

3 Regarding this particular text, see, for instance, Marshall Leicester's *The Disenchanted Self: Representing the Subject in the* Canterbury Tales (Berkeley, CA: University of California Press, 1990), 66.

4 Arlyn Diamond, "Chaucer's Women and Women's Chaucer," in *The Authority of Experience*, ed. Arlyn Diamond and Lee R. Edwards (Amherst, MA: University of Massachusetts Press, 1977), 83.

5 R.W. Frank's *Chaucer and the Legend of Good Women* (Cambridge, MA: Harvard University Press, 1972), 25. On the "legend of Chaucer's boredom" see 189–210.

6 Elaine Tuttle Hansen, *Chaucer and the Fictions of Gender* (Berkeley, CA: University of California Press, 1992), 2. She is, in fact, narrating a position that she would partially move on from in her monograph.

7 D.W. Robertson, Jr., *A Preface to Chaucer: Studies in Medieval Perspective* (Princeton, NJ: Princeton University Press, 1962), 271, 498, 499.

8 For landmark works on feminist criticism and Chaucer, see Carolyn Dinshaw's *Chaucer's Sexual Poetics* (Madison, WI: University of Wisconsin Press, 1989), and Hansen's *Chaucer and the Fictions of Gender*.

9 Jonathan Sidnam, *A Paraphrase upon the three first Bookes of Chaucers Troilus and Cressida* (MS 1630) in *Geoffrey Chaucer: The Critical Heritage, Vol. 1, 1385–1837*, ed. Derek Brewer (London: Routledge, 1978), 149–51, here 151.

10 R. Howard Bloch, *Medieval Misogyny and the Invention of Western Romantic Love* (Chicago, IL: University of Chicago Press, 1991).

Myth 11

CHAUCER WAS GUILTY OF RAPE

On 4 May 1380, in the Court of Chancery, Cecily Chaumpaigne, daughter of the late William Chaumpaigne and his wife Agnes, had a deed of release enrolled in the close rolls in which she

> remitted, released, and entirely quitclaimed on behalf of myself and my heirs in perpetuity Geoffrey Chaucer, esq., all manner of actions such as they relate to my rape [*de raptu meo*], or any other thing or cause, and of whatever condition they are, that I ever had, have, or could have, from the beginning of the world down to the day of making the present things.[1]

The document was witnessed by five of Chaucer's friends and affixed with Cecily Chaumpaigne's seal. It then sat in the Tower of London, presumably unnoticed, until 1856 when it was transferred to the Public Records Office. Sometime in 1873, F.J. Furnivall (with the help of the antiquary William Floyd) discovered the document and, in a column that went by the name "Literary Gossip," it was announced not only that Furnivall had found it, but almost immediately afterwards that there was nothing to see, "that this deed may have merely set at rest an unfounded claim is more than possible, otherwise the release would have been compounding a felony, if the law was then as it is now, and would hardly have been witnessed by the deed enrolled."[2]

Furnivall probably would have been satisfied to leave it there, but it is apparent that his discovery had piqued the curiosity of his fellow Chaucerians and he was obliged to print the document in a supplement to his work on Chaucer's minor poems.[3] He also included a treatment of the laws governing rape in the medieval period, as well as a gloss on the word used by Chaumpaigne in the deed of release, *raptus*: it "was used

30 Great Myths About Chaucer, First Edition. Thomas A. Prendergast and Stephanie Trigg.
© 2020 John Wiley & Sons, Inc. Published 2020 by John Wiley & Sons, Inc.

for the abduction of an heir, of a man's wife and goods, &c., as well as for the rape of a virgin, &c."[4] Furnivall concludes:

> While I wish this record about Cecilia Chaumpaigne had not been on the Close Roll, yet, as it was there, I feel much obliged to Mr Floyd for pointing it out; as, if we take the worst possible view of it—violent rape not being possible—it only shows that a thing happend, which any one, from certain of Chaucer's Tales, must have known might well have happend, and which was hardly considerd a fault in the gentleman of his day.[5]

One wonders how much Furnivall was really grateful to Floyd, as his response to the document is almost immediately to mitigate the charge of rape, both by suggesting that the word *raptus* might mean only abduction and that the charge might merely have resulted from the fact that Chaucer "lay with her" – hardly a fault in a "gentleman of his day."[6] We barely need point out that Furnivall's assertion – "violent rape not being possible"– is merely that: the critic's insistence that he does not believe Chaucer would be capable of rape.

As we might expect, most Chaucerian biographers and scholars are, like Furnivall, reluctant to say definitively that Chaucer was a rapist. We may compare the similar charges of rape against Thomas Malory, the author of the *Morte Darthur*. His biographer Christina Hardyment, in 2005, claimed that this charge "collapses like a house of cards" under pressure of "serious scrutiny." Her circular logic is very similar to Furnivall's: "His role in the Joan Smith affair was exactly what we would expect of the author of the *Morte Darthur*: that of a knight chivalrously embarking on the rescue of a damsel in distress, and succeeding after a first, failed attempt."[7] The biographer's temptation to extrapolate a life from an author's narrative fictions and his or her fictional voices is indeed immense.

In Chaucer's case, it is often suggested that the "quality" of the friends Chaucer calls on to witness this deed of release are further evidence of his innocence. How could such important men – so clearly part of a powerful homosocial friendship group – be wrong about the character of the poet?[8] D.S. Brewer even suggested we might wonder or marvel at the "powerful passions" the incident evokes.[9]

It is fair to say that contemporary critics have taken a much more jaundiced view of this particular document. The word *raptus*, for instance, may seem to shade into the meaning for abduction rather than forced coitus – reflecting a legal attempt "to prevent women and men from using accusations of rape to manipulate or avoid marriage strictures."[10] But as Christopher Cannon has demonstrated, in this form, and in the way in which it appears in the deed of release, it pretty clearly connotes what we would consider rape. Other documents, in fact, enrolled in the court of the mayor and aldermen of London in June and July of the same year, but clearly bearing on the Chaumpaigne matter, suggest a complicated legal workaround whereby Chaucer made a payment of ten pounds to Cecily Chaumpaigne through associates (a very large amount – over half of what Chaucer received yearly for being Controller of Customs), thus managing to keep his name out of any direct connection with the payment.[11] It is difficult at such a far remove to ascertain precisely what was going on, but it certainly looks like Chaucer was interested in secretly paying off Chaumpaigne.

We may get some clue from another document discovered by Christopher Cannon that is dated three days after the initial deed of release was recorded in the close rolls. On 7 May 1380, a "memorandum" was copied in the Court of King's Bench that was purportedly the original deed of release that had been entered into the close rolls. But there was a significant difference: this copied document omitted the phrase *de raptu meo*.[12] The suggestion is that Chaucer went to some lengths to have that phrase retracted (perhaps with the complicity of Chaumpaigne, as she herself was present at the enrolling). Why go to so much trouble to suppress the reference in this document since it was already enrolled elsewhere? As Cannon shows, the memoranda at the Court of King's Bench were much more accessible and more often referenced than the close rolls. The implication is that Chaucer used his connections to suppress a phrase in a publicly available document that would have been as controversial in the fourteenth century as it is in the twenty-first.

Of course, all this really proves is that Chaucer was accused of rape and went to great lengths to prevent the case from coming to trial, and that Chaumpaigne seems to have made some kind of settlement that led her to release Chaucer from any actions pertaining to her rape. In her recent biography of Chaucer, Marion Turner spends relatively little time – two pages, at most – on the topic of Cecily's accusation. She acknowledges that the "raptus" charge was almost certainly an accusation of sexual rape, but quickly moves to an agnostic position. "We don't know," she writes, about the precise nature of the incident, though she does not hesitate later to describe Chaucer's relations with Cecily as "disastrous."[13] More recently, Sebastian Sobecki has suggested that Chaucer might have abducted Cecily Chaumpaigne in order to arrange a marriage with his ward Edmund Staplegate. But he also acknowledges that

> just because he was legally entitled to arrange a marriage for his ward between 1377 and 1382 does not mean that Cecily Chaumpaigne was not a victim of Chaucer's sexual aggression. If the legal documents associated with her were linked to Chaucer's interest in arranging a marriage for

Edmund Staplegate, then a new interpretive trajectory emerges. But if her case was not linked to Chaucer's guardianship, then *raptus* meaning rape remains the empirically strongest interpretation of the Chaumpaigne records.[14]

So, a number of questions remain. What was the precise nature of the act that led to Chaumpaigne's deed of release? Why did she agree to it? To what extent did Chaucer believe or not believe that he was guilty of rape? By rape, do we mean medieval notions of rape or late modern understandings of the word?

To the first question, absent some spectacular discovery of additional documents, we will never know what the action was that led to the description of the act from which Chaucer was quitclaimed. So, too, we will never know why Cecily Chaumpaigne agreed to release Chaucer from any actions against him for the offense. It is possible, for instance, as one biographer has argued, that Chaumpaigne actually threatened to bring a charge of rape against Chaucer to win compensation from him, and that the original charge was not the offense named in the deed.[15] But this, like Furnivall's attempts to mitigate the charges against Chaucer, has to reside in the space of mere conjecture. Did Chaucer believe he was guilty? This too remains unknown. It is evident that he did not want the charges brought against him, and it is also evident that he understood that their nature was explosive. He might have believed he was guilty, or he might have simply wished to avoid the calumny of being charged with rape.

The last question is more complicated and thus gets to the heart of the matter. In many ways the question of what constitutes rape seems relatively simple – it is non-consensual sex. There might be different kinds of non-consensual sex (statutory rape, violent rape), but they all involve the unwillingness or incapacity of one party or another to consent to coitus. But establishing what constitutes consent, in a legal sense, is more difficult. Contemporary laws rely on the notion that an interior state of consent be exteriorized in an action: "positive cooperation." Yet there can also be a conflicting attitude that can be hidden by a cooperative act. The result is that certainty about an interior consensual status or act of willingness cannot be ascertained. There are, thus, "acts of rape that remain unknown to the law."[16]

If modern legal conceptions of rape are at worst faulty or at best uncertain, medieval notions of rape were no less problematic. There were, of course, differences in how rape was defined (the possibility of spousal rape, for instance, is modern). At the same time, there is no doubt about the nature or definition of violent rape that clearly violates the consent of one of the partners. We see an example in the *Wife of Bath's Tale* when a "mayde" is taken by a knight "maugree hir heed" (against her will). Chaucer is clear here: "By verray force, he rafte hire maydenhed" (III.887–8). As consent is so very clearly not given, the entire tale might well be seen as a meditation not on the definition of rape, but on the understanding of how to respect the exercise of another's free will.

Moreover, what about those moments when free consent is difficult to recognize? Or seems to come retrospectively? The law's confusion between abduction (or ravishment) and rape makes it difficult here, but there does seem to be some suggestion that consent after the act would be seen as different than if there had been no consent (though, as already noted, if force is used there can be no retrospective consent).[17] In terms of thinking about how all of this might affect our understanding of Chaucer and his works, critics have turned to his own meditations on the nature of rape or, in one case, an instance where he did not label something as rape.

In the denouement to Chaucer's *Reeve's Tale* (discussed briefly in Myth 9), two clerks, desiring revenge on a miller who had cheated them, conspire to "swyve" his wife and daughter. The wife, being tricked into believing one clerk to be her husband, has no objection to the act, though she presumably would if she knew the truth. The situation of the daughter is more difficult. When the other clerk sneaks into her bed, it is reported,

> This wenche lay uprighte and faste slepte,
> Til he so ny was, er she myghte espie,
> That it had been to late for to crie,
> And shortly for to seyn, they were aton.
>
> (I.4194–7)

In modern terms both of these actions would be categorized as rape, but medieval law is less clear. The daughter, in particular, initially has no time to consent, but then later refers to the clerk as her "dear lover" and even gives him a going-away present. Is this post-coital consent? And does it mitigate the charge of rape? Medieval law would seem to suggest that it might, unless force was used, which remains unclear.

Nevertheless, whether this tale can tell us anything about Chaucer's understanding of the nature of rape or consent or about his own encounter with a rape charge is more problematic. For one thing, the literary genre of the tale makes it difficult to subject the represented acts of coitus to legal interpretation. Chaucer was working within the tradition of the fabliau genre and was, in fact, only retelling a tale (or, importantly, having a literary character within his literary fiction retell a tale) that had been told elsewhere. This does not mean that we should ignore the fact that the tale contains sex that we would consider non-consensual, nor does it mean that we should conveniently forget the existence of a certain document from 4 May 1380. It means that we should acknowledge the uncertainty of whether his representation of coitus here, or elsewhere in his works, has any bearing on what happened with Cecily Chaumpaigne because of what that deed of release does not tell us – the nature of the act that she calls *raptus*.

Notes

1 "remisisse, relaxasse, et omnino pro me et heredibus meis imperpetuum quietum clamasse Galfrido Chaucer, armigero, omnimodas acciones, tam de raptu meo, tam [sic] de aliqua alia re vel causa, cuiuscumque condicionis fuerint, quas vnquam habui, habeo, seu habere potero, a principio mundi vsque in diem confeccionis presencium." Martin M. Crow and Clair C. Olson, eds., *Chaucer Life-Records* (Oxford: Oxford University Press, 1966), 343.

2 *The Athenaeum* 2405 (29 November 1873), 698.

3 F.J. Furnivall, *Trial Forewords to my "Parallel Text Edition of Chaucer's Minor Poems"* (London: N. Trübner, 1871), 136–44.

4 Ibid., 136.

5 Ibid., 143.

6 Ibid., 142.

7 Christina Hardyment, *Malory: The Knight Who Became King Arthur's Chronicler* (New York: Harper, 2006), 304.

8 Stephanie Trigg, *Congenial Souls: Reading Chaucer from Medieval to Postmodern* (Minneapolis, MN: Minnesota University Press, 2002), 36–37.

9 D.S. Brewer, *A New Introduction to Chaucer*, 2nd ed. (London: Longman, 1998), 118.

10 Christopher Cannon, "*Raptus* in the Chaumpaigne Release and a Newly Discovered Document Concerning the Life of Geoffrey Chaucer," *Speculum* 68 (1993), 74–94, here 81.

11 Derek Pearsall, *The Life of Geoffrey Chaucer: A Critical Biography* (Cambridge, MA: Blackwell, 1992), 136–7.

12 Cannon, "*Raptus* in the Chaumpaigne Release," 90–94.

13 Marion Turner, *Chaucer: A European Life* (Princeton, NJ: Princeton University Press, 2019), 211, 271.

14 Sebastian Sobecki, "Wards and Widows: *Troilus and Criseyde* and New Documents on Chaucer's Life," *English Literary History* 86, no. 2 (Summer, 2019), 423.

15 Pearsall, *Life of Geoffrey Chaucer*, 137.

16 Christopher Cannon, "Chaucer and Rape: Uncertainty's Certainties," in *Representing Rape in Medieval and Early Modern Literature*, ed. Christine Rose and Elizabeth Robertson (New York: Palgrave, 2001), 255–79, here 258. Much of what follows is indebted to Cannon's careful consideration of the problem of Chaucer and rape, though we disagree a little with his conclusions.

17 *Statutes of the Realm* (London: Dawsons of Pall Mall, 1810–28), I:87.

Myth

12

CHAUCER HAD A FALLING OUT WITH HIS BEST FRIEND

Sometime around 1540, the antiquary John Leland wrote a life of Geoffrey Chaucer that (despite its shortcomings) proved to be a principal source of Chaucerian biographies at least until the nineteenth century. In it Leland claimed that no sooner had the writer John Gower "perceived and proved the genius and worth of Chaucer than he made of him an intimate friend, took him to his embrace, looked upon him as one of his noblest delights—in short honored him almost as if he were some divinity."[1] Leland would seem to have had good evidence for his claim, as Gower has the character of Venus (from his *Confessio Amantis*) praise Chaucer:

> As mi disciple and mi poete
> For in the floures of his youthe
> In sondri wise, as he wel couthe,
> Of Ditees and of songes glade,
> The whiche he for mi sake made,
> The lond fulfild is overall:
> Wherof to him in special
> Above alle othre I am most holde.[2]

Leland interpreted Venus's voice as Gower's own, and read Venus's high regard as an indication of Chaucer's own discipleship to Venus, but also to Gower himself.

30 Great Myths About Chaucer, First Edition. Thomas A. Prendergast and Stephanie Trigg.
© 2020 John Wiley & Sons, Inc. Published 2020 by John Wiley & Sons, Inc.

Chaucer, for his part, seemed to have reciprocated the praise, famously dedicating his *Troilus and Criseyde* to Gower (and Ralph Strode):

> O moral Gower, this book I directe
> To the and to the, philosophical Strode,
> To vouchen sauf, ther nede is, to correcte,
> Of youre benignites and zeles goode.
>
> (V.1856–9)

The printer Thomas Berthelette affixed these words to his 1532 version of the *Confessio Amantis* and wrote of them: "by the whiche wordes of Chauser, we may also vnderstande that he and Gower were bothe of one selfe tyme, both excellently lerned, [and] both great frendes to gether."[3] While the evidence might seem slim for this grand assertion of poetical amity (especially as it understands Venus's words as Gower's own), even contemporary commentators suggest that the dedication demonstrates that Gower and Chaucer formed part of a small group whose moral, philosophical and aesthetic capacities enabled them to operate as a "special interpretive community."[4]

Yet in 1775, Thomas Tyrwhitt, in his commentary on Chaucer's Man of Law's Tale, argued that something must have gone amiss with this relationship. Tyrwhitt points out that in the prologue to his tale, the Man of Law rejects stories of incest like the "wikke ensample of Canacee, / That loved hir owene brother synfully / ... Or ellis of Tyro Apollonius, / How that the cursed kyng Antiochus / Birafte of his doghter hir maydenhede" (II.79–80; 82–4). Further, the Man of Law remarks that Chaucer never wrote of such things because they were "unkynde abhomynacions" (II.88). Tyrwhitt points out that if Chaucer did not relate such stories, Gower did and

> if the reflection ... upon those who relate such stores as that of *Canace*, or of *Appollonius Tyrius*, was leveled at Gower, as I very much suspect, it will be difficult to reconcile such an attack to our notions of the strict friendship, which is generally supposed to have subsisted between the two bards.[5]

Tyrwhitt also notes that "in the new edition of the *Confessio Amantis*, which Gower published after the accession of Henry IV, the verses in praise of Chaucer are omitted."[6] The suggestion is that Gower, angry at Chaucer for taking a literary potshot at him, redacted the verses.

This is a pretty thin rationale for a full-fledged quarrel, so perhaps it was to be expected that critics sought a more substantial reason for their purported "breakup." Attention turned to the possibility of a more serious rivalry that was both professional and poetic in nature. Critics seized on the fact that in the versions of the *Confessio Amantis* where Venus's compliments to Chaucer were excised, so too was the dedication altered from Richard II to his eventual usurper, Henry of Lancaster. And so in the mid-nineteenth century, one anonymous critic asked:

> Was Gower's homage to the son of Chaucer's early patron [John of Gaunt] the cause of this hostility? Did the poet, so highly esteemed by John of Gaunt, deem himself sole laureate of the house of Lancaster, and therefore resent, with the keen sense of actual wrong the dedication of the *Confessio Amantis* to the heir of that house?[7]

As suggested by the interrogative nature of these suggestions, literary jealousy as a rationale for "the quarrel" was at best highly speculative. Nonetheless, the broad outlines of this rationale continued to be repeated well into the twentieth century and they were joined by other explanations. Chaucer and Gower split along political lines: Chaucer favoring Richard while Gower was busy rededicating the *Confessio* to his usurper. Or, Chaucer was a critic of the Catholic Church, inclining towards Wycliffism, while Gower was a resolute supporter of the Church.[8]

As might be clear, these explanations, far from affirming the quarrel, only highlighted the extent to which any corroboration for it was circumstantial. As John Fisher put it, "the evidence for an association between the two men is external as well as internal. The evidence for a quarrel depends exclusively upon interpretations placed upon possible allusions in their works."[9] Chaucer certainly esteemed and trusted Gower – we know as much from his use of Gower as his lawyer in 1378, and from his dedication of the *Troilus* to the older poet. Chaucer may have been poking fun at his friend in the *Man of Law's Tale*, but if he was, it is something of a stretch to claim that it resulted in or was the result of a quarrel. Gower seems to have reciprocated Chaucer's esteem. Though it is Venus rather than Gower himself who gives the encomium to Chaucer, it is hard not to read her praise as a reflection of Gower's own. The omission of this passage from a later version of the work could be the result of any number of reasons. Perhaps the revision was a simple aesthetic choice, or maybe it would have been less timely to have Venus suggest that Chaucer finish his "testament of love" while he was working on the *Canterbury Tales*. And while we cannot be sure about the level of interaction between Chaucer and Gower, it is even possible that Chaucer himself suggested the revision.[10] In short, the explanations for the quarrel are all built on the unsupported assumption that there was a quarrel.

By the end of the twentieth century, the idea that the two men had a "quarrel," a disagreement that was serious enough to abrogate their relationship, had faded away. It was never "disproven," but rather down-graded. As one of Chaucer's biographers put it, the lines in the *Man of Law's Tale* were part of a

> private joke directed at Gower ... an audience of their poetical friends must have found this funny, and it is funny enough still; whether Gower thought it was funny is another question. He and Chaucer had a real disagreement, and it may have caused some tension between them, but the old notion that they quarreled is clearly not true.[11]

As Carolyn Dinshaw has pointed out, this diminution of the antagonism of the two men transforms the quarrel into a rivalrous exchange, but it does not quite lay the "ghost" of the myth to rest.[12] So why does this idea of poetic antagonism remain?

We see the roots of the impulses behind the myth in a biography of Chaucer published some thirty years after Tyrwhitt's initial assertion that there was a quarrel. William Godwin opines that "the breach between Chaucer and Gower has resemblance to that between Shakespear [sic] and Jonson, two of the most eminent English geniuses of the six-teenth century."[13] In an anachronistic move, Godwin transfers the rival-rous emulation of the Elizabethan playwrights back into the fourteenth century. There is, apparently, something in the recognition of "genius" that generates a narrative of poetical antagonism. There are two reasons for this imaginative antagonism. First, in a rivalry, one person must nec-essarily come out on top. In the "contretemps" between Shakespeare and Jonson, Godwin leaves no doubt that he believes it is only the death of Shakespeare that enables Jonson to escape his persistent (and by Godwin's lights, justified) feelings of inferiority and celebrate the play-wright in the First Folio as "not of an age but for all time!"[14] So too, with Gower, the imagined rivalry never redounds to his benefit. Throughout the nineteenth century and well into the twentieth, "Gower was to play the lumbering fall guy to the nimble and free-spirited Chaucer."[15] The antagonism, in other words, raises Chaucer above the supposed quotidian dullness of medieval complaint poetry (of the kind that Gower wrote) and makes him someone, like Shakespeare, who tran-scends his age.

Alternatively, or perhaps additionally, rivalry tends to consolidate identity – making clear the differences between two rivals. In the case of Chaucer and Gower, the establishment of a coherent Chaucerian identity tended to focus on the "manly" qualities of Chaucer. In large part, of course, this was the result of Chaucerian reading communities in the eighteenth, nineteenth and twentieth centuries that themselves tended to be largely masculine. What made Chaucer canonical was the ability of those in these reading communities to identify with him. And given the makeup of these communities, it is perhaps unsurprising to see Chaucer's masculinity so obviously stressed by editors, readers and critics like F.J. Furnivall, Leigh Hunt and Derek Brewer.[16] The supposed quarrel with Gower enabled readers to see Chaucer as one who triumphed over his lesser, secondary and thus feminized foe. As Dinshaw puts it, "traditionally feminine traits—timidity, dependency, secondariness, sycophancy, insincerity, fickleness, dullness—were adduced only to be explicitly expelled. ... most often the manly Chaucer was purged of Gower's femininity."[17] Thus, even in the absence of any positive, historical evidence the specter of the quarrel subsisted, not because there was any epistemological justification, but because a certain set of ideologies – Chaucer the transcendent poet, Chaucer the man – formed the quarrel and were themselves incompletely expelled from critical discourse.

Notes

1 Derek Brewer, ed., *Chaucer: The Critical Heritage, Volume I: 1385–1837* (London: Routledge and Kegan Paul, 1978), 91–2.

2 John Gower, *Confessio Amantis*, 8:2942–9, in *The English Works of John Gower*, Vol. II, ed. G.C. Macaulay, EETS e.s. 82 (Oxford: Clarendon Press, 1900–02, reprinted 1971).

3 Quoted in Caroline Spurgeon, *Five Hundred Years of Chaucer Criticism and Allusion 1357–1900* (Cambridge: Cambridge University Press, 1925), I:77–8.

4 The phrase is Paul Strohm's from *Social Chaucer* (Cambridge, MA: Harvard University Press, 1989), p. 59.

5 Thomas Tyrwhitt, *The Canterbury tales of Chaucer: to which are added, an essay on his language and versification; an introductory discourse; and notes*, 5 vols. (London, 1775–78), 4:147.

6 Ibid., 4:147–8.

7 "John Gower and his Works," *British Quarterly Review* 27 (1858), 3–36, here 11.

8 John Fisher's treatment of the development of the idea of the quarrel remains the most authoritative: *John Gower: Moral Philosopher and Friend of Chaucer* (New York: New York University Press, 1964), 1–36.

9 Ibid., 28.

10 For an intriguing hypothesis that Chaucer and Gower were based in Southwark at the same time, see Sebastian Sobecki, "A Southwark Tale: Gower, the 1381 Poll Tax and Chaucer's *Canterbury Tales*," *Speculum* 92 (2017), 630–60.

11 Donald R. Howard, *Chaucer: His Life, His Works, His World* (New York: Dutton, 1987), 420.

12 Carolyn Dinshaw, "Rivalry, Rape and Manhood: Gower and Chaucer," in *Chaucer and Gower: Difference, Mutuality, Exchange*, ed. Robert F. Yeager (Victoria, BC: University of Victoria, 1991), 130–52, here 131.

13 William Godwin, *Life of Geoffrey Chaucer* (London: 1804), 4:84.

14 Ben Jonson, "Preface to the First Folio," in *Mr. William Shakespeares Comedies, Histories, & Tragedies* (London: E. Blount, William and Isaac Jaggard, 1623).

15 Dinshaw, "Rivalry, Rape and Manhood," 132.

16 Stephanie Trigg, *Congenial Souls: Reading Chaucer from Medieval to Postmodern* (Minneapolis, MN: University of Minnesota Press, 2002), xxi, 167–8, 183.

17 Dinshaw, "Rivalry, Rape and Manhood," 133.

Myth
13
CHAUCER LIVED IN THE MIDDLE AGES

What could be more obvious? Of course Chaucer lived in the Middle Ages and it would be one of the most well-known things about him. Indeed, as we suggest a number of times, it is sometimes hard to disentangle our ideas about Chaucer from our ideas about the Middle Ages; so much so that the phrase "the age of Chaucer" is sometimes used to describe the second half of the fourteenth century. So why would this count as a myth?

Many historians and literary critics take issue with the widespread cultural appropriation and abjection of words like "medieval" to describe anything that is perceived as old-fashioned or outmoded; or the careless use of the phrase "dark ages" to describe the many centuries between early Latin and Greek scholarship and their so-called re-birth or "renaissance" in fifteenth-century Europe. On those grounds alone we might well resist the easy identification of Chaucer with the Middle Ages. But in this "myth," we discuss the somewhat different question of Chaucer's experience of his own temporality. Viewed in this light, it is immediately apparent that Chaucer did not live in the middle of anything, since of course he had no sense that his historical period would come to be seen as squeezed between two more highly valued cultural formations.

Medieval views about time and periodization were very complex. In a symptom of the abjection of the medieval as primitive, naïve and superstitious in comparison to the "new science" of the Renaissance, it is sometimes argued that medieval people experienced time as a kind of continuous present that would come to an end only with the millennial apocalypse in the year 1000. It is true that medieval culture had a greater tolerance of what we would call historical anachronism. In some respects this understanding of time subtended medieval religion and faith, in that the events

30 Great Myths About Chaucer, First Edition. Thomas A. Prendergast and Stephanie Trigg.
© 2020 John Wiley & Sons, Inc. Published 2020 by John Wiley & Sons, Inc.

of Christ's life, for example, are often represented as if taking place in a kind of continual present. Christ's passion and forgiveness, the joy of his mother in his birth and childhood, and her grief at his death: all these emotional events are celebrated and commemorated in the regular liturgical cycles of the church year, and are also available as a powerful emotional resource at other times, especially in the later Middle Ages when a stronger affective response was often elicited in literary works and spiritual writings. But this temporal immediacy was also layered against a strong sense of historical or linear time, which stretched from the creation of the world and which was fundamentally changed by the advent of Christ.

In the famous opening to the *Canterbury Tales*, Chaucer shows how he is able to weave several of these temporal strands together quite effortlessly, even knowingly: the seasonal cycles of the natural world; the historical event of St. Thomas's martyrdom in the Cathedral; and the mixed forms of religious and secular observation in his own time and seasons, as he plays with our expectations of amorous and erotic poetry and the mixed devotional and entertainment imperatives of pilgrimage.

In other texts, Chaucer's approach to time and his attitude to what we describe as medieval culture is much more complex. His *Troilus and Criseyde*, for example, offers a very nuanced version of cultural and temporal layering, though it is not without contradictions. The poem is set in ancient Troy, in the city under siege by the Greeks. The poet, the audience and some of the characters are aware that Troy will be destroyed, while others are ignorant of that future, and so there is already the customary narrative tension of telling a well-known story. Towards the end of the poem, when Criseyde realizes her future reputation will be as a faithless woman, this temporal distinction begins to disintegrate. The narrator, too, seems to find it hard to proceed with this aspect of the story, since the narrative destiny of the characters seems increasingly shaped by the inevitable twisting and turning of the wheel of Fortune.

Initially, Trojan urban culture is presented as fully and interestingly pagan, as the citizens pay honor to Athena. And yet, in so many other respects the dominant cultural forms and expectations of behavior in this poem are modeled on late medieval English culture: the form of discussion and debate in the parliament; the domestic interior scenes in the houses of Criseyde, Pandarus and Deiphebus, or the palace of Troilus; even the presiding ethos of courtly love that insists the love affair be kept secret. The narrative and conversational exchanges of the poem, too, are framed in the discourse of late medieval London: sophisticated banter; Christian allusions; and a high degree of self-consciousness about forms of behavior. Let us take one example: Pandarus suggests Criseyde put aside her nun-like veil (mourning for her husband, or contrition for her father's abandonment) and dance to "do observaunce" to May. She is horrified at the prospect of drawing such attention to herself, and says he is mad, wild and raving. She knows very clearly what she should do:

> It satte me wel bet ay in a cave
> To bidde and rede on holy seyntes lyves;
> Lat maydens gon to daunce, and yonge wyves.
>
> (II.117–19)

Criseyde is conscious of the appropriate behavior for a widow (and indeed, for all three traditional categories of women), while her allusion to an anchoress's seclusion and devotion is of course tied to the idea of the Christian saints. It is a small but telling example of Chaucer's high tolerance for cultural and historical anachronism in his fiction; here, the psychological and emotional "truth" of Criseyde's shocked response is more important to his fictional project than researching what the appropriate forms of behavior for Trojan women might be. (This is also the kind of behavioral anachronism that is often found in medievalist fiction, where it is equally met with various degrees of tolerance from readers.)

There is another way of thinking about Chaucer's medievalness and his temporality, through the problematic lens of cultural history and periodization. These somewhat arbitrary narratives attempt to make sense of cultural history and change, dividing history into manageable epochs, for both pedagogical and more general historical reasons. It is a not unreasonable approach, but it is inevitably beset by a number of problems. First, cultural change does not occur evenly across different countries and cultures, even in the same broad geographical region; and such change is also experienced with tremendous differences according to factors such as age, gender, education, urban or rural setting, and whether one participates in the work of cultural and linguistic elites and religious majorities or not. There is no obvious "beginning" or "end" of the Middle Ages, for example. Second, it has come to seem almost inevitable that each era promotes itself as a vast improvement on the previous one; and of all the eras in Western history that tell this story about themselves, the most successful at it was the Renaissance. Even this term names the period's sense of itself as recovering the forgotten learning of the ancient world, which it argued was lost to obscurity and ignorance during the Middle Ages. Those facts are disputed, but without re-visiting this much-discussed issue, let us focus on Chaucer's own situation in relation to cultural change and his sense of his own temporality.

While Chaucer is undoubtedly a "medieval" writer in terms of his deep embeddedness in medieval religious culture, he was far from insular or disconnected from the writers and thinkers associated with the "Renaissance," particularly in Italy, where artists and writers were experimenting with different forms of perspective, spatial relationships and subjectivity. Marion Turner emphasizes Chaucer's experiences in Genoa and Florence and his participation in this new urban and mercantile aesthetic: "the same broad social and economic factors enabled the production both of visual art and of poetry that was especially interested in partiality, in incompletion, in imperfect perspectives."[1] Chaucer was familiar with the works of Petrarch, Dante and Boccaccio, for example, from his trips to Italy in the 1370s. He knew how to move between the "Virgilian" and the "Ovidian" versions of the story of Dido and Aeneas in his *The House of Fame*: the first favoring the development of imperial power; the second focusing on the history of personal, individual feeling. And in *The Parlement of Foules* he stages the kind of dialogue with the ancient figure (in this case Scipio Africanus) that is often associated with Renaissance humanism. In the same poem he also seems to align himself with newer forms of knowledge, gained from a return to older, classical books, when he describes reading the *Somnium Scipionis* of Cicero:

> For out of olde feldes, as men seyth,
> Cometh al this newe corn from yer to yere,
> And out of olde bokes, in good feyth,
> Cometh al this newe science that men lere.
>
> (ll. 22–5)

As an indication of their significance for the Renaissance recognition of Chaucer, these four lines appear on a cartouche as part of the elaborate framing at the top of the title page of Speght's 1598 edition of Chaucer's *Collected Works*, where they are paired with a brief quotation from Ovid in the frame along the lower edge.

Chaucer also seems to participate in many of the intellectual and bookish practices we associate with the Renaissance. For example, at the end of his *Troilus and Criseyde*, while he submits his work to his friends Gower and Strode for correction, he also sends off his book in its envoi to keep company in some kind of timeless celestial realm with the classical authors, Virgil, Ovid, Homer, Lucan and Statius. And it is worth reminding ourselves, as many commentators point out, that Chaucer had substantial exposure to Italian *quattrocento* culture, in a way that pre-figured many of the discoveries of this world that are so often taken as characteristic of sixteenth-century English culture. Perhaps the most celebrated example of this temporal and cultural pleat or warp in conventional narratives is Chaucer's translation of Petrarch's famous sonnet, "S'amor non è," in Book

I of his *Troilus and Criseyde*. The poem as a whole is an expanded and altered translation of Boccaccio's *Il Filostrato*, but at this moment, when Troilus has retreated to his chamber to lament his confusion and hopeless feelings of love towards Criseyde, he speaks in a lyrical rendition of Petrarch's sonnet, in three stanzas of "rhyme royal." C.S. Lewis famously argued that Chaucer "medievalized" Boccaccio's text, particularly through his introduction of Boethian themes, but Paul Strohm suggests that Chaucer's attitude to Boccaccio and Petrarch was not conditioned by any such consciousness of epistemic difference: "Chaucer presumably never thought to consider Boccaccio and Petrarch as anything *but* perfectly plausible near-contemporaries, sharing diversely, like himself, in various aspects of fourteenth-century literary culture."[2] Strohm offers a different reading of this translated sonnet, as a curious "temporal archive" that has the effect of troubling these conventional narratives of medieval into Renaissance. This English translation of Petrarch has the effect of anticipating by nearly two centuries the Petrarchan fashion among Elizabethan poets that seems such a feature of the English Renaissance. The sonnet is thus, in Strohm's phrase, "'nonsynchronous' with its surroundings."[3] Strohm argues that the terms medieval and Renaissance help us "identify and appreciate the exceptional excitement of moments like Petrarch-in-Chaucer,"[4] but that they "work" for us only insofar as they help us index temporal complexity, not as signposts that might try to regiment time into an orderly march or succession, with one period or school trimly following another in sequence.

The debate about periodization is a lively one in contemporary medieval studies, and shows no sign of abating. Many scholars take issue with the way the medieval period is routinely and persistently characterized as homogenous, orthodox and intellectually incurious, while some others such as James Simpson have proposed a more proactive approach, controversially seeing the medieval period as one of resistance and revolution, in contrast to the reformation movements that followed.[5] And in more recent popular culture there is an urgent critique of the apparent appropriation of medieval signs and symbols by white supremacists and other right-wing political movements. In so far as the "Middle Ages" are still being re-invented and re-imagined, Chaucer lived in them only in the most contingent and arbitrary way.

Notes

1 Marion Turner, *Chaucer: A European Life* (Princeton, NJ: Princeton University Press, 2019), 162.
2 Paul Strohm, *Theory and the Premodern Text* (Minneapolis, MN: University of Minnesota Press, 2000), 94.

3 Ibid., 85.
4 Ibid., 94.
5 James Simpson, *Reform and Cultural Reformation*, Oxford English Literary History, vol. 2, 1350–1547 (Oxford: Oxford University Press, 2002); Patricia Clare Ingham, *The Medieval New: Ambivalence in an Age of Innovation* (Philadelphia, PA: University of Pennsylvania Press, 2015), 15, 20.

Myth 14

CHAUCER WAS A PROTO-PROTESTANT

In 1570, some twelve years after Queen Elizabeth I succeeded to the throne, the great martyrologist John Foxe wrote that Chaucer "saw into religion as much as even we do now, and uttereth in his works no less, and seemeth to be a right Wicklevian."[1] The "we" in this quotation refers specifically to those sixteenth-century reformers who rejected the authority of the Catholic Church. And by identifying the poet as someone who followed the teachings of the religious dissident John Wycliffe, Foxe at once locates Chaucer in a previous temporal moment (Wycliffe died in 1382) and makes his own ability to "see" as timeless as the poet's. Foxe seems to delight in using this affinity with Chaucer in order to further his reformist agenda. Indeed, he included in his influential *Acts and Monuments* a work that he attributed to Chaucer entitled *Jack Upland* – a bitter attack on the friars and most likely a text that had connections with those known as Lollards (a sometimes derogatory term used to describe the followers of John Wycliffe).

To be fair, Foxe undoubtedly felt himself justified in making Chaucer a reformer before the fact. *Iack vp Lande* (*Jack Upland*) had been attributed to "famous Geoffrey Chaucer" perhaps as early as 1536,[2] and another Wycliffite text, *The Plowman's Tale* (an attack on the clergy), had been included in William Thynne's 1542 edition of Chaucer. Moreover, others saw Chaucer as a precursor to the Reformation insofar as he was a persistent critic of the Church. The antiquarian John Leland claimed that Chaucer wrote the alliterative poem *Piers Plowman* (not The *Plowman's Tale* as had long been thought) and said that it had been suppressed in successive editions of Chaucer because it dealt with the bad morals of priests. And the zealous reformer John Bale (expanding on Leland's notes) asserted that Lollard divines such as William White reported that "Chaucer by no means approved of the

30 Great Myths About Chaucer, First Edition. Thomas A. Prendergast and Stephanie Trigg.
© 2020 John Wiley & Sons, Inc. Published 2020 by John Wiley & Sons, Inc.

idleness of that great crowd of mumblers, the monks, nor of their unintelligible prayers, their relics and ceremonies."[3]

This proto-Protestant reading was enshrined in the biography appended to Thomas Speght's 1598 edition of Chaucer (and retained in the 1602 and 1687 editions), wherein he claimed that Chaucer attended Oxford "with *John Wickelife*, whose opinions in religion he much affected."[4] This belief that Chaucer had "some little Byas towards the Opinions of *Wycliff*," as the poet John Dryden put it, would continue throughout the seventeenth and eighteenth centuries, nourished by the notion that Chaucer must be partial to Wycliffe's ideas or he would never have written such anti-clerical works as *The Plowman's Tale* and *Jack Upland*.[5] It was not until John Urry's 1721 edition of Chaucer that doubts began to be expressed about Chaucer's authorship of these "tales." John Dart, the author of the biography attached to the edition, said, "I cannot go so far as to suppose that either the *Plowman's Tale* or *Jack Upland* were written by him." Yet even so, he claimed that Chaucer was a "Favourer of the Lollards," and later the edition reframed Leland's claim about *Piers Plowman*, saying that *The Plowman's Tale* had been suppressed by the Church in early Chaucer editions, and repeated Foxe's ascription of *Jack Upland* to Chaucer.[6] The death knell for Chaucer's reputation as a proto-Protestant should have come some fifty-seven years later when Thomas Tyrwhitt (in his landmark edition of Chaucer) decisively rejected both works, claiming that not even Wycliffe would have gone so far as *The Plowman's Tale*. Yet somehow, even after these works were declared non-Chaucerian, the legend of a Protestant Chaucer persisted, continuing at least through the late twentieth century and probably further.[7]

Why and how did this legend persist in the absence of the texts that gave rise to it? One could argue that even without *Jack Upland* and *The Plowman's Tale*, the image of a "liberal apostle of rationalism" who cast "the fourteenth-century Church as totalitarian, foreign power" would be congenial to late nineteenth- and twentieth-century readings of Chaucer as a "rational skeptic."[8] After all, his treatment of friars in the *Summoner's Tale*, his portrayal of the Pardoner (see Myth 20), the Summoner in the *Friar's Tale* and perhaps even his portrait of the Prioress all suggest an attitude towards the Church that, if not reforming, would seem to be a kind of protest against ecclesiastical abuses that might accord well with the religious revolutions that followed in the early modern period. Of course, protest does not equal Protestant. Any number of writers in the Middle Ages criticized abuses of the Church without being seen as agents of the Reformation *avant la lettre*, yet there are some small clues to indicate that Chaucer had, if not a reforming interest, then at least an interest in reformers (and they in him).

The most interesting and also the most frustrating piece of evidence that links the poet with Lollards comes from 1464, when John Baron of Amersham (member of a group of suspected Lollards from the Chiltern Hills) was investigated for having, among other books, a copy of the *Canterbury Tales*.[9] While it is not completely clear why this particular book would have been produced for Baron's prosecution (hence the frustration), it seems likely that it had to do with the fact that it was in English and seems consonant with the Lollards' interest in texts produced in the vernacular. One of the tenets of Lollardy had to do with the belief that texts, religious texts and especially the Bible should be translated into English. And the biblical citations in texts such as the *Pardoner's Tale* or the *Parson's Tale* would have been sufficient under a rigorous reading of Archbishop Arundel's Constitutions (which governed the definition of heresy) to be seen as heterodox.[10] Yet it was not only that Chaucer "translated" parts of the Bible that made it possible for him to be seen as Lollard.

One would not want to make too much of guilt by association, but it has become clear that those within what scholars have come to call "Chaucer's circle" were interested in writing and collecting vernacular religious literature, including Wycliffite texts. And we can demonstrate that some of them (for instance, Sir John Clanvowe, one of the so-called Lollard knights) actually owned Wycliffite material.[11] It appears, then, that Chaucer had social and literary connections with writers who, at the very least, would have been considered suspicious after Wycliffe had been found guilty of heresy in 1382, and had they been discovered in possession of such texts after Arundel's Constitutions (1407–09) might have found themselves in real danger.

But did any of these ideas make their way into Chaucer's own works? He was critical of the Church, of course, but his only overt mentions of Lollardy initially seem negative. In the endlink to the *Man of Law's Tale* from the *Canterbury Tales,* the host, Harry Bailly, commands the Parson "for Goddes bones, / Telle us a tale." The Parson, as Wycliffites were wont to do, chastises him for swearing and Harry responds, "O Jankin, be ye there? / I smelle a Lollere in the wynd" (II.1166–7; 1172–3). Facetiously, the Host goes on to tell the pilgrims that they would get no tale from the Parson but "for Goddes digne passioun /... a predicacioun [sermon]; / This Lollere heer wil prechen us somwhat" (II.1175–7). How we interpret this passage depends on our subject position. Do we think Harry is rightfully puncturing the Parson's inflated self-importance, or do we think Harry's derision tells us more about the frivolous nature of pilgrimage (as Wycliffites believed)? As in so many things, Chaucer gives us no clear answer and, in fact, has an entirely different pilgrim chime in, to uncertain effect.

In the few references to Church doctrine from Chaucer's works that might have a Lollard cast, the poet's position remains equally unclear. He seems to have both the Summoner and the Pardoner appropriate Lollard discourse in the service of humor, but whether he is making of fun of Lollards or providing voices of Lollard dissent within his works is difficult to discern.[12] So, too, might the Wife of Bath be seen as the very image of a female Lollard preacher, but whether this portrait licenses what she has to say and her right to say it, or is an embodiment of English fears of Lollardy, remains debatable.[13] What seems clear, however, is that whether or not Chaucer was a proto-Protestant, he operated within an environment, both textual and cultural, in which he and others engaged with ideas that were seen by many as heterodox and even dangerous. The level and manner of his engagement, however, resist the easy binaries of orthodox/heterodox.

Notes

1 John Foxe, *The Acts and Monuments of the Christian Martyrs*, 4th edn., ed. Josiah Pratt, 8 vols. (London: Religious Tract Society, 1877), 4:248–50.
2 *Iack vp Lande Compyled by the famous Geoffrey Chaucer* (Southwark: Prynted by J. Nicolson for Ihon Gough, 1536), A1r.
3 It remains unclear what sources, if any, Bale has consulted. Caroline Spurgeon, *Five Hundred Years of Chaucer Criticism and Allusion 1357–1900*, 3 vols. (Cambridge: Cambridge University Press, 1925), 3:21. For *The Plowman's Tale* see William Thynne's edition of *The Workes of Geffray Chaucer newly imprinted* (London, 1542), CXIXr–CXXVIv.
4 Thomas Speght, ed., *The Workes of our Antient and Learned English Poet, Geffrey Chavcer, newly Printed* (London, 1598), B3r.
5 Kathleen Forni, *A Chaucerian Apocrypha: A Counterfeit Canon* (Tallahassee, FL: University Press of Florida, 2001), 95.
6 John Urry, *The Works of Geoffrey Chaucer* (London: B. Lintot, 1721), c1r, f2r. Dart was understandably irked (Forni, *Chaucerian Apocrypha*, 210, n.3).
7 Linda Georgianna, "The Protestant Chaucer," in *Chaucer's Religious Tales*, ed. C. David Benson and Elizabeth Robertson (Woodbridge: D.S. Brewer, 1990), 55–6.
8 Ibid., 60.
9 Anne Hudson, *Lollards and Their Books* (London: Hambledon Press, 1985), 142.
10 Ibid., 149.
11 Andrew Cole, *Literature and Heresy in the Age of Chaucer* (Cambridge: Cambridge University Press, 2008), 79–80.
12 Frances McCormack, "Chaucer and Lollardy," in *Chaucer and Religion*, ed. Helen Phillips (Woodbridge: Boydell and Brewer, 2010), 35–40, here 38.
13 Ibid., 39.

Myth 15

CHAUCER WAS ANTI-SEMITIC

Just before Chaucer tells his famously interrupted *Tale of Sir Thopas*, Harry Bailly turns to one of the other pilgrims and asks:

> "My lady Prioresse, by youre leve,
> So that I wiste I sholde yow nat greve,
> I wolde demen that ye tellen sholde
> A tale next, if so were that ye wolde.
> Now wol ye vouche sauf, my lady deere?"
>
> (VII.447–51)

She agrees, and what follows is perhaps the most controversial tale in the entire *Canterbury Tales*. The tale concerns a certain young boy who loves the Virgin Mary so much that he sings a song called *Alma Redemptoris Mater* ("Loving Mother of Our Savior") as he walks to and from school. His journey takes him through the Jewish quarter of the city and when the Jewish residents hear him, they decide (egged on by Satan) to do something about it, because the song is contrary to their teachings. They conspire to murder the boy and hire someone to slit his throat. When the boy is missed by his mother, she goes searching for him and is led by the intervention of Christ to a privy into which the boy's body has been dumped. She calls out and he miraculously begins to sing. The Jewish perpetrators are found, tortured, hanged and drawn by wild horses. The miraculous singing, enabled by Mary with a grain she places on the boy's tongue, ends when the grain is removed, and the boy is celebrated as a martyr. The Prioress concludes by asking for prayers from "yonge Hugh of Lyncoln" (VII.684) – a boy who was celebrated as a martyr in 1255 because he (like

---

30 Great Myths About Chaucer, First Edition. Thomas A. Prendergast and Stephanie Trigg.
© 2020 John Wiley & Sons, Inc. Published 2020 by John Wiley & Sons, Inc.

the little boy in her tale) had supposedly been killed by Jews, though he had actually died by falling into a Jewish well. This notorious incident led to the execution of at least nineteen Jewish men by Henry III.

When the Prioress finishes her tale, the pilgrims remain silent. The pilgrim Chaucer refers to it only as a "miracle" and remarks that it was a wonder to see the pilgrims look so sober. Early reception of the tale makes it clear that the work was primarily seen as part of a genre of Marian "miracle tales."[1] In fact (except for one gloss), it is not until 1602, in Thomas Speght's edition, that there is any reference to Jewish characters in the tale ("A Miracle of a Christian Child murthered by the Iewes").[2] And it is not until 1765 that there is any condemnation of the story as being anti-Semitic. Bishop Percy, comparing an analogue of the story to Chaucer's version, remarks that these narratives concerning the blood-libel were circulated "in excuse for the cruelties exercised upon that wretched people, and probably never happened in a single instance …. We may reasonably conclude the whole charge to be groundless and malicious."[3] Thomas Tyrwhitt, in his magisterial edition some ten years later, agrees with Percy, saying "this was one of the oldest of the many stories, which have been propagated, at different times, to excite or justify several merciless persecutions of the Jews, upon the charge of murthering Christian children."[4]

Only occasionally, however, in the nineteenth century would critics suggest that it was Chaucer himself who was "not without his touch of bigotry … in Hugh of Lincoln [sic]."[5] More often than not it was the Prioress who was seen as indulging in anti-Semitic prejudice. Thomas Lounsbury might be seen as emblematic of this approach, whose basic outline would continue well into the twentieth century:

> We need not suppose that Chaucer himself had the least belief in the absurd story that forms the groundwork of this pathetic piece. … Still, one cannot but regret that a man with evident broad mindedness should have allowed his genius to pander, for the sake of literary effect, to a cruel slander which could hardly fail to extend and aggravate the hatred already felt for a wretched and hunted race.[6]

The anti-Semitism here is the product of an attempt to create a particular literary effect – most likely the sentimentality and pathos (so valued by nineteenth-century critics) of a small boy whose innocent devotion to the mother of God got him killed.

The early twentieth century saw an increased focus on the character of the Prioress, often treating her anti-Semitism as distasteful, but not a true reflection of her character or, alternatively, as an expression of a generalized portrait of those who might have been hostile to Christianity. As we might expect, approaches to the tale changed radically after the Second World War and the Shoah. R.M. Lumiansky omitted the tale from his edition, suggesting that

> though anti-Semitism was a different thing in the fourteenth-century [sic] from what it is today, the present day reader has modern reactions to literature, no matter when it was written ... for most of us, "The Prioress's Tale" is ruined by the similarity between this kind of story and some of the anti-Semitic propaganda which was current in Nazi Germany, and which is still in operation, not only in numerous foreign countries but also here at home.[7]

As Heather Blurton and Hannah Johnson have suggested, Lumiansky's response was an "early bellwether, registering a newly felt sense of the tale's troubling implications."[8] With a recently realized understanding of the ethical concerns surrounding the tale, attention turned to who was ultimately to be held responsible for the kind of prejudice that could no longer be seen as simply a distasteful relic of the Middle Ages.

Predictably, the focus on the Prioress as a character in Chaucer's work rather than an expression of Chaucer's own views was renewed. In this reading, Chaucer was not complicit in the Prioress's anti-Semitism, but was, in fact, satirizing anti-Semitism. As one critic put it, "in the tale which Chaucer assigned to the Prioress, the widely held ritual murder legend is held up for implicit condemnation as vicious and hypocritical."[9] Many of these views focused less on the tale itself than on the portrait of the Prioress in the *General Prologue*. There she is characterized as fussy, more concerned with her dogs or the fate of a mouse than with her fellow human beings. Chaucer, then, is presenting a woman who (depending on the reading) callously narrates a hateful tale, or unknowingly replicates the base and backward views of her age. Chaucer himself, on the other hand, transcends the common beliefs of his time and exhibits the cosmopolitan qualities of tolerance and understanding that we would expect of England's first poetic genius.

As might be evident, this profoundly timeless Chaucer is based on notions of genius and canonical authorship that carry their own ideological baggage. And it fits ill with historical understandings of medieval literature. If Chaucer meant the tale told by the Prioress to be seen as satirical, indicating a profound rejection of anti-Semitism, there seems to be little evidence that his audience would have understood it this way. As we have already seen, the tale's representation of its Jewish characters is barely noted until the beginning of the seventeenth century. Its inclusion in a number of Marian collections suggests that the focus of medieval readers was on the miraculous Marianism that was reinforced by the miracle of the Virgin within the tale. As Blurton and Johnson suggest,

"the story of reception significantly undermines arguments that empha-
size the satirical edge of the *Prioress's Tale*."[10]

So how do we approach a Chaucer who might well be anti-Semitic? It
depends, finally, on how one reads. Some have argued that we need to
approach the Chaucerian canon with a disinterested aestheticism that
abjures the temptation to deploy ethical readings of the tales more congen-
ial to contemporary audiences. The advantages of this kind of reading seem
to be that we recover the medieval context and meaning of the work rather
than "literature's ... and criticism's ideological participation in the injus-
tices of the past."[11] Against this seemingly disinterested recuperation of the
tale's historical meaning, others such as Emily Stark Zitter have argued that

> Chaucer's anti-semitism is frightening and repugnant, both in medieval and
> certainly in modern times. Historical critics apologize for it; critics favoring
> a wholly ironic "hard" reading try—ultimately with little success—to deny
> it completely. ... I would like to conclude by arguing for a stronger and
> more explicitly moral approach to interpreting and especially to teaching a
> dangerously effective anti-semitic tale.[12]

How to adjudicate these two *seemingly* incompatible positions? It is
important to note (as Zitter does) that the choice between historical and
ethical readings is a false dichotomy. Chaucer's contemporaries may not
have read the tale in ways that seem overtly anti-Semitic, but that does
not mean that they were not complicit in a broader cultural anti-Semitism
that had serious ethical consequences in the medieval period, just as it has
had (and continues to have) serious consequences for late modernity. So,
too, Chaucer's inclusion of an anti-Semitic tale in his collection cannot
simply be explained away as satire or excused as a historical accident of
his times. To understand and appreciate how this prejudice operated in
the Middle Ages and to acknowledge that it operates in an analogous
fashion in the contemporary period is not to engage in a reductionist,
presentist form of criticism. Rather it is, in the words of Blurton and
Johnson, to remove Chaucer "from some rarefied atmosphere of apothe-
osis ... and render him more three-dimensional, to recognize him, in some
respects, as a worthy subject of the type depicted in some of his poems."[13]

Notes

1 Mary F. Godfrey, "The Fifteenth-Century *Prioress's Tale* and the Problem of
  Anti-Semitism," in *Rewriting Chaucer: Culture, Authority and the Idea of the
  Authentic Text, 1400–1602*, ed. Thomas A. Prendergast and Barbara Kline
  (Columbus, OH: Ohio State University Press, 1999), 93–115.

2 The gloss appears in the Hengwrt Chaucer (Hg) and Cambridge University Library MS Dd.4.24 (Dd) and offers a précis of a version of the tale from John of Garland's *Stella Maris* that interestingly pre-dates Hugh of Lincoln's death. See Beverly Boyd, ed., *A Variorum Edition of the Works of Geoffrey Chaucer, 2: The Prioress's Tale* (Norman, OK: University of Oklahoma Press, 1987), 63–64.

3 Thomas Percy, *Reliques of ancient English poetry: consisting of old heroic ballads, songs, and other pieces of our earlier poets, (chiefly of the lyric kind.) Together with some few of later date*, 3 vols. (London, J. Dodsley, 1765), 1:32.

4 Thomas Tyrwhitt, ed., *The Canterbury tales of Chaucer to which are added, an essay upon his language and versification; an introductory discourse; and notes*, 5 vols. (London, 1775–78), 4:173–4.

5 Henry Hart Milman, *History of Latin Christianity; Including that of the Popes to the Pontificate of Nicolas V*, 3rd ed., 9 vols. (London: John Murray, [1855] 1872), 9:247.

6 Thomas R. Lounsbury, *Studies in Chaucer*, 1892, 3 vols. (New York: Russell & Russell, 1892), 2:491.

7 R.M. Lumianksy, ed. and trans., *The Canterbury Tales of Geoffrey Chaucer* (New York: Simon and Schuster, 1948), xxiii.

8 Heather Blurton and Hannah Johnson, *The Critics and the Prioress: Antisemitism, Criticism, and Chaucer's* Prioress's Tale (Ann Arbor, MI: University of Michigan, 2017), 22.

9 R.J. Schoeck, "Chaucer's Prioress: Mercy and Tender Heart," in *Chaucer Criticism*, ed. R.J. Schoeck and Jerome Taylor (Notre Dame, IN: University of Notre Dame Press, 1960), 245–58, here 249.

10 Blurton and Johnson, *Critics and the Prioress*, 184.

11 Michael Calabrese, "Performing the Prioress: 'Conscience' and Responsibility in Studies of Chaucer's Prioress's Tale," *Studies in Literature and Language* 44, no. 1 (2002), 66–91, here 66.

12 Emily Stark Zitter, "Anti-semitism in Chaucer's *Prioress's Tale*," *Chaucer Review* 25, no. 4 (1991), 277–84, here 277.

13 Blurton and Johnson, *Critics and the Prioress*, 186.

Myth 16

CHAUCER WAS A SPY

On 23 November 2003 Terry Jones, of Monty Python fame, unveiled a blue plaque at the former site of the Tabard Inn in Talbot's Yard, Southwark, honoring both the inn as a historical site and Chaucer himself as "England's greatest medieval poet." Jones's remarks that day included the following summary: "He was a famous man, a poet, a spy, a diplomat and Clerk of the King's Works."[1] One could argue about whether Chaucer was famous in the fourteenth century (at least in the same way that we think of fame in the twenty-first century), but it is true that he was a diplomat, Clerk of the King's Works and, of course, a poet. But whether or not he was a spy is more difficult to determine. It is hard to pinpoint precisely where or when this myth originated. Perhaps unsurprisingly, it is repeated in Terry Jones's 2003 book—but it remains unreferenced.[2] It exists on the internet, shows up in various teaching guides and has a lively presence in a number of medieval mysteries, but the ultimate source remains shadowy and elusive.

Even if we do not quite know where this myth originated, we know quite a bit about the circumstances that might have generated it. Chaucer traveled a great deal on the king's behalf and conducted business for him both openly and secretly. In 1372, for instance, he traveled to Genoa and Florence in order to negotiate the appointment of a special seaport for the use of Genoese merchants, and perhaps to negotiate a loan for Edward III from the Compagnia dei Bardi, one of the most powerful banks in the fourteenth century.[3] And in 1376 he traveled on the king's secret business (*secretis negociis domini regis*) with Sir Thomas de Burley, former Captain of Calais, perhaps to negotiate a marriage between the future Richard II

30 Great Myths About Chaucer, First Edition. Thomas A. Prendergast and Stephanie Trigg.
© 2020 John Wiley & Sons, Inc. Published 2020 by John Wiley & Sons, Inc.

and Marie, the daughter of Charles V of France.[4] Similarly, he traveled in 1377 with Sir Thomas Percy on secret business for the Crown. In both cases he was the junior member of the party, but given the work he had done for the king on his other travels, it is clear that he was trusted and carried a fair amount of authority.[5] It is possible that the secret nature of the king's business in which he was engaged led to a belief that, as he was acting in secret for the king, he must have been something of an intelligencer.

Would this secret work have extended to spying for the king? The fifteenth-century writer Phillipe de Commynes was purported to have said that messenger, spy and diplomat amount to the same thing.[6] Under this rubric, it would be easy to think Chaucer a spy, but it may perhaps be too general to be of much help. In thinking about whether Chaucer would have been considered a spy in the late Middle Ages, it is important to realize that the late medieval idea of a spy might be seen as analogous to modern notions of the spy, since his or her job (there were female spies) was to collect intelligence, particularly military intelligence for a government. But there were, obviously, differences. When thinking about the medieval spy we are not talking about post-Cold War notions of spycraft involving dead drops and sleeper agents (though there were ciphers). Medieval notions of the spy more often involved direct intelligence about the disposition of military forces.

In her *Book of Deeds of Arms and of Chivalry*, the early fifteenth-century writer Christine de Pizan distinguishes between a number of different tasks of the spy. Referencing the fourth-century Roman military writer Vegetius, who wrote the standard work about war, she says that spies might be used as disposable scouts – they might dress "as pilgrims or laborers, to search day and night for ambushes. If these spies do not return, the commander should follow another route if possible, for this is an indication that they have been captured."[7] Spies might also insinuate themselves into the councils of the enemy and uncover their plans: "it is profitable to have wise spies who know well how to discover the strategy of the adversaries. For such as these know how by gifts and promises to intervene and by ruse to attract one or several, even from the council of the other side, if possible, so that they can learn the whole plan of action."[8] Or they might act as *agents provocateurs*: "it is very profitable to find ways of sowing dissension in the enemy ranks, so that they do not deign to obey their commander."[9] All spies would not necessarily carry out all of these tasks – the spying undertaken was driven by need, and the work of spying would most likely dovetail with the primary professions of the spy, as soldier, diplomat, messenger and so on.

So, given the medieval definition of the spy, can we claim that Chaucer was engaged in spying for either Edward III or Richard II, or any other high-ranking government official or general? Chaucer was involved in a military campaign; he was in the company of Lionel, Earl of Ulster, in the French campaign of 1359–60. Intriguingly, he was captured and ransomed by the king for a large sum of money. Was he one of the disposable scouts that Christine de Pizan talked about as being "spies"? There is no evidence of this, and the force of which Chaucer was a part was comparatively small and liable to capture. In addition, ransoming one's captured forces was a relatively common occurrence: Chaucer's position in Lionel's household would have made it remarkable if they had thought of him as dispensable, and unremarkable that he was ransomed (although others were ransomed for more).

Was he in a position to offer bribes to opposing forces in order to secure military intelligence? Could he have been an *agent provocateur*, managing to undermine the governments of foreign enemies? As we saw earlier, he was involved in diplomatic work and so had access to the kinds of government officials who might have sensitive military or political knowledge. But his diplomatic record more often suggests that he was seen as someone who was an accomplished mediator. He was sent by the king to facilitate trade deals, ensure that property that had been seized by English officials would be returned to its foreign owners, or treat with potential military allies.[10] We cannot, of course, be sure of what happened on those journeys in which he carried out the secret business of the king, but his general diplomatic profile seems much more in tune with a negotiator who facilitated making arrangements in difficult situations, rather than one who was attempting to suborn others to give up sensitive information or convince them somehow to work against their government.

Finally, did Chaucer ever use his diplomatic position in order to gain military intelligence? Before the mid-twentieth century there was no real evidence that this was the case. But in 1955 it was discovered that a certain document in a Spanish archive that apparently referred to someone called "Geffroy de Chanserre" was actually a safe-conduct (issued by the King of Navarre) for the English poet for 22 February through to 24 May 1366. The document does not specify why Chaucer would need a safe-conduct, but one of his biographers suggested that he was on an "unofficial, even secret mission."[11] Most of the speculation surrounding this mission centers on the affairs of Pedro of Castile, King of Castile and Leon, to whom Chaucer refers in the *Monk's Tale*. At the time, Pedro was involved in a conflict with his half-brother over the throne; a conflict that, in the early part of 1366, was going badly for Pedro. In February 1367, the Black Prince (son of Edward III) intervened and, fighting on behalf of Pedro, won a decisive victory at the Battle of Najera later that year, which led to the reinstallation of Pedro on the throne.

Chaucer's presence in Spain at a time of crisis that deeply concerned the English Crown could be accounted for by a number of different reasons. It is possible that he was there to dissuade certain Gascon knights from fighting against Pedro. Or, he could have been scoping out the situation and reporting back to Edward III about the feasibility of fighting for the erstwhile King of Castile and Leon. More likely, however, he was in the service of the prince, and it is here that he might have been gathering intelligence, both military and political, in order to better inform the prince's actions.[12] Some have even claimed that in doing so, he may have enlisted in Pedro's brother's camp "as a spy of the English Crown."[13] While this is unlikely, it would make sense that Chaucer, having been in Navarre, would report on the situation to his superiors, and this report might have had an impact on the decisive battle in Najera, the capital of Navarre.

Does this make Chaucer a spy? As we have already discussed, it depends on what we mean by "spy." It might be better to think this way. Chaucer may well have been an intelligence gatherer. We know that he acted as an agent of the Crown and we know that sometimes he acted secretly. If we think of him as acting as a "secret agent" of the Crown at various points in his career, then this might be a better description than "spy." What remains unexplained is why there would be the desire to define him as a spy. Chaucer held many jobs during his life – page, personal attendant, diplomat, Collector of Customs, Clerk of the King's Works, Forester – but these all lack the romance of thinking about the greatest medieval English poet as a spy. It is possible that the subtlety, intelligence and deception seemingly required for spywork more pleasingly fit our notion of the man whose work is routinely seen as subtle, intelligent and difficult to decode.

Notes

1 Leigh Hatts, "Terry Jones Unveils Chaucer Plaque at Copyprints," *London SE1: Community Website* (23 November 2003), http://www.london-se1.co.uk/news/view/737, accessed 27 November 2018.

2 Terry Jones, Alan Fletcher, Terry Dolan, et al., *Who Murdered Chaucer? A Medieval Mystery* (New York: St. Martin's Press, 2003).

3 Martin M. Crow and Clair C. Olson, eds., *Chaucer Life-Records* (Oxford: Clarendon Press, 1966), 39.

4 The historian Jean Froissart, though not to be completely trusted, says as much (ibid., 49–51).

5 Ibid., 42, 44.

6 Ian Arthurson, "Espionage and Intelligence from the Wars of the Roses to the Reformation," *Nottingham Medieval Studies* 35 (1991), 134–54, here 134.

7 Christine de Pizan, *The Book of Arms and of Chivalry*, ed. Charity Cannon Wilson, trans. Sumner Willard (University Park, PA: Pennsylvania State University Press, 1999), 49.

8 Ibid., 47.

9 Ibid., 47.

10 Crow and Olson, *Chaucer Life-Records*, 31–66.

11 Derek Pearsall, *The Life of Geoffrey Chaucer* (Oxford: Blackwell, 1992), 51.

12 For a review of these various positions, see R.F. Yeager, "Chaucer Translates the Matter of Spain," in *England and Iberia in the Middle Ages*, ed. María Bullón-Fernández (New York: Palgrave, 2007), 189–214, here 206, n. 15.

13 Antonio R. León Sendra and Jesús L. Serrano Reyes, "Chaucer and Montserrat," *Selim* 9 (1999), 123–43, here 127.

Myth 17

CHAUCER WAS A CROOK

Over one hundred years ago, the great Chaucerian critic George Lyman Kittredge, referring to Chaucer's day job in the Port of London, made this famous pronouncement: "Now few facts of history, be it sacred or profane, are more solidly established than that Geoffrey Chaucer, in his habit as he lived was not naïf. ... a naïf Collector of Customs would be a paradoxical monster."[1] Kittredge's rather jaundiced view of the medieval customhouse was well deserved. As David Carlson put it, "The potential for abuse that characterizes this system was so great that the conflicts of interest built into it, structurally even, come to seem, not accidental by-products, but necessary components without which the system could not have been kept functioning. The customs system was corrupt by design."[2]

Was Chaucer involved in the corruption? We should start by clearing up Kittredge's uncharacteristic slip: Chaucer was not Collector, but Controller of Customs. Had he been a Collector, chances are that he would have engaged in practices that we would consider crooked. But the difference between the positions of Collector and Controller was significant. The Collector of Customs was often a man of substance and the position was not compensated, most likely because it was understood that the Collectors had other means by which to profit from their posts. These means varied and were often not above board. For instance, in between quarterly deliveries to the Exchequer, Collectors had access to the custom collected and could use it for their own purposes. Responsible for the weighing of the wool (which generated by far the greatest amount of custom), the Collector could add or subtract weight surreptitiously, or even fail to note a shipment at all – in return, of course, for a healthy kickback.

30 Great Myths About Chaucer, First Edition. Thomas A. Prendergast and Stephanie Trigg.
© 2020 John Wiley & Sons, Inc. Published 2020 by John Wiley & Sons, Inc.

The Controller of Customs, on the other hand, was a paid position that was meant as a check on the Collector. The duties of the Controller were to ensure that the dues were properly collected and accounted for. The Controller was to keep the records in his own hand, which meant that he had to be in attendance at the Wool Quay on a daily basis.[3] The Controller and the Collector were to work together and each had half of a mold that when combined would produce what was known as the Cocket Seal. This seal was to be attached to each wool sack or bundle of hides. The idea behind the two halves was that each would ensure the other's honesty.

In reality, of course, things did not always work out this way. First, the Controller of Customs very rarely had the same social or political standing as the Collector. In Chaucer's case, the Collectors included the merchants Nicholas Brembre, William Walworth and John Philipot. All were knighted, all became Lord Mayor of London, and all abused their positions for gain.[4] Chaucer would not have been in a very strong position to oppose any of them, despite his connections with John of Gaunt. In fact, it was probably because of his connection to Gaunt and the court that Chaucer was appointed. It is doubtful that Chaucer desired the job. The movement out of the royal household probably seemed "like a setback or a stall in his social ascent."[5] And the work was time-consuming and difficult. It is much more likely that Chaucer got the job because someone wanted him in the position.

Paul Strohm has argued that this supposition is backed up by a series of events that surrounded Chaucer's appointment to the position. In February 1374, Nicholas Brembre was appointed Collector. In April of the same year, Chaucer received a grant from the king that was to be collected each day at the Port of London. In May, he was granted a lease from the mayor and alderman of London to a property ten minutes from the Wool Quay. In June, he became Controller, not through a bill from the treasurer of the realm, but through royal appointment, and five days later Gaunt conferred a life annuity on Chaucer and his wife. This evidence is all circumstantial, but it suggests a coordinated effort by a person or persons in the king's entourage to get someone into the position who would "work well" with Brembre.[6]

Would Chaucer have understood that this was the expectation? The Custom House was not exactly considered a beacon of honesty in the fourteenth century. John Gower says as much in his *Mirour de L'omme* in what has been termed his paean to wool, "Fraud, who has plenty of money governs your warehouse" ("Triche, q'ad toutplein d'argent / De ton estaple est fait regent").[7] There were, in addition, constant attempts to regulate unauthorized profiteering. Three years before Chaucer became

Controller, Parliament suggested that the Controllers were demanding fees above and beyond what Parliament had explicitly authorized and attempted to eliminate them. Eight years later Parliament petitioned that Controllers be limited to annual terms. The endless attempts to control corruption on the docks suggest widespread knowledge of how intractable the problem was.

But if Chaucer was well aware of what was expected of him, the extent of his complicity once he obtained the position is difficult to determine. Given the power, wealth and standing of the Collectors, it is unlikely that he would have confronted Brembre and the others directly. In fact, for part of the time he lacked the means to do so. The wool trade was enormously lucrative and the funds flowing from it were a major source of the Crown's income. But sometimes the funds flowed too slowly and the Crown needed a loan. In order to ensure the loan, the Crown would assign the entirety of the wool subsidy to the lending party until the loan was paid off. In order to guarantee this, one half of the Cocket Seal was given to the lender. In 1374, when Chaucer first came to the Wool Quay, the Collector was Nicholas Brembre. He was also at that time alderman of London and participated in a large loan from the city to the king. As part of the collective, he, along with others, was given half of the Cocket Seal – Chaucer's half. Thus, he had his own half of the seal and access to Chaucer's half.[8] The mechanism that was to ensure the honesty of the process now resided completely with the one person most likely to profit from its dishonesty. A similar set of events occurred a number of times during Chaucer's twelve-year tenure (often involving Brembre), leaving him without the seal for as many as a hundred months.

Of course, Chaucer still would have had to oversee and certify the Collector's accounts. But if Chaucer was working hand in glove with Brembre and the other Collectors, he seemed not to have profited from it. Less than two years after he resigned his position of Controller, a series of actions were initiated against Chaucer to recover debts. The first was initiated by a Collector in April 1388 and extended at least until June. The sum (£3. 6s. 8d.) involved in the action would seem to indicate that Chaucer was having significant financial difficulties. It was during this period that Chaucer transferred his Exchequer annuities to John Scalby – these kinds of transfers were not unusual and they usually indicated a desire to "obtain ready money."[9] Yet if this is what Chaucer was attempting to do, it did not extricate him from his difficulties, since another action was brought against him in November of the same year and extended into 1390. It seems clear that if there was wrongdoing, it failed to enrich the poet and was rather more a case of going along with men who were much more powerful than he.

The circumstances surrounding his departure from the position suggest as much. Even though he was not financially secure, he resigned on 4 December 1386. He had served for a long time (the second longest since 1351), so perhaps it was simply time for him to move on. Or it may be that he grew weary of the work. We know that he was assigned a permanent deputy to handle part of the workload. However, Strohm argues that political pressures may have led Chaucer to make a "constrained choice."[10] Two months before Chaucer resigned his position, the Commons petitioned Parliament to annul all of the port Controllers' lifetime appointments because "they were oppressing the people with extortions."[11] The day after Chaucer resigned the post, he lost the lease to his apartment over Aldgate. And finally, the Collector, Nicholas Brembre, with whom he had apparently had an understanding, was well on his way to creating the circumstances that would lead to his execution two years later, and thus was in no position to help Chaucer. Marion Turner challenges Strohm's reading of Chaucer's close relationship with Brembre, though, arguing that they were not necessarily always close allies, "just as it is a mistake to see Brembre as consistently the ally of the Crown during these years."[12] What *is* clear, though, is that Chaucer's employment was never simply a job; rather, it necessarily involved engagement in the murky world of court politics and international trade. In any case, after he resigned his post, Chaucer then left London for Kent, apparently having served his purpose – not so much a crook as a minor official caught in the great game of late fourteenth-century English politics.

Notes

1 George Lyman Kittredge, *Chaucer and his Poetry, Lectures delivered in 1914 on the Percy Turnbull Memorial Foundation in the Johns Hopkins University, by George Lyman Kittredge* (Cambridge, MA: Harvard University Press, 1915), 45.

2 David Carlson, *Chaucer's Jobs* (New York: Palgrave, 2004), 11.

3 Ibid., 11.

4 Derek Pearsall, *The Life of Geoffrey Chaucer* (Cambridge, MA: Blackwell, 2002), 100.

5 Carlson, *Chaucer's Jobs*, 6.

6 Paul Strohm, *Chaucer's Tale: 1386 and the Road to Canterbury* (New York: Viking, 2014), 92–7.

7 John Gower, *Mirour de l'omme*, in *The Complete Works of John Gower*, ed. G.C. Macaulay (Oxford: Clarendon Press, 1899), 1:281, lines 25399–400. As Strohm points out, "staple" has a double meaning here: it refers to the actual building on the wool wharf and the entire enterprise of the wool trade – the Wool Staple.

8 Strohm, *Chaucer's Tale*, 119.
9 Martin M. Crow and Clair C. Olson, eds., *Chaucer Life-Records* (Oxford: Oxford University Press, 1966), 38.
10 Strohm, *Chaucer's Tale*, 183.
11 Crow and Olson, *Chaucer Life-Records*, 269.
12 Marion Turner, *Chaucer: A European Life* (Princeton, NJ: Princeton University Press, 2019), 181.

Myth
18 CHAUCER WAS A POLITICAL OPPORTUNIST

Those leveling charges of political opportunism against Chaucer tend to rely heavily on five lines from what may be the poet's final poetic production:

> O conquerour of Brutes Albyon,
> Which that by lyne and free eleccion
> Been verray kyng, this song to yow I sende,
> And ye, that mowen alle oure harmes amende,
> Have mynde upon my supplicacion.
> ("The Complaint of Chaucer to His Purse," lines 22–6)

These lines, from the envoi to the poem known as "The Complaint of Chaucer to His Purse," seem innocent enough, especially in the context of the rest of the poem, which embodies his purse as a lover and playfully enjoins her not to be "lyght," rather "Beth hevy ageyn, or elles mot I dye" (lines 7, 14, 21). Its intent, to get the king to make his purse heavy (or at least heavier), could be seen as completely conventional. After all, poets had routinely addressed their sovereigns in the interest of receiving patronage, or in the case of Chaucer to receive payment on a deferred annuity (see Myth 26).

Yet these lines have been seen as unusual because they addressed Henry IV, the son of John of Gaunt who usurped the throne from Richard II, and they did so less than six months after Henry's coronation. In addition, there is a suspicion that the poem originally lacked the five-line envoi, but was "dusted off" and re-purposed (and perhaps had even been intended for Richard).[1] Had Chaucer been completely divorced from the political

30 Great Myths About Chaucer, First Edition. Thomas A. Prendergast and Stephanie Trigg.
© 2020 John Wiley & Sons, Inc. Published 2020 by John Wiley & Sons, Inc.

world of the fourteenth century, one might take little note of his poem, but Chaucer had been a long-time Ricardian loyalist. He was granted an uninterrupted continuation of an annuity from Edward III that he had held since 1367. He had secured a royal appointment as Controller in the Port of London for wool and petty customs in 1374 (see Myth 17). In 1389 he was appointed Clerk of the Works and had been abroad "on the king's business" any number of times from the 1370s to the 1390s (see Myth 16). True, he had minimized his royal connections during the period from 1385 to 1387 when Richard's power was seemingly on the wane, but given what was happening to Ricardian adherents at this time (some dead, others in grave peril), this might be seen as prudent self-protection rather than political opportunism.[2]

So how do we interpret his seeming move from loyal adherent to Richard II to petitioner of his usurper? The key lies in how we interpret the five-line envoi to his "Complaint." There is little question that the poem offers a defense of Henry's rise to the throne. In it, Chaucer employs a tripartite approach to justifying the accession that mirrors Lancastrian sources. Henrician propaganda attempted to establish the legitimacy of Richard's deposition by insisting that there had been some funny business during the reign of Henry III, when Henry IV's ancestor had been displaced as the eldest son by Richard II's ancestor. It was, therefore, actually Henry who should have been crowned king in 1377, not Richard. Chaucer borrows this idea, claiming that Henry was the true king "by line," though he suppresses the conspiracy theory (not widely believed), perhaps thinking the less said about it the better.[3] The Lancastrians also made the claim that Henry had to accede to the throne because the kingdom was about to be lost through bad governance; a claim that Chaucer modifies and makes more forthright – proclaiming that Henry was conqueror, but then softening a seemingly discordant sense that "might makes right" by noting the connection with the legendary founder of England, Brutus, who himself had to conquer the island's original inhabitants in order to establish "Albyon." Finally, Chaucer adapts the less familiar notion that the estates wanted Henry to become king and acclaimed him so, and thus he could claim "free eleccion" as well as right by lineage and conquest.

It is doubtful that early modern and later readers of the poem were as aware of the close connections between Lancastrian propaganda and Chaucer's "Complaint" as we have become.[4] But, historically, the poem and its envoi were seen as extremely problematic. It is likely that Thomas Speght, the editor of two editions of Chaucer's works (1598 and 1602), altered the attribution of this poem to Thomas Hoccleve in his second edition because it did not accord with what he knew (or thought he knew) about Chaucer – that he was not the kind of poet who would switch allegiances so easily.[5] Even after 1721, when the poem was re-attributed to Chaucer by John Urry, doubts remained about Chaucer's authorship. In 1804, William Godwin, for instance, insisted that the poet "felt too deeply the sacredness of the muse, to be able to lend his talents to the temporizing politics of the day ... we must ... by no means hastily conclude that this compliment to the usurper, slight as it is, was penned by Chaucer."[6] According to the Life attached to Urry's edition (much quoted throughout the nineteenth century),

> the respect Chaucer retained for his former master, Richard, and gratitude for the favours he had received from him, kept him from trampling upon his memory, and basely flattering the new king; as most of his contemporaries did, and particularly Gower, who, notwithstanding the obligations he had to Richard II ... basely insulted the memory of his murdered master, and as ignominiously flattered his murderer.[7]

Though the attack on Gower is unfair, it suggests the extent to which Chaucer was seen as *sui generis* in his desire to keep his poetry pure – far from the prince-pleasing verses in which others might indulge.

Even after the verses were universally acknowledged as being Chaucer's, twentieth-century critics distanced the poet from charges of opportunism by claiming that the envoi was a slight thing (as would befit a begging poem), a half-hearted copy of one of Henry's own proclamations – "not markedly enthusiastic," as one critic put it.[8] But as we have seen, whatever the origin of the rest of the poem, the envoi is most certainly "a fresh and energetic refashioning of elements" in a particular textual environment.[9] Can we say that this "refashioning" reveals Chaucer to be a political opportunist? It is important to keep in mind that Chaucer elected not to repeat some of the more outrageous claims that the Lancastrians put about (such as that Richard resigned his throne with a "happy face" [gladde chere]).[10] And some critics have even read Chaucer's envoi as, to say the least, reticent about Henry's accession to the throne. It does not, for instance, mention one of the primary claims for any king – that he is so by the grace of God – and it is possible that the reference to "conquest" rather than (as Lancastrian sources tended to have it) "recovery" suggests the more problematic aspects of the deposition of Richard.[11] Yet, even if we reject these interpretations of the poem as reading too much into the absence of sustained panegyric (and it is well to note that Gower used the same tripartite justification in his *Cronica Tripertita*), it does seem the case that this is the type of poem Chaucer might be expected to produce. He was, after all, a petitioner who was apparently in serious financial trouble – the kind that can land one in prison (see Myth 26). As his annuity could only be confirmed by the king, it was advisable to acknowledge that Henry was, and should be seen as, the new king. Some might see this as opportunism, but to us it seems more like the pragmatic actions of a poet who, after all, was not addressing a stranger, but the son of his patron John of Gaunt, a man he not only knew, but had worked for and who had been generous to him five years before Chaucer addressed him as "verray king."[12]

Notes

1 Sumner Ferris, "The Date of Chaucer's Final Annuity and of the 'Complaint to his Empty Purse,'" *Modern Philology* 65 (1967), 45–52, here 45.
2 Paul Strohm, "Politics and Poetics: Usk and Chaucer in the 1380s," in *Literary Practice and Social Change in Britain: 1380–1530*, ed. Lee Patterson (Berkeley, CA: University of California Press, 1990), 91–7.
3 Paul Strohm, "Saving the Appearances: Chaucer's 'Purse' and the Fabrication of the Lancastrian Claim," in *Hochon's Arrow: The Social Imagination of Fourteenth-Century Texts* (Princeton, NJ: Princeton University Press, 1992), 75–94, here 84.
4 Due mostly to the intervention of Paul Strohm.
5 Thomas A. Prendergast, "Politics, Prodigality and the Reception of Chaucer's 'Purse,'" in *Reinventing the Middle Ages and the Renaissance: Constructions of the Medieval and Early Modern Periods*, ed. William Gentrup (Turnhout: Brepols, 1998), 70.
6 William Godwin, *Life of Geoffrey Chaucer*, 4 vols. (London: Printed by T. Davison for R. Phillips, 1804), 4:142, 145.
7 John Dart and Rev. Timothy Thomas, "Life of Geoffrey Chaucer," in Geoffrey Chaucer, *The Canterbury Tales of Chaucer*, ed. John Urry (London: B. Lintot, 1721), E1r–E1v.
8 Strohm is quoting V. J. Scattergood here, *Hochon's Arrow*, 93.
9 Strohm, "Saving the Appearances," 93.
10 Ibid., 80.
11 R.F. Yeager, "Chaucer's 'To His Purse': Begging, or Begging Off?" *Viator* 36 (2005), 373–414. Yeager argues elsewhere that Chaucer's reticence might have had mortal consequences.
12 Ibid., 410, n.162.

Myth 19

THE WIFE OF BATH MURDERED HER HUSBAND

In 1948, Vernon Hall, Jr., a professor of English at Dartmouth, published a piece called "Sherlock Holmes and the Wife of Bath" in the organ of the so-called Baker Street Irregulars, a group of Holmes enthusiasts founded by the writer Christopher Morley. In this fanciful short story, Holmes remarks to Watson, "if the murder in the *Wife of Bath's Prologue* has not been discovered before, it is because I had never read that part of the *Canterbury Tales* until a fortnight ago."[1] His assertion was largely based on her description of her relationship with her future fifth husband, Jankyn, while she was still married to her fourth husband. She reports that they were walking in the fields "Til trewely we hadde swich daliance, / This clek and I, that of my purveiance / I spak to hym and seyde hym how that he, / If I were wydwe, sholde wedde me" (III.565–8). She tells him that she had a dream (though this is false) in which he had come to kill her and "al my bed was ful of verray blood" (III.579). Yet, her interpretation of the dream is not that he is a threat, "But yet I hope that ye shal do me good, / For blood bitokeneth gold, as me was taught" (III.580–81). For Holmes, this is clearly an entreaty to Jankyn that he aid her in disposing of her fourth husband in order to marry and profit from his death (especially as she tells him that if she were a widow, they could marry). The truth of this noirish plot seems supported by the fact that the fourth husband mysteriously passes away, freeing Jankyn to marry the Wife.

It is likely that this confection of a fictional detective reading about the fictional Alisoun and attributing a murder to her equally fictional lover was initially meant as a bit of ludic Holmesian fun. After all, one of the

30 Great Myths About Chaucer, First Edition. Thomas A. Prendergast and Stephanie Trigg.
© 2020 John Wiley & Sons, Inc. Published 2020 by John Wiley & Sons, Inc.

guiding principles of the Irregulars was what was known as "the game" – maintaining that Holmes and Watson actually lived and that Arthur Conan Doyle was only their literary agent. Yet games have a way of getting out of hand and so it was with this one. Some twenty-five years after Holmes's encounter with the Wife, a noted medievalist and future president of the New Chaucer Society, Beryl Rowland, made the startling claim that, in fact, Holmes was right – there had been foul play involved in the "abrupt demise of Alice's fourth husband."[2]

In particular, Rowland argues that "the deliberate ambiguities, the abstruseness of some of the allusions, the frequent ellipses, the shifts in patterns and in mood … suggest a pathological state."[3] Unable to control her confessional nature, Alisoun allusively betrays that she killed her fourth husband, while not, of course, directly admitting it. When, for instance, she talks of her "dream" and tells us it is false, it was because "it … was true literally: she did dream the event; it actually happened."[4] That Jankyn knew of the murder and was complicit becomes evident to us when he begins to read to Alisoun from his book of "Wicked Wives." Five of the stories narrate the untimely death of husbands through the working of their wives. And the most damning evidence comes when Jankyn begins to generalize in terms that purportedly come closest to the circumstances that might best match the Wife's situation:

> … somme han slayn hir housbondes in hir bed,
> And lete hir lecchour dighte hire al the nyght,
> Whan that the corps lay in the floor upright.
> And somme han dryve nayles in hir brayn,
> Whil that they slepte, and thus they had hem slayn.
> Somme han hem yeve poysoun in hire drynke.
> He spak moore harm than herte may bithynke.
>
> (III.766–72)

Shortly thereafter Alisoun famously tears his book, socks him on the cheek and he retaliates, striking her on the head. When she falls down as if dead, he turns to flee, at which point she says, "O! hastow slayn me, false theef? … / And for my land thus hastow mordered me?" (III.800–1). Rowland sees in this asseveration a reference to the murder, for Jankyn already possesses all of the Wife's property: "She is alluding to the way in which he has already acquired it."[5] His total capitulation at the end of the *Prologue* results from his fear both that she would expose him and/or that she might not cavil at repeating her crime with him as her victim.

In an essay conceived separately from Rowland's, though appearing later, Dolores Palomo takes a somewhat different tack. She cites a good deal of evidence that Rowland herself had used – the sudden death, the "dream," the hesitancy in relating events, the murderous wives from Jankyn's book – but then suggests that "Alisoun conspired with Jankyn to murder the reveler and that though she may have later backed out of the scheme, Jankyn carried it out and Alisoun cannot deny her moral culpability."[6] Her justification for relieving Alisoun of the actual killing (if not culpability) is that Jankyn appears also to have died suddenly. Palomo concludes that the Wife (who talked extensively about her "gossib" with whom she shared everything) had, in fact, revealed the terrible secret, with the result that Jankyn was found out and executed for it.

While Rowland's and Palomo's arguments gained traction with some critics, most scholars found them unconvincing.[7] T.L. Burton argued that the whole basis for their suspicion – the suddenness of the death of the fourth husband – was anachronistic because

> both writers forget how close death was in the Middle Ages, and especially so in a century which saw the population of Europe repeatedly devastated by wars and plague. It is a closeness which is everywhere apparent in the literature of the period: in sermons; in morality plays; in proverbs stressing how death strikes young and old alike and how the time of its striking cannot be predicted.[8]

In addition, Burton asserts that to see the Wife as murderous is to completely ignore "the comic spirit in which most of her monologue is delivered."[9] And finally, he makes the point that in the "dream" that the Wife reports to Jankyn, the wording makes it clear that it cannot be the fourth husband's blood in the bed. It is the Wife who is at risk of being stabbed and the blood in her oneiric fiction is clearly her own – most probably (as Rowland herself points out) because stabbing is meant to be symbolic of sexual relations.

Some ten years later, Susan Crane wrote a tongue-in-cheek defense of the Wife arguing that not only was the evidence against her insubstantial (and would never hold up in a court of law), but also even the suspicion that she might have murdered her fourth husband was not justified. Rowland's belief, for instance, that the elliptical and abstruse narration of Alisoun's courtship of Jankyn results from the fact that she has something to hide does not hold up, because the entire *Prologue* is written in a similar manner. Unless we read the sudden stops, starts and hesitations that occur elsewhere in a similar vein, we have to acknowledge that this is the style of the Wife's narrative, rather than evidence that she is covering something up. The fact that Jankyn's book contains so many wifely murderers might seem suspicious, and it seems to be the thing that triggers Alisoun's violence towards Jankyn, thus suggesting a guilty conscience. But it is worth remembering that the Wife boxes Jankyn on the cheek not after the reading of the murders, but after "the book's testimony on women's chiding and sensuality."[10]

More to the point, Crane argues that those suspicious of Alisoun make a fatal category error – they treat her "as a person who has a complete life that we can recover by conjecture."[11] She goes on to assert that "of course, literary characters resemble living people, but the reality of fictional characters is enclosed in and determined by their texts."[12] To make the mistake of not respecting the differences between art and life is not only to be profoundly naïve, but also "to invent more of her life than Chaucer has already given us." It is "to take ourselves for poets."[13] Crane also points out that to accuse Alisoun of murder is to fall into the trap of reading Alisoun as merely a misogynistic stereotype out of Jankyn's book. It is to impoverish what Chaucer is trying to do in the *Wife of Bath's Prologue*, which is not to confirm antifeminist expectations but to shake the foundations of these expectations.

Crane's essay more or less demolished the case against the Wife of Bath. Yet suspicions persisted. D.J. Wurtele acknowledged that the fourth husband may not have been murdered, but argues that the evidence adduced by Rowland suggests that if Alisoun was innocent of murder, she (and maybe Jankyn with her) was not innocent of intending to murder. It just so happened that the fourth husband died by a "fortuitous intervention of Providence" rather than murderous action.[14] And Martin Puhvel, enlarging on a claim he made in an earlier essay, argues that Alisoun managed to get away with murder because she used poison (perhaps more than once). He cites in particular a historically real Alice (Kyteler) who allegedly killed her fourth husband and fled to the Bath area, arguing that Chaucer may have associated "Alys of Bath with a figure real and historical, thus attempting to lend verisimilitude and credibility" to his character.[15] Puhvel's insistence that behind the Wife lies a genuine historical character is, of course, simply another version of what Crane warns us against – understanding the Wife of Bath as being somehow "a real person" (see Myth 8). But perhaps this is to be expected. After all, the charge of murder was first brought against the Wife of Bath in a journal whose stated purpose is "the game": to treat literary characters as if they are real. "The rule of the game," as Oxford alumna and mystery novelist Dorothy L. Sayers once put it, "is that it must be played as solemnly as a county cricket match at Lord's: the slightest touch of extravagance or burlesque ruins the atmosphere."[16]

Notes

1 Vernon Hall, Jr., "Sherlock Holmes and the Wife of Bath," *Baker Street Journal* 3 (1948), 84–93, here 85.

2 Beryl Rowland, "On the Timely Death of the Wife of Bath's Fourth Husband," *Archiv für das Studium der neueren Sprachen und Literaturen* 209 (1972–73), 273–82, here 273.

3 Ibid., 273–4.

4 Ibid., 281.

5 Ibid., 280.

6 Dolores Palomo, "The Fate of the Wife of Bath's 'Bad Husbands,'" *Chaucer Review* 9 (1975), 303–19, here 309.

7 Notably, Donald B. Sands, "The Non-Comic, Non-Tragic Wife: Chaucer's Dame Alys as Sociopath," *Chaucer Review* 12 (1978), 171–82.

8 T.L. Burton, "The Wife of Bath's Fourth and Fifth Husbands and Her Ideal Sixth: The Growth of a Marital Philosophy," *Chaucer Review* 13 (1978), 34–50, here 47n.

9 Ibid., 35.

10 Susan Crane, "Alison of Bath Accused of Murder: Case Dismissed," *English Language Notes* 25 (1988), 10–15, here 10.

11 Ibid., 11.

12 Ibid., 11.

13 Ibid., 12.

14 D.J. Wurtele, "Chaucer's Wife of Bath and the Problem of the Fifth Husband," *Chaucer Review* 23 (1988), 117–28, here 126.

15 Martin Puhvel, "The Death of Alys of Bath's 'Revelour' Husband," *Neuphilologische Mitteilungen* 103, no. 3 (2002), 328–40, here 338. Puhvel is not the only critic to propose that there might be a historical antecedent involving poison. Mary Hamel suggests that Chaucer had another murder in mind when he was composing the Wife's prologue, and used it to suggest not that the Wife murdered, but that Jankyn suspected she had murdered; "The Wife of Bath and a Contemporary Murder," *Chaucer Review* 14 (1979), 132–9.

16 Dorothy L. Sayers, *Unpopular Opinions* (London: Victor Gollancz, 1946), 7.

Myth
20 CHAUCER "OUTS" THE PARDONER

In 1926, Walter Clyde Curry argued that the Pardoner had a dark secret that was revealed in the well-known description of the pilgrim from the *General Prologue*: "A voys he hadde as smal as hath a goot. / Ne berd hadde he, ne nevere sholde have; / As smothe it was as it were late shave. / I trowe he were a geldyng or a mare" (I.688–91). Curry argued that the physiognomy of the Pardoner as described by Chaucer indicated that the Pardoner was "most unfortunate in his birth. He carries upon his body and has stamped on his mind and character the marks of what is known to mediaeval physiognomists as a *eunuchus ex nativitate*."[1] Further, he averred that the "gentlefolk" on the pilgrimage "are doubtless well acquainted with the current physiognomical lore" and "recognize the type immediately."[2] Thus when the Host, enraged at the Pardoner's behavior after his tale, threatens to cut off his "coillons," it draws attention to the fact that he has none. The Pardoner's attempts to conceal his lack are, Curry asserted, pathetic:

> he goes about singing in concert with the Summoner a gay little song, "Come hider love, to me" (A, 672), and boasts with brazen effrontery that he will drink wine "And have a jolly wenche in every toun" (C, 453). He sings and brags like a real man; but one suspects that most of his *affaires d'amour* result in chagrin and disappointment like that in which he engages with Kitt the Tapster in the *Tale of Beryn*.[3]

It was perhaps inevitable that Curry's thesis would lead other critics to understand lines like "I trow he were a geldyng or a mare" in more figurative terms. Muriel Bowden was the first to suggest a bit coyly that

30 Great Myths About Chaucer, First Edition. Thomas A. Prendergast and Stephanie Trigg.
© 2020 John Wiley & Sons, Inc. Published 2020 by John Wiley & Sons, Inc.

"Chaucer's description of the physical attributes of the Pardoner mark this figure explicitly as the kind of person we immediately suspect him to be."[4] Reflecting the bias of her times, she comments that the song he sings does not demonstrate, as Curry claims, a boast about his heterosexual prowess, but a come-on to the Summoner who, "far from being unresponsive to depraved and unnatural advances, trumpets forth a bass accompaniment ('burdoun') to emphasize his perverted friendship with the Pardoner."[5] Bowden's thesis was amplified a few years later by a number of critics who saw in the line "This Somonour bar to hym a stif burdoun" (I.673) a pun on "burdoun" that not only carries a musical sense, but is also the word for a staff. As one critic put it, this meaning "added to the Pardoner's being a *geldyng or a mare* bears out the suggestion that these two worthies were homosexuals and point to the obscene pun."[6] By the latter part of the twentieth century, the homosexuality of the Pardoner was seen to be so obvious that Jill Mann remarked "after [the description of the Pardoner in the *General Prologue*] one wonders how the Pardoner's 'secret' could ever have been thought to be concealed; the modern stereotype is identical in every respect."[7]

Perhaps reacting to what she saw as Mann's (and other critics') presentist tendencies, Monica E. McAlpine attempted to make a more historically sophisticated argument about the Pardoner's homosexuality. While acknowledging that the term "homosexual" did not enter the language until 1869, she nonetheless argued that the most accurate gloss for the Middle English term "mare" "would probably be a slang term for the effeminate male homosexual."[8] Why did Chaucer not simply come out and address the Pardoner's sexuality? McAlpine argued that it was Chaucer's method to involve the reader in a hermeneutic that prevented a reductive treatment of the character. Readers were thus engaged in a reading that, through interpretive means, became a moral exercise. McAlpine's ingenious ability to turn uncertainty to her own advantage might have seemed to settle the fact that we are (at least) meant to wonder about the Pardoner's sexuality and suspect (if not decide) that he must be gay. But far from settling the debate, it only encouraged demurral.

Just two years after McAlpine's essay, C. David Benson made the case that the evidence usually adduced to "prove" that the Pardoner was gay was at best imprecise. The term "mare," for instance, could simply refer to an effeminate man. The "stif bourdon" that the Summoner "bar" to the Pardoner could simply be a literal reference to the bass part that he sang. In any case, Chaucer tells us that "I *trow* he were a geldyng or a mare," so it is not even clear that we are to trust Chaucer the Pilgrim's opinion. Benson takes seriously the Pardoner's claim that he has a wench in every town and (addressing Curry's thesis) argues that the Host's threat to castrate the Pardoner actually confirms that he has testicles and thus normalizes his sexuality. More tellingly, he suggests that curiosity about the Pardoner's sexuality can easily become ridiculous, because the character has no existence off the written page. As with the Wife of Bath (see Myth 19), he cannot have a secret because he is not a real person. Chaucer cannot "out" him because he does not exist.[9]

This final, pragmatic, rhetorical move is appealing because it fits into a series of binaries (real/fictional; true/false) that offer a certain resolution to the problem by suggesting that it is not a problem at all. But Benson's own treatment of the Pardoner's sexuality buys into these binaries less than it might initially appear. Near the end of his essay, he says:

> I do not mean to deny there is definitely something odd about the Pardoner as described in the General Prologue, but I would suggest that his sexuality remains too imprecise to serve as a reliable guide to his entire performance and Tale. Chaucer throws out several hints, but he does not define. He may have aroused our suspicions, but he does not indicate any exact condition that can be used as a sure foundation on which to build an interpretation.[10]

Benson frames his argument in oppositional terms, but he is not as far from McAlpine's position as he makes out. In most of the essay, he stresses that the Pardoner's sexuality is not beside the point, but uncertain. There is something "odd" about the Pardoner. Chaucer gives us "hints." We might "suspect." All of these are terms used to describe something that demands interpretation, which is something with which McAlpine would agree.

This focus on the uncertain nature of the Pardoner's sexuality and its function as a metacommentary on the work of interpretation provided the focus for many of the critical treatments of the pilgrim at the end of the twentieth century. Carolyn Dinshaw, for instance, returns to Curry's thesis about the eunuchry of the Pardoner, but also notes that eunuchry and other physical and sexual conditions (including homosexuality) "were conflated in the Middle Ages."[11] The result is a radical instability in the description of the Pardoner in the *General Prologue*. The narrator knows that there is something strange about the pilgrim: "something is lacking, either the physical equipment or masculine gender-identification," but it remains unclear what.[12] This, she argues, is precisely the point. To identify the lack certainly is to penetrate to "the naked truth" and engage in what she calls a "heterosexual hermeneutic."[13] She instead suggests that we embrace a "eunuch hermeneutics" – an admission that even as we strive for full understanding, representation is partial and so it is well to understand that the search for meaning and knowledge is bound to be multiple.

Glenn Burger, while mounting a powerful critique of Dinshaw's work (he argues that she essentializes the Pardoner as "absolute other"), nonetheless agrees that definitively categorizing the Pardoner as homosexual (or eunuch, or effeminate, etc.) is reductive. It is to "reproduce the strategies of containment the pilgrims use to maintain active control of what the pilgrimage means."[14] By this he means that the Pardoner is understood only to be how Chaucer the Pilgrim describes him, or what the Host implies he is. His otherness, then, "constitutes the worth of someone else's active voice" and can be true only if we "remain locked within a single, unified level of discourse."[15] Critics, of course, have long maintained that to read any pilgrim's voice as conveying absolute meaning in the *Tales* is, to say the least, problematic. But these approaches to the Pardoner indicate that if there is (as Curry suggested so long ago) a secret about the Pardoner, it is not about whether his genitals are present *or* absent, nor whether he is straight *or* (as Burger puts it) perverse. It is that reading the Pardoner requires us to acknowledge the reductiveness of these binaries (at least as we understand them).[16]

If, then, "outing" is representing the Pardoner as certainly gay, then this is probably not quite what Chaucer meant to do. One of the assumptions that many of these interpretations make is that there is much that remains unspoken by the pilgrims – hence critics speak of the secret, or to be more accurate, the open secret, something everyone knows but no one explicitly reveals. Most medieval readers and scribes were similarly circumspect about the Pardoner's "secret." There is, however, manuscript evidence that a few medieval readers may have believed that the secret was a bit too open. Some sixty lines before the Pardoner remarks that he had "a jolly wenche in every toun" occur two lines that reflect his ability to generate revenue through his false relics: "By this gaude have I wonne, yeer by yeer, / An hundred mark sith I was pardoner" (VI.389–90). In three manuscripts, "wonne yeer by yeer" is replaced with "wommen every yer." Elizabeth Allen has argued that these alterations may indicate a discomfort with the ambiguity attending the Pardoner's sexuality.[17] Perhaps even more tellingly, another manuscript replaces the line "I trowe he were a geldyng or a mare" with "I trowe he *had* a geldyng or a mare." Allen believes that given the level of scholarly engagement in the Pardoner's "secret," it is surprising that we do not find many more attempts to smooth out his sexuality in the manuscript tradition. But maybe the reverse is actually true. Maybe medieval scribes and readers understood that even an open secret is not really *out* in the open.

Notes

1 Walter Clyde Curry, *Chaucer and the Mediaeval Sciences* (New York: Oxford University Press, 1926), 59.

2 Ibid., 65.

3 Ibid., 68. Properly speaking, it is in the prologue to the *Tale of Beryn* that the episode takes place. This prologue is a spurious treatment of the pilgrims' arrival in Canterbury that is extant in one eccentric manuscript (Alnwick Castle, Northumberland, Duke of Northumberland 455).

4 Muriel Bowden, *A Commentary on the General Prologue to the Canterbury Tales* (New York: Macmillan, 1948), 274.

5 Ibid., 274.

6 Paull F. Baum, "Chaucer's Puns," *PMLA* 71, no. 1 (March 1956), 225–46, here 232.

7 Jill Mann, *Chaucer and Medieval Estates Satire* (Cambridge: Cambridge University Press, 1973), 145–6.

8 Monica McAlpine, "The Pardoner's Homosexuality and How it Matters," *PMLA* 95, no. 1 (1980), 8–22, here 20, n.11.

9 C. David Benson, "Chaucer's Pardoner: His Sexuality and Modern Critics," *Mediaevalia* 8 (1982), 337–46.

10 Ibid., 344.

11 Carolyn Dinshaw, "Eunuch Hermeneutics," *ELH* 55, no. 1 (1988), 27–51, here 30.

12 Ibid., 30. Although, she notes, the Host at least seems pretty certain that the Pardoner has no balls (53).

13 Ibid., 27.

14 Glenn Burger, "Kissing the Pardoner," *PMLA* 107, no. 5 (1992), 1143–56, here 1152, n.1.

15 Ibid., 1145, 1152, n.1.

16 Not everyone is so quick to dispense with the idea that we are to understand the Pardoner as gay. See, for instance, Stephen F. Kruger's fine article, "Claiming the Pardoner: Toward a Gay Reading of Chaucer's *Pardoner's Tale*," *Exemplaria* 6 (1994), 113–39. And, more recently, some have seen these approaches as "threatening to erase the Pardoner's body altogether." See Elspeth Whitney, "What's Wrong with the Pardoner? Complexion Theory, the Phlegmatic Man, and Effeminacy," *Chaucer Review* 45 no. 4 (2011), 357–89, here 359.

17 Elizabeth Allen, "The Pardoner in the 'Dogges Boure': Early Reception of the 'Canterbury Tales,'" *Chaucer Review* 56, no. 2 (2001), 91–127, here 100.

Myth
21
CHAUCER NEVER FINISHED THE CANTERBURY TALES

As everyone knows, the frame narrative of the *Canterbury Tales* is set up in the *General Prologue* as a kind of game. The Host, Harry Bailly, says that, at the end of the pilgrimage, he will choose the best tale-teller and that pilgrim "shall have a soper at oure aller cost" (I.799). Further, Harry's decision will not be based on one tale, but rather

> ... ech of yow, to shorte with oure weye,
> In this viage shal telle tales tweye
> To Caunterbury-ward, I mene it so,
> And homward he shal tellen othere two,
> Of aventures that whilom han bifalle.
>
> (I.791–95)

Yet by the time we get to the *Parson's Tale*, Harry Bailly turns to the Parson and asks him to "knytte up wel a greet mateere" because "every man ... hath toold *his tale*" (X.28, 25). In 1775, the great eighteenth-century editor Thomas Tyrwhitt, commenting on Harry Bailly's plan, articulated what would have been blazingly obvious to anyone who had access to a "complete" version of the *Tales*:

> From this passage we should certainly conclude, that each of them was to tell *two tales* in the journey to Canterbury, and two more in the journey homeward; but all the other passages, in which mention is made of this agreement, would rather lead us to believe, that they were to tell only one tale in each journey ... and therefore the reader, if he is so pleased, may consider this as one of those inconsistencies, hinted at above, which prove too plainly that the author had not finished his work.[1]

---

30 Great Myths About Chaucer, First Edition. Thomas A. Prendergast and Stephanie Trigg.
© 2020 John Wiley & Sons, Inc. Published 2020 by John Wiley & Sons, Inc.

Chaucer's original conception of the scope of the work (if that is what it was) was massive. There were, if one counts the Canon's Yeoman who enters late, thirty pilgrims, and if each told four tales, the original conception of the work would have comprised one hundred and twenty tales (or an English great hundred). This is not to say that Chaucer was competing with his probable model for the *Tales*, but the work would have surpassed Giovanni Boccaccio's *Decameron* by twenty.

So what happened? Even if one takes the *Prologue* to the *Parson's Tale* as the final word (one tale from each pilgrim), we still come up six tales short. And Chaucer famously tells two tales (though one is interrupted), so seven of the pilgrims have yet to tell their tales at the completion of the work. And there are other difficulties. References to the tale-telling game by Harry Bailly in other parts of the *Tales* suggest that what is expected is "a tale or two" (V.698), and one pilgrim even threatens to tell "tales too or thre" (III.846). The number of tales that the pilgrims are supposed or threaten to tell seems remarkably fluid. In addition, the *Tales* end before we reach Canterbury and so we are deprived of the homeward tale-telling action promised by the Host.

Early scholars attempted to mitigate the problem by suggesting that even if Chaucer did not fulfill his promise, he never meant for the pilgrims to tell four tales. With just a bit of emendation, the text, at least, could offer a consistent plan of one tale each way. So, for instance, the line which reads "And homward he shal tellen othere two" might be emended to read "And homward he shal tellen o *thereto*." These kinds of emendation offer the advantage of resolving an inconsistency, but they suffer from the fact that they never appear in any of the manuscripts that contain the *General Prologue*. Later commentators, influenced by ironic readings of the *Tales*, offered more radical solutions, suggesting that we are wrongly conflating Chaucerian motivation with the motivation of Harry Bailly. In fact, Chaucer's plan might actually involve the "humorous deflating" of the Host, or the desire to demonstrate the gap between intent and outcome, rather than any definitive statement of how long Chaucer's own work might be.[2]

Despite all of these attempts to explain away the gap between what the Host promised and what actually appears in the *Tales*, the broad consensus is that Chaucer's own idea of the shape and size of the *Canterbury Tales* changed during the course of the writing of the work. Whether he initially intended for it to be a longer work and then later revised his ideas remains unknown, because it is quite possible that the *General Prologue* was composed after many of the tales.

In addition, there are other markers of incompleteness. Some of the tales that do make their way into the work are no more than fragments.

Famously, the *Cook's Tale* ends mid-tale, just as a riotous apprentice has lodged with a friend of his whose wife "swyved for hir sustenance" (I.4422). Some scribes, disconcerted about the non-ending of the tale, composed a new ending; others inserted a long romance in rhymed couplets called the *Tale of Gamelyn*; and in one of the most important manuscripts within the tradition, the tale is followed by a simple note: "Of this cokes tale maked Chaucer na moore."[3] Finally, though some tales are grouped together, the collection as a whole lacks links between many of the groupings. The result is that the most influential edition of Chaucer's work, *The Riverside Chaucer* (currently reprinted as *The Wadsworth Chaucer*), breaks the work up into ten fragments. This state of affairs led one influential critic to suggest that "this is how ideally it [the *Canterbury Tales*] should be presented, partly as a bound book (the first and last fragments are fixed) and partly as a set of fragments in a folder, with the fragmentary information as to their nature and placement fully displayed."[4]

So does the unfinished nature of the work really make any difference to our interpretation of it? One critic suggested that the focus on its unfinished nature was actually harmful, because it subordinated the idea of the *Canterbury Tales* to some *faux*-genuine idea of pilgrimage; the obsession with how long the pilgrimage would have taken (three and a half days); where, precisely, the pilgrims were at any given time (leading to a notorious re-ordering of the *Tales* along geographical lines); and whether the pilgrims were "real" people was more the product of nineteenth-century novelistic realism than any medieval understanding of the *Canterbury Tales*.[5] What we needed to understand is that the work was "*unfinished but complete*," constituting the definitive record of Chaucer's intent.[6]

This sounds like a way to move forward and has the virtue of being sensible because it deals with a text that seems to exist – the *Canterbury Tales* – even if it is unfinished. And this "unfinished" text would appear to be that within the pages of the *Riverside Chaucer*. But to think of the *Canterbury Tales* this way is to make the mistake of thinking that medieval texts maintain their "urn-like integrity in entering the ocean of textual transmission."[7] The *Canterbury Tales*, or portions of it, exists in over eighty manuscripts, all of them (except perhaps one) produced after Chaucer's death. And even a cursory glance at these different versions of the *Tales* shows us that it is not just that the *Canterbury Tales* is unfinished, it is unfinished in a multitude of different ways by the people who copied it. And these scribes were themselves attempting to come to terms with the nature of the unfinished work. Further complicating the understanding of this unfinished work is that we do not know the state in which Chaucer left his papers at the end of his life, so we do not know *how* it was unfinished. So, for instance, we have two early and important manuscripts (Ellesmere and Hengwrt) that were produced quite close to one another. Both were copied by the same scribe (who may or may not be the famous Adam Scriveyn to whom Chaucer addresses a poem). And yet this single scribe produces two texts that have different tale orders and even, in some places, different content. The governing assumption has generally been that the scribe was attempting to reconstruct the text as Chaucer would have intended (even as he undertook this project at different times).

Chaucer's own thinking, then, would seem more or less analogous to the thinking of modern readers, like the critic mentioned, who are trying to get at the author's intent. The fact that he produced two texts that are so different might simply be the product of historical accident. Maybe he did not have all of the materials to hand when he produced the first manuscript and then this was later (partially) remedied. Yet even here the understanding of the intent of the author, or *intentio auctoris*, complicates matters. Recent work on the understanding of authorial intent suggests that texts in the Middle Ages were conceived to have "considerable agency separate from the human, historical author."[8] It is not that the scribes did not believe in human intention, it is just that the intention of the human author was available only insofar "as it [was] displaced into the work" and the "*intentio auctoris* refers most often to the intention of the work."[9] Scribes, then, who produced manuscripts often aspired to produce more complete versions of the *Tales* than were available to them. As we have seen, they would sometimes confect small or large stretches of text in order to make good the absence of a text (like the *Cook's Tale*) that the work apparently promised.

We would think of this wholesale invention as false – an inauthentically "finished" text. But it is not at all certain that all scribes or all readers of the *Tales* would have thought the same way. It is quite possible that when scribes invented links between the tales (or re-purposed already existing links), they were "finishing" a text in a fundamentally medieval way, adhering not to "an authorial original, nor any historical reconstruction of the text at one point in its transmission," but to a sense of the text that existed outside of the material forms of the text that they inherited.[10] In this sense, then, they might not have understood the statement "Chaucer never finished the *Canterbury Tales*" in quite the same way that we do. The text had an end or *telos* towards which it tended and it was up to the writer (whether the original author or the copyist) to discover what it was.

Notes

1 Thomas Tyrwhitt, ed., *The Canterbury Tales of Chaucer to which are added, an essay upon his language and versification; an introductory discourse; and notes*, 5 vols. (London, 1775–78), 4:130–31.

2 Malcolm Andrew, Charles Moorman and Daniel J. Ransom, eds., *A Variorum Edition of the Works of Geoffrey Chaucer, 2: The Canterbury Tales: The General Prologue* (Norman, OK: University of Oklahoma Press, 1993), 581–2.

3 John Bowers, ed., *The Canterbury Tales: Fifteenth-Century Continuations and Additions* (Kalamazoo, MI: Medieval Institute Publications, 1992), 33–9. In addition, the *Squire's Tale* breaks off abruptly. It remains unclear, however, whether the interruption of the Franklin that purportedly ends the tale is Chaucer's or someone attempting to make Chaucer's work "seem" more complete.

4 Derek Pearsall, "Editing Medieval Texts: Some Developments and Some Problems," in *Textual Criticism and Literary Interpretation*, ed. Jerome J. McGann (Chicago, IL: University of Chicago Press, 1985), 92–106, here 97.

5 Donald R. Howard, *Writers and Pilgrims: Medieval Pilgrimage Narratives and Their Posterity* (Berkeley, CA: University of California Press, 1980), 119–21.

6 Donald Howard, *The Idea of the Canterbury Tales* (Berkeley, CA: University of California Press, 1977), 1, emphasis in original.

7 David Wallace, ed., *The Cambridge History of Medieval English Literature* (Cambridge: Cambridge University Press, 1999), xx.

8 Mary Carruthers, *The Experience of Beauty in the Middle Ages* (Oxford: Oxford University Press, 2013), 53.

9 Ibid., 171.

10 Daniel Wakelin, *Scribal Correction and Literary Craft: English Manuscripts 1375–1500* (Cambridge: Cambridge University Press, 2014), 155.

Myth
22

CHAUCER IS OBSCENE

Until relatively recently, the creation of obscenity as a crime or as an offense to public morals was seen to be synonymous with the rise of modernity. The "rude" Middle Ages was viewed as a time when bawdiness was accepted and accommodated.[1] The editor of the first expurgated version of Chaucer's *Canterbury Tales*, William Lipscomb, for instance, writes in 1795 of "the grossness and indelicacy of Chaucer's times." He acknowledges Chaucer's greatness, but argues that "our veneration for his great and various excellencies is rather the more testified, by purging him from his impurities, and exhibiting him to a more refined age a safe as well as a brilliant example of native genius."[2] This line of thinking leads him to omit the *Miller's Tale* (a story that involves extramarital sex, the kissing of an ass and the forcible insertion of a "hoote kultour" into an anus) and the *Reeve's Tale* (which arguably tries to make a joke out of rape; see Myth 11). Lipscomb argues that the omission of these tales (as well as some other "improper passages") will thus enable "readers of every denomination" to have "safe access" to Chaucer. This strange emphasis on safety was generated by the idea that indelicate reading could lead to moral atavism.

Yet, as even a casual reader of the *Tales* knows, Lipscomb's totalizing assumption about the "indelicacy and grossness" of the Middle Ages ignores the fact that Chaucer records his own hesitations about the matter of the Miller's and Reeve's tales. He (somewhat disingenuously) defends himself as a simple recorder of the pilgrims' tales, saying that since the Miller actually told the tale, he had the obligation to include it, but warns the reader that "The Millere is a cherl; ye knowe wel this. / So

30 Great Myths About Chaucer, First Edition. Thomas A. Prendergast and Stephanie Trigg.
© 2020 John Wiley & Sons, Inc. Published 2020 by John Wiley & Sons, Inc.

was the Reve eek and othere mo, / And harlotrie they tolden bothe two"
(I.3182–4). The term "harlotrie" generally refers to low talk or speech
about things that are scurrilous and obscene; in fact, around the same
time that Chaucer was working on the *Tales*, one medieval writer actu-
ally used the word to translate the Latin *obscenitas*.[3]

Medieval understandings of obscenity varied. So, for instance, "obsce-
nus" comes from "*ob* (on account of) and *cenum* (dirt or filth)"; and
"anything shameful is called *obscaenum* because it ought not to be said
openly except on the *scaena*," which refers to a small building attached to
ancient Greek theaters, but just offstage.[4] What this shameful, filthy
obscenity might consist of is difficult to determine, but Isidore of Seville
suggests that it may relate to different kinds of "love." The love of a wife
is just and the love of children pious, but the love of a prostitute is
obscene.[5] That which is obscene, then, is unclean, should not be openly
talked about, and probably involves some kind of illicit fornication.

Like Lipscomb, however, some contemporary critics have argued that
it seems as if "medieval culture lacks a sense of the obscene since it
diverges markedly from modernity in the level of publicity and respecta-
bility it accords to certain displays of sexuality and body parts."[6] For
example, one Anglo-Norman manuscript contains the fabliaux *Les trois
dames qui trouverent un vit* (the three women who found a penis) and *Le
chevalier qui fist parler les cons* (the knight who could make cunts speak),
as well as "an English translation of the 'Sayings of St. Bernard' ... and
the English religious verse piece *The Way of Christ's Love*."[7] This mixture
of religious with bawdy works would suggest that, at the very least, the
medievals had very different ideas about the separation of spiritual from
"fleshly" texts. And the open dissemination of these mixed compendia
would also suggest that the medievals either did not understand the
obscene in the way we would, or that they did not see such stories as
obscene.

Yet, as Nicole Nolan Sidhu points out, to think about the dissemina-
tion of these sacred and profane works in manuscripts as in any way
analogous to the contemporary dissemination of textual and pictorial
material is to ignore the fact that access to manuscripts was actually quite
circumscribed. In a sense, these ribald stories (and their intermixture with
more "appropriate" reading) did remain "offstage" and thus their ability
to subvert medieval "community standards" would be limited to those
elites who were actually already invested in maintaining these
standards.[8]

Chaucer's own metacommentary on the Miller's and Reeve's tales, of
course, suggests the opposite. The intermixture of "cherls" and "gentles"
and the oral nature of the fictive tale-telling game seems to make that

which is hidden accessible to all. In fact, what is really transgressive about the frame narrative is not that the illiterate "cherls" have access to the subversive fabliaux (because they themselves are the tale-tellers), it is that the gentles are forced to listen to them. Similarly, what is objectionable is not really the material of the stories, but the fact that those from the upper classes are *seen* to be hearing the tales. The pilgrim Chaucer, making a representation of the tale-telling, has the luxury of making it possible for the reader to avoid this indignity. After he warns his readers about the fact that the Miller and Reeve ("and othere mo") were "cherls", he famously suggests that if the reader does not wish to "hear" the tale, "Turne over the leef and chese another tale; /... / Blameth nat me if that ye chese amys" (I.3183, I.3177, I.3181). Other writers, like Ovid, have used similar disclaimers, but for Chaucer, of course, the transgressive nature of the situation is mitigated by the private experience of reading rather than hearing the tales. In the fictional frame of the *Canterbury Tales* the pilgrims and Chaucer have no choice but to hear the fabliaux, while the reader is in a position to choose. But as the reader's choice will not be witnessed (unless someone is reading over her shoulder), the possibility for embarrassment at finding delectation in the obscene is almost completely absent.

In one sense Chaucer generates obscenity by creating a fictional situation where that which should remain hidden is made public. At the same time, he makes it possible for the reader to avoid obscenity because she can self-censor. As we saw in Lipscomb's comments, modern conceptions of obscenity became somewhat more capacious. Warnings about the explicit nature of the material were not enough. The availability of the supposedly obscene work became the problem, because access to it was so much more widespread than it had been in pre-print culture. "Readers of every denomination" (as Lipscomb put it) need to be safeguarded from making the wrong choice that Chaucer's work gives them. These anxieties crested in the middle of the nineteenth century when anti-obscenity laws went into effect in the USA and Great Britain. And even though the courts relented at the end of the century, specifically exempting Chaucer's works from being considered obscene (on the grounds that they constituted great literature), bowdlerized versions of Chaucer continued to be produced well into the twentieth century.

In the USA, at least, this desire to protect the reader persisted until quite late – with a special emphasis on the danger Chaucerian obscenity posed to minors.[9] In the 1980s and 1990s, American high schools went so far as to ban or expurgate certain parts of Chaucer's works because of sexual explicitness, vulgar language and the fact that "the community's standards are violated."[10] This last phrase is a direct reference to the

Supreme Court's attempt in *Miller vs. California* (1973) to define what is obscene, and thus is not protected by the First Amendment of the Constitution that guarantees free speech. Like earlier judicial decisions, the Court explicitly exempts works that have "serious literary, artistic, political, or scientific value." In Chaucerian terms, if there is enough "sentence" then the work can contain prurient "solaas" as well. In contemporary American legal terms, Chaucer's poetry is deemed not to be obscene primarily because any potential obscenity is outweighed by its overall literary merit.

Yet, taking this narrow, legalistic (and American) view of obscenity ignores the extent to which obscenity also functions in the social realm. George Shuffleton argues that Chaucer is obscene (though not pornographic), and this is precisely why he remains in the literary canon: "generations of students are taught how to be high-minded about obscenity, how to distinguish between a dirty joke and a respectable tale. The classroom asks readers to respond to obscenity with something other than titillation, scandalized outrage, or giggles."[11] Ultimately this leads to the development of an "'aesthetic disposition': an ability to make cultural distinctions that in turn reinforce social distinctions."[12] In a sense, Shuffleton returns to Chaucer's own linkage between class and obscenity, arguing that just as he distinguishes between stories told by "cherls" and those told by gentles, so too is he used to policing the boundary between obscenity and good taste. Yet, if this is so, it is also true that Chaucer's naughtiness is often used as a kind of lure for students, just as his own disclaimers, far from preserving his reader's modesty, actually serve to incite a desire for that which purportedly should be hidden.

Notes

1 Nicola McDonald, "Introduction," in *Medieval Obscenities*, ed. Nicola McDonald (Woodbridge: York Medieval Texts, 2014), 1.

2 William Lipscomb, ed., *The Canterbury Tales of Chaucer; Completed in a Modern Version*, 3 vols. (Oxford, 1795), 1:vii–viii.

3 John Trevisa, trans., *Polychronicon Ranulphi Higden, Monachi Cestrensis*, ed. Joseph Rawson Lumby, 9 vols. (Cambridge: Cambridge University Press, 1874), 5:36–7.

4 Alastair Minnis, "From *coilles* to *bel chose*: Discourses of Obscenity in Jean de Meun and Chaucer," in *Medieval Obscenities*, ed. Nicola McDonald (Woodbridge: York Medieval Texts, 2014), 156.

5 Ibid., 156.

6 Nicole Nolan Sidhu, *Indecent Exposure: Gender, Politics, and Obscene Comedy in Middle English Literature* (Philadelphia, PA: University of Pennsylvania Press, 2016), 17.

7 Ibid., 17.

8 Explicit representations of the body could, of course, be seen by a much wider audience in medieval churches (corbel sculptures etc.), but these being produced at the behest of religious authorities were often used to regulate culture rather than subvert it. See ibid., 23.

9 George Shuffleton, for instance, has argued that Chaucer's supposed "obscenity has dominated readers' perceptions … [in the USA] … in peculiar ways that it has not elsewhere"; "Chaucerian Obscenity in the Court of Public Opinion," *Chaucer Review* 47, no. 1 (2012), 1–24, here 2.

10 Dawn B. Sova, *Banned Books: Literature Suppressed on Social Grounds* (New York: Facts on File, 2006), 76–8.

11 Shuffleton, "Chaucerian Obscenity," 22.

12 Ibid., 22.

Myth
23

CHAUCER WAS SKEPTICAL OF CHIVALRY

After the Prioress finishes her tale about the murder and (temporary) resurrection of a little clergeon, the Host, seemingly looking for something a little less "sobre," turns to Chaucer and asks him to "telle us a tale of myrthe" (VII.706). Chaucer responds with the *Tale of Sir Thopas*, "a rym" he says, "I lerned longe agoon" (VII.709). What follows is no old rhyme, but "a brilliant parody of everything that can go wrong" in chivalric romance.[1] Its childish hero rides through a forest inhabited by "many a wilde best" – deer and rabbits. When he encounters a giant named "Elephant," Thopas threatens him and then runs away because he is not wearing his armor. The meter and matter are so lame that one critic characterizes Chaucer's contribution as "a tale that gallops about without ever really arriving."[2] Harry Bailey, unable to take any more of this "rym dogerel," stops him mid-stride, saying "Namoore of this, for Goddes dignitee … / Thy drasty ryming is nat worth a toord!" (VII.919–20).

By and large, the critical response to Chaucer's tale understood that he was parodying or burlesquing the aesthetic excesses of chivalric romances such as *Sir Beves of Hampton*, *Guy of Warwick* or *Horn Child* (all of which Chaucer mentions in his tale).[3] This idea probably began with Thomas Warton who, in his *History of English Poetry* (1774), claimed:

> Genuine humour, the concomitant of true taste, consists in discerning improprieties in books as well as characters. We therefore must remark under this class another tale of Chaucer, which till lately has been looked upon as a grave heroic narrative. I mean the Rime of Sir Thopas.[4]

30 Great Myths About Chaucer, First Edition. Thomas A. Prendergast and Stephanie Trigg.
© 2020 John Wiley & Sons, Inc. Published 2020 by John Wiley & Sons, Inc.

Warton was probably wrong about the prevailing belief concerning the tale. Some might have seen the tale as a "morall" piece, but most understood Thopas as a "figure of fun."[5] Warton's innovation was to suggest that Chaucer's object was to critique not the character of Thopas, but the books that contained other chivalric romances. Laura Hibbard Loomis even believed that she had discovered the book that he had in mind (and in hand) when he was writing his parody or burlesque of these chivalric romances.[6] A quick glance through these romances would seem to confirm the idea that Chaucer is parodying the genre. He constructs his tale by borrowing from these works and deforming their characteristic tail rhyme so that his chivalric romance barely scans.

Yet, as Joseph Dane argues, to see Chaucer's tale as a parody or burlesque is to import categories of literature into our interpretation of Chaucer that were only invented in the eighteenth century.[7] It is also to restrict the understanding of Chaucer's tale as a metatextual response to a literary genre. Some critics have understood the object of Chaucer's scorn as not only the romances that seemed to laud chivalric ideals, but the chivalric ideals themselves. V.J. Scattergood, for instance, acknowledges that "Chaucer's satire in *Sir Thopas* is made largely in terms of style," and goes on to say:

> but it is not simply style that he intends to discredit. Romances implicitly assume an endeavor. To the extent that heroes of romance are exemplary, romances prompt their readers to believe in the value of amazing feats of arms, of unthinking, sworn commitment to grand causes, to flamboyant, asocial behavior. For Chaucer this view of life is rather ridiculous, and inappropriate to contemporary needs and capabilities. By giving his romance an unheroic, mundane setting, and by making his hero the product of an urban, bourgeois, mercantile and essentially contemporary culture, Chaucer is emphasizing the irrelevance in the late fourteenth century of the values romances traditionally celebrate. And by making his story an old one, told in an outmoded form, he appears to be implying that if romances ever had any real relation to life, it was at sometime in the distant past.[8]

The belief that Chaucer was not simply mocking a form of literature, but the thing that that form celebrated, arose (at least partially) from readings of the long prose tale that Chaucer told after Harry Bailey unceremoniously stopped his "drasty rhyming." This tale, a translation of Reynaud de Louens's *Livre de Melibée et de Dame Prudence*, is a moral prose treatise that advocates peace instead of war and reconciliation instead of vengeance. In concert with the *Tale of Sir Thopas* it seems to take issue with chivalric excess, specifically the "martial honor" that characterizes knightly behavior. Alcuin Blamires, for instance, claims that Chaucer, "in order to register his objections to that cult ... takes advantage of his presence among the pilgrims of the *Canterbury Tales* to present what amounts to a personal critique on the subject. *Thopas* and *Melibee* are, I believe, the game and earnest of Chaucer's opposition to the current definition of chivalric honor."[9]

But if we understand Chaucer's tale as a critique of late fourteenth-century chivalric practices, what about Chaucer's "verray, parfit, gentil knight"? The Knight's portrait in the *Canterbury Tales* would seem to be quite positive. And, in fact, critics would claim that the Knight was a paragon of chivalric virtue which, at its best, was a civilizing force: "chivalry and romantic love, often called courtly love, were the two great victories of the spirit in the secular civilization of Christendom over the two most powerful male impulses, aggression and an omnivorous sexuality."[10] Some critics were less than convinced, however, that Chaucer meant for his portrait of the Knight to be wholly positive. Terry Jones attempted to make the case that Chaucer "described a typical mercenary of his day, whose career has been one of bloodshed and oppression .... In the Knight's Tale, he presents a chivalric romance, seen through the eyes of a mercenary captain, which consequently turns into a hymn of tyranny."[11] Even the future of his son (the Squire) seems dark, as he has already participated in a "chyvachie" (a particularly brutal form of warfare) that was directed against fellow Christians.[12] What Chaucer purportedly means to critique in his portrait of the Knight (as well as his tale) is the replacement of feudal order based on loyalty with "a callous money relationship."[13] Chivalry, then, has fallen off from what it formerly was, and, according to Jones, Chaucer's representation of the Knight is at once an indictment of chivalry and a nostalgia for an earlier chivalric ethic. Yet, as David Aers points out, there is very little evidence "to flesh out his highly generalized commonplaces about this present but fading 'feudal' age."[14] In fact, Chaucer himself was very much a part of the bourgeois, mercantile economy, and the Church had been employing mercenaries for over a hundred years in the Crusades.

More recently, Helen Phillips has made a more nuanced argument about chivalry, claiming that the romances that Chaucer was making fun of were not seen as antiquated, nor were they simply a nostalgic recollection of an idealized chivalric past. Instead, she argues that "they were core forms at the centre of an established and powerful canon of English narrative—socially powerful and nationally powerful, with claims to occupy already the role of national narrative."[15] In parodying these romances, Chaucer is taking issue with chivalric ideals that were "associated with regional power and the entrenched interests ... of great dynasties" that were "alien to the late medieval political climate Chaucer worked in, with Richard II's policies of forging more centralist and personal support, aimed (unsuccessfully) at countering baronial power."[16] Chaucer, in other words, was writing in support of Richard and against a chivalric ideal that bolstered baronial resistance to sovereign power. Does this mean that he rejects chivalry out of hand? Phillips does not quite say so, but points out that his other (non-parodic) romances tend to focus on love rather than chivalry, and are meant for those in Richard's circle who were denigrated as "knights of Venus, not Bellona" by one particularly dismissive chronicler.[17]

If Phillips's argument seems speculative, it nonetheless does appear pretty certain that Chaucer at the very least meant to ask probing questions about the nature of chivalric identity. Even if we accept Lee Patterson's suggestion that Chaucer's literary mode "is a discourse that insists upon its autonomy from both ideological programs and social appropriations," we need not read this insistence as decisive.[18] So, if the pilgrim Chaucer simultaneously mocks both "literary ambition and chivalric achievement" in his *Tale of Sir Thopas*, we may be sure that the writer Chaucer wants his audience to interrogate the nature of both, even as it remains unclear whether his ambition was to deliver a withering critique of chivalry or a gentle love tap.[19]

Notes

1 Helen Cooper, *Oxford Guides to Chaucer*: The Canterbury Tales (Oxford: Oxford University Press, 1991), 301.
2 Alan Gaylord, "Chaucer's Dainty 'Dogerel': The 'Elvyssh' Prosody of *Sir Thopas*," *Studies in the Age of Chaucer* 1 (1979), 83–104, here 89.
3 See, for instance, Laura Hibbard Loomis, "Chaucer and the Auchinleck MS: 'Thopas' and 'Guy of Warwick' in *Essays and Studies in Honor of Carleton Brown*, ed. P.W. Long (New York: New York University Press, 1940), 111–28, here 128.
4 Thomas Warton, *The History of English Poetry from the Close of the Eleventh to the Commencement of the Eighteenth Century, to which are prefixed two Dissertations I: On the Origin of Romantic Fiction in Europe II: On the Introduction of Learning into England*, 3 vols. (London, 1774–81), 1:433.
5 J.A. Burrow, "Sir Thopas in the Sixteenth Century," in *Middle English Studies Presented to Norman Davis in Honour of his Seventieth Birthday*, ed. Douglas Gray and E. G. Stanley (Oxford: Clarendon Press, 1983), 69–91, here 89.
6 Loomis, "Chaucer and the Auchinleck MS," 128. On the skepticism attending this claim (as well as its enduring nature), see Ann Higgins, "*Sir Tristrem*, a Few Fragments, and the Northern Identity of the Auchinleck Manuscript," in

The Auchinleck Manuscript: New Perspectives, ed. Susanna Fein (York: York Medieval Press, 2016), 108–26, here 113–14.

7   Joseph A. Dane, "Genre and Authority: The Eighteenth-Century Creation of Chaucerian Burlesque," *Huntington Library Quarterly* 48 (1985), 345–62. Warton writes with the benefit of a critical hindsight that has as its assumption the idea of "taste," which was not a concept that would have been recognizable to the medievals.

8   V.J. Scattergood, "Chaucer and the French War: *Sir Thopas* and *Melibee*," in *Court and Poet: Selected Proceedings of the Third Congress of the International Courtly Literature Society*, ed. Glyn S. Burgess (Francis Cairns: Liverpool, 1981), 287–96, here 290.

9   Alcuin Blamires, "Chaucer's Revaluation of Chivalric Honor," *Mediaevalia* 5 (1979), 245–69, here 257. See also Scattergood, "Chaucer and the French War," 291–3.

10   Nevill Coghill, *Chaucer's Idea of What Is Noble* (London: English Association, 1971), 14.

11   Terry Jones, *Chaucer's Knight: The Portrait of a Medieval Mercenary* (Baton Rouge, LA: Louisiana State University Press, 1980), 222.

12   Lee Patterson, *Chaucer and the Subject of History* (Madison, WI: University of Wisconsin Press, 1991), 189.

13   Jones, *Chaucer's Knight*, 12.

14   David Aers, "Review of Terry Jones' *Chaucer's Knight: The Portrait of a Medieval Mercenary*," *Studies in the Age of Chaucer* 4 (1982), 169–75, here 171.

15   Helen Phillips, "Auchinleck and Chaucer," in *The Auchinleck Manuscript: New Perspectives*, ed. Susanna Fein (York: York Medieval Press, 2016), 139–55, here 148–9.

16   Ibid., 152.

17   *The St Albans Chronicle: The 'Chronica maiora' of Thomas Walsingham I: 1376–1394*, ed. John Taylor, Wendy R. Childs and Leslie Watkiss (Oxford: Oxford University Press, 2003), 814–15.

18   Lee Patterson, "'What Man Artow?': Authorial Self-Definition in the *Tale of Sir Thopas* and the *Tale of Melibee*," *Studies in the Age of Chaucer* 11 (1989), 117–75, here 173.

19   Ibid., 133.

Myth 24

CHAUCER DESCRIBED HIMSELF IN HIS WORKS

Who was Geoffrey Chaucer? What did he look like? Throughout this book we have tried to suggest that there is often a very close relationship between traditional ideas and readings of Chaucer's poetry and the growth of the various "myths" about Chaucer's own life and his personality. One of the presiding structural myths about canonical literary authors is that their works are in some way co-extensive with, and expressive of, their "real" personalities, and Chaucer is no exception. When we use the familiar phrase "in Shakespeare," "in Austen" or "in Chaucer" to describe patterns of imagery, narrative or ideological structure in their works, for example, we are drawing a kind of equivalency between the perceived character of the author and the "character" of the works themselves. This equivalency works powerfully to flatter our sense that we can know and recognize an authorial personality; such affectionate familiarity is crucial to the ideology of modern authorship as an interpretive principle and organizational category. Indeed, we suggest that Chaucer is one of the first writers in English to develop, quite self-consciously, a program of constructing a relatively consistent voice across all his works. Not only is that voice consistent enough to make us feel a sense of familiarity that eases our passage from one work to the next, it is also an attractive and likable voice that encourages identification and affinity.

The myth that is the subject of this chapter – that Chaucer describes himself consistently in mind, body and soul – is of a slightly different order. What does Chaucer tell us about himself? And how does this information correlate to the early visual representations of the poet?

30 Great Myths About Chaucer, First Edition. Thomas A. Prendergast and Stephanie Trigg.
© 2020 John Wiley & Sons, Inc. Published 2020 by John Wiley & Sons, Inc.

Certainly there are a number of places in his poetry where Chaucer does seem to describe himself, although as we might expect, he sometimes conflates physical attributes with personality traits and psychological conditions. For example, in his earliest narrative poem, *The Book of the Duchess*, the narrator describes his physical ailments of insomnia and depression, and hints that these derive from unrequited love (Myth 3). This is consistent with other representations of himself as an "unlikely" or unhappy lover.

Similarly, in the prologue to *The House of Fame*, and its disquisition on the different categories of dreams and visions, Chaucer follows Macrobius and links physical states such as humoral complexions, illness, deprivation or too much study and anxiety to the production of vivid dreams. This prepares the ground for his own dream, and especially the episode in Book II in which a golden eagle picks him up from one dream landscape and carries him through the skies to another, to visit the temple of fame. The narrator is dazed and numbed with fear, but the eagle addresses him sharply (see our discussion of this passage in Myth 4), restores his wits and eventually gets his heart beating again. As they converse, the eagle explains that he has been sent by Jupiter to reward the narrator for his long and fruitless service to Cupid and Venus and for having set his scant wit ("that in thy hed ful lyte is," 621) to work in making poems and songs of love. Moreover, the eagle describes how "Geffrey" gives himself a headache ("thou wolt make / A-nyght ful ofte thyn hed to ake," 631–2) writing about love even though he has no success in this matter. Indeed, he has become almost socially dysfunctional, in that after a long day at his books at work with his "rekenynges" (653), he does not seek diversion or anything new, but goes home to sit with another book, "also domb as any stoon" (656), living solitary like a hermit, though without practicing any abstinence. These are the bookish habits of a medieval nerd, whose obsession with books has made him both ill and incurious; too old, he says to the eagle, to bother learning how to identify the stars he sees on his magical flight. In terms of his physical description, the eagle says he is "noyous for to carye" (574); while some commentators assume this means the poet is suggesting he is overweight, the context suggests rather that he might equally be "troublesome" or "difficult" to carry through his dazed unresponsiveness and fear – as the eagle says, there is no need to be afraid. We also note that this word "noyous" is used only thirty-odd lines after he describes the eagle carrying him as easily as if he has been a lark (546).

As we have discussed, in several other poems Chaucer describes himself as unsuccessful or "unlikely" in love, and again, while the idea has grown that Chaucer was unsuccessful in love in part because he was plump, there is very little evidence of this in the poetry. In *The Parliament of Foules*, for example, the narrator is characterized more as an insomniac, inexperienced in love and worried about it, but not overweight. Rather, his dream-guide Scipio suggests his doubt, uncertainty and even his stupidity about love are like a sickness.

In the *Canterbury Tales*, however, there is a more specific description of the narrator, offered by the Host:

> And thanne at erst he looked upon me,
> And seyde thus: "What man artow?" quod he;
> "Thou lookest as thou woldest fynde an hare,
> For evere upon the ground I se thee stare.
>
> "Approche neer, and looke up murily.
> Now war you, sires, and lat this man have place!
> He in the waast is shape as wel as I;
> This were a popet in an arm t'enbrace
> For any womman, smal and fair of face.
> He semeth elvyssh by his contenaunce,
> For unto no wight dooth he daliaunce."

(VII.694–714)

This is the clearest self-account of Chaucer as seen by the other pilgrims and, like his own "portraits" of the pilgrims, it combines physical, behavioral, psychological and social aspects. It is as if the Host has only just noticed him as part of the company and realizes Chaucer has been riding along with his head down, listening carefully and not even showing his face. It is a most deliberate moment of self-revelation, drawing attention for the first time since the end of the *General Prologue* to Chaucer's role as reporter, silently observing the other pilgrims and listening attentively to their tales and self-presentations. The Host's joke about Chaucer's portly waist is offset by the rest of his description of his body in feminized, unthreatening, rather cuddly terms, especially as a "poppet," a small person or even a doll. The phrase "small and fair of face" is particularly telling: Chaucer is telling us how attractive he is, though as ever, the tone is uncertain. The phrase "gent and small" is used several times in Middle English to describe attractive men and women,[1] and while "small" often means "thin," its dominant use in physical descriptions evokes positive connotations, while the "fair" face of Chaucer is unambiguous. Chaucer has the Host describe him as attractive and cuddly, though his expression is also "elvyssh," an unusual word in this context, meaning somewhat otherworldly. This is backed up by the last line of the Host's characterization: "unto no wight dooth he daliaunce."

This is a rather contradictory description: Chaucer is sexualized as someone who should be attractive, in an unthreatening manner, to women; but he also appears to be someone who does not welcome human interaction. This strikes a contrasting note to the convivial, chatty pilgrim who makes a point of talking with all his fellow travelers in the *General Prologue*, while this attractive Chaucer is also inconsistent with the unhappy, unlikely lover-narrator of the dream-visions and the *Troilus*. Indeed, the Host's last phrase – "unto no wight dooth he daliaunce" – echoes the refrain of Chaucer's parodic love poem "To Rosemounde," in which the poet laments the failure of his love suit with this beautiful woman, whom he begs to allow him to love her, even if she will not speak or flirt with him: "Thogh ye to me ne do no daliaunce" (24).

As ever with Chaucer, the question of tone is always problematic, and we can easily call on the customary appeal of Chaucer's "irony" or his cultivation of a deliberately naïve "persona" to reconcile these potential contradictions.

In our consideration of Chaucer's self-descriptions, we must also think about the circumstances in which Chaucer read and circulated his works. Although we do not have any firm records of Chaucer reading his poetry aloud, it seems likely that on at least some occasions he would have done so, at least to his own small coterie, if not larger gatherings. And in such contexts, allusions to a cultivated public persona and references to his own body take on another layer of complexity and potential humor. We observe too that Chaucer's self-presentation in his poetry is often structured around the question of heterosexual relationships: whether he is likely to appear attractive or unattractive to women. While women may have read his poetry, or heard him read in public as they do in the Corpus Christi manuscript frontispiece to the *Troilus*, for example, they would certainly have been in the minority (though that frontispiece is increasingly read as depicting a fictional scene of courtly narration, not as any kind of historical record). And while many of the narrative addresses in his poetry, to the young people, "he or she," in the last stanzas of the *Troilus and Criseyde*, or the irony-laden or provocative remarks about marriage in the tales of the Merchant, Wife of Bath or Clerk, when Chaucer addresses individual readers by name, these are always male: his son, Louis, or his friends Bukton, Strode, Gower or Vache.

An additional source of information is in the early manuscript portraits of Chaucer: the Ellesmere manuscript where he appears riding his horse opposite the opening of the *Tale of Melibee*; the *Troilus* frontispiece; and the portraits added into the several manuscripts of Hoccleve's *Regement of Princes*, against the stanza where the poet laments Chaucer's death and says he has commissioned this portrait to remind us of what his friend and master looked like.[2] Chaucer's face does not appear particularly small here, and the size of his waist is not really discernible. Other features, such as his forked beard, are not mentioned in his poetry, nor are the floppy hat, the rosary and the pen case around his neck that become quasi-iconographical features in later portraits.

Thus, while Chaucer gives the impression of addressing us directly in a personal voice, the clues he offers are strongly mediated by the genre and form in which he is writing: a lovelorn melancholy is appropriate for love poetry; a studious torpor suits a comically visionary flight through the heavens; a taciturn, disengaged pilgrim can best report on the human variety of the company of pilgrims; while a jokey irony affirms a conversation among equals in the shorter lyrics; and, as we have seen, a penitential mode of voice is appropriate at the conclusion of a life's work.

Notes

1 *Middle English Dictionary*: small 3[b]. https://quod.lib.umich.edu/m/middle–english–dictionary/dictionary.
2 For a discussion of early representations of Chaucer, see David R. Carlson, "Thomas Hoccleve and the Chaucer Portrait," *Huntington Library Quarterly* 54, no. 4 (1991), 283–300. For a list of pre-1700 likenesses, and a discussion of the Chaucer portraits, see Derek Pearsall, *The Life of Geoffrey Chaucer* (Oxford: Blackwell, 1992), 285–305.

Myth
25
CHAUCER WROTE THE FIRST NOVEL IN ENGLISH

In 1938, for Karl Young it was already a commonplace that Chaucer's *Troilus and Criseyde* was considered to be like a novel, or was indeed the "first psychological novel."[1] This view was most influentially expressed by George Lyman Kittredge, who wrote in *Chaucer and His Poetry*, in 1915:

> The Troilus is not merely, as William Rossetti styles it, the most beautiful long narrative poem in the English language: it is the first novel, in the modern sense, that ever was written in the world, and one of the best.[2]

The characterization and praise of this poem as a novel constitute a complex act of literary criticism that still influences the way we speak and write about Chaucer's *Troilus and Criseyde*. Such a description may well ease the path of students who might otherwise be put off by the poem's dense syntax, deep mythological allusions and digressions into philosophical and theological debates about predestination and the virtues of detachment from worldly concerns. The expectations of the novel form, on the other hand, direct the reader's interest to more familiar elements such as narrative progression and character development. The license to think of Troilus, Criseyde and Pandarus as characters who might behave like those in novels by Jane Austen or Ian McEwan, for example, may help readers feel they "know" them and thus develop readings and interpretations using the insights of modern psychology and character study. This is almost inevitable in the more informal contexts of the classroom. And in some respects the comparison makes sense, especially in the conversational way the three main characters interact

30 Great Myths About Chaucer, First Edition. Thomas A. Prendergast and Stephanie Trigg.
© 2020 John Wiley & Sons, Inc. Published 2020 by John Wiley & Sons, Inc.

with each other, and discuss each other against the backdrop of a social world that is realized in considerable detail.

Nevertheless, in formal terms, the work's primary allegiances might well be seen as lyrical or dramatic, rather than novelistic. Articulated into five books that mimic the structure of ancient tragedy, most with a formal invocation to a muse or a presiding spirit, *Troilus and Criseyde* begins with a distinctive voice of poetic complaint: as a text that might provide other lovers with a voice to express their own courtly sufferings. The narrator takes center stage in the opening stanzas, positioning himself carefully with an attitude of humble deference to his courtly audience, but also as a bookish scholar working through a primary text. Neither of these narrative stances has much in common with the conventional novel. Indeed, *Troilus and Criseyde* is treasured for the fluid and flexible way it moves between epic and romance modes, while its Boethian framework and ending – rejecting all the triumphs, joys and sorrows of human life – hardly seem to look forward to, or anticipate, the development of the realist novel. Eugene Vance argues, moreover, that the poem is constructed as a narrative organized around a sequence of lyrical cores and the story is there to make links between these powerful moments of lyrical intensity: "what has not been properly understood is that these lyrical cores are not merely ornamental but generative with regard to the narrative in which they occur."[3] In this reading, the "novelistic" aspects of the poem are merely incidental.

So why do people continue to believe that *Troilus and Criseyde* is the first novel? In his summary, Young quotes a number of critics who remark upon the poem's verisimilitude to "the world of every day,"[4] or "a sense of ordinary life"[5] or, more tellingly, "a page out of the book of modern everyday life."[6] This idea of the poem's responsiveness to everyday life is paired with a sense that it is not a romance; that, in Ker's words, Chaucer "leaves all romantic convention behind."[7] At least three ideas are linked here: first, that novels are tied to realism; second, that romance is incommensurate with the novel and inferior to it; and third, that when we say *Troilus and Criseyde* is a novel, we are really wanting to say that Chaucer was a modernist, like us, and that the "everyday" life he delineated was comparable to our own. But here, critics do not really mean that Trojan life is like our life, though they may well be developing the idea that the life in Troy that Chaucer depicts bears more than a passing resemblance to fourteenth-century London life. Once more, it appears to be the conversational dialogue in the domestic interiors they really mean, or the easy, sophisticated play between Criseyde and Pandarus as recognizably "modern" subjects. This is the closest thing perhaps to the idea of the poem as "psychological" realism. As encoded signs of such realism, we might cite Pandarus's little cough before he begins to explain Troilus's love to Criseyde (II.254), even Troilus's nervousness when he first speaks to her (III.92–8), or Criseyde's singular "monobrow" that is the only flaw to her golden beauty (V.813), or her resistance to Troilus's attempt at mastery by saying he has "caught" her: "Ne hadde I er now, my swete herte deere, / Ben yolde, ywis, I were now nought heere!" (III.1210–11).

We focus on Criseyde here because it seems to us that when people write about this poem as a psychologically realized novel, they are principally thinking of the character of Criseyde, though this association between novelistic form and complex female characters is not always remarked. Criseyde is the first place Karl Young goes to find an example of the "persistent study of the poem as a novel," when he writes: "Patient and sympathetic inquiry into the reflections and feelings of Criseyde, for example, has disclosed her essential traits with something like finality."[8] We may set aside Young's optimism that Criseyde's character might be fully accounted for by 1938, but his next sentence is telling more of the issues that a novelistic approach opens up: "Although analysis and formula can never capture the living unity of her personality, they have now, I should think, made permanently visible about all the significant psychological elements in her nature."[9]

The idea that Criseyde's personality might have a "living unity" is already to assume the illusions of realist fiction – that literary characters might be as "real" as people. Even though the main burden of Young's essay is to emphasize the dominance of romance features in the poem (he argues that while Boccaccio's *Il Filostrato* is a novella, Chaucer transformed it into a romance), his understanding of character is still structured and conditioned by the conventions of the novel.

Young mistakenly thought the character analysis of Criseyde was pretty much finalized in 1938. Subsequent generations of critics – and not just feminist critics – would prove him wrong. In 1993, Carolyn Dinshaw explored the dynamics of interpretive mastery in the drive to understand and explain this female character, notoriously described by Chaucer as "slydynge of corage" (V.825). Dinshaw contrasts the super-realist and humanist reading of E. Talbot Donaldson, who confessed his own "love" for Criseyde, with the stern Augustinian exegetical reading of D.W. Robertson, who on the other end of this spectrum, in Dinshaw's reading, regards Criseyde as little more than the symbolic object of Troilus's own flawed solipsism and narcissism.[10] Feminist critics such as Arlyn Diamond and Elaine Hansen drew careful attention to the way Criseyde's choices are dramatically circumscribed at every point, but Gretchen Mieszkowski offered a more bracing view in 1991: "The most famous medieval English heroine and the most extravagantly admired woman in all of English literature has no strength, courage, determination, or selfhood. She agrees instead of deciding, submits instead of controlling, and is so insubstantial that at times she seems more nearly a mirage than a person." And again, "She has no personal substance .... She responds to the men around her and mirrors them, but she is not someone herself."[11] Mieszkowski's reading works from the opposite assumption to the idea of the "living unity" of a person. She also draws attention to the consistent ways in which Chaucer *diminishes* Criseyde's agency at every turn, in comparison with Boccaccio's text: "Situations conjured up by Chaucer's Pandarus replace all the decisions Boccaccio's Criseida makes."[12]

Mieszkowski revisits Charles Muscatine's analysis of Criseyde's spoken discourse as it mediates between Troilus's high romance style and Pandarus's more homely fabliau style: "To the degree that woman is a mirror [earlier in the essay she discusses Simone de Beauvoir's *The Second Sex*], she cannot have values of her own"; as Criseyde changes from being like Troilus or Pandarus, she becomes "without substance altogether."[13] Mieszkowski is not discussing the novelistic aspects of the poem here, but, as for Young and many other critics, it is the "knowable" figure of Criseyde that becomes the test case for the poem's realism and its politics.

It is worth speculating on the extent to which we might think of this text as a novel if it were *not* for Criseyde's apparent verisimilitude; if the main characters on which we based such assessments and comparisons were Troilus and Pandarus. We suggest the comparison would quickly collapse. Pandarus's role as a mere narrative functionary, mediating between the prince's chambers and Criseyde's apartment, would be foregrounded; while Troilus's emotional behavior would quickly be exposed as uncompromising, unrealistic and stylized. And although his famous conversion to love in Book I after offending Lord Cupid can be read as an allegory of narrative personification, this hardly gives us as sense of Troilus as a "living unity."

Of course, there are many different kinds of novel, from epistolary fiction through to domestic comedies, sweeping epics, satires and post-modern experiments, though "psychological" is the most common qualifier when this word is used to describe *Troilus*. But Chaucer's poem has not generated any modern medievalist novels: indeed, the most suc-cessful modern adaptation is Lavinia Greenlaw's astonishing *A Double Sorrow*, which in effect takes up Eugene Vance's reading of the poem as a succession of intense lyrical moments.[14] *Troilus and Criseyde* is not a novel, though we comprehend and are sympathetic with the general critical desire to explain Criseyde as if she were a fully realized person; a desire that is sustained by the idea that she is drawn as if she were a character in a realist novel.

Moving away from Criseyde as a key idea in this comparison, though, there is another sense in which Chaucer's poem might be read as a novel: that is, as an example of historical fiction, a genre that at least since Walter Scott's *Ivanhoe* (1819) has offered a series of imaginative pathways into the medieval past. Chaucer's poem offers many such pathways: his play of anachronisms; his mixture of Trojan and Christian beliefs; his self-consciousness about social, cultural and linguistic change; his struggles with the historical "facts" of the story he has chosen to tell. These are all typical features of historical fiction that depend less on the possibility of transhistorical emotional realism and more on the potential of a literary work to show how differently our lives might have played out in the past.

Notes

1 Karl Young, "Chaucer's 'Troilus and Criseyde' as Romance," *PMLA* 53, no. 1 (1938), 38–63.
2 George Lyman Kittredge, *Chaucer and His Poetry* (1915; Cambridge, MA: Harvard University Press, 1970), 109.
3 Eugene Vance, *Mervelous Signals: Poetics and Sign Theory in the Middle Ages* (Lincoln, NE: University of Nebraska Press, 1990), 271.
4 E. de Selincourt, *Oxford Lectures on Poetry* (Oxford: Oxford University Press, 1934), 50.
5 W.P. Ker, *Form and Style in Poetry* (London: Macmillan, 1929), 78–9.
6 de Selincourt, *Oxford Lectures*, 50.
7 W.P. Ker, *Epic and Romance* (London: Macmillan, 1926), 369.
8 Young, "Chaucer's 'Troilus and Criseyde,'" 38.
9 Ibid., 38–9.
10 Carolyn Dinshaw, *Chaucer's Sexual Poetics* (Madison, WI: University of Wisconsin Press, 1989), 33.
11 Gretchen Mieszkowski, "Chaucer's Much Loved Criseyde," *Chaucer Review* 26, no. 2 (1991), 109–32, here 109.
12 Ibid., 114.
13 Ibid., 123.
14 Vance, *Mervelous Signals*, 270–71.

Myth 26

CHAUCER WAS IN DANGER OF BEING THROWN IN DEBTOR'S PRISON

Stories about Chaucer, debt and prison have been circulating since at least the sixteenth century. Taking as a point of departure the poet's "begging poem," the editor Thomas Speght said:

> in that complaint which he maketh to his empty purse, I do find a written copy, which I had of John Stow (whose library hath helped many writers) wherein ten times more in that is adioined, then is in print. Where he maketh great lamentation for his wrongfull imprisonment, wishing death to end his daies.[1]

This connection was expanded upon in the eighteenth century and in the nineteenth, led by William Godwin (father of Mary Shelley), who claimed that in the latter stages of his life Chaucer was a "prisoner, embarrassed in his circumstances."[2] Ultimately, it was demonstrated that this particular iteration of the legend was based on works that were falsely ascribed to Chaucer, but the myth of the impoverished and debt-ridden poet remained durable and was aided by the discovery of a series of actions against him to recover debts that stretched from 1388 to 1399.

During this period there were four separate suits that named Chaucer as a defendant, but the most serious was a fifth suit involving a series of actions brought against him by the widow of a former business colleague (Isabella Buckholt) from 1398 to 1399. We do not know how the case was resolved (if it was), but the final document we possess terminates in a demand that Chaucer appear in court or be declared outlaw.[3] The case represents the only occasion we know of in which Chaucer appointed an attorney to represent him in the Court of Common Pleas, and it is likely

30 Great Myths About Chaucer, First Edition. Thomas A. Prendergast and Stephanie Trigg.
© 2020 John Wiley & Sons, Inc. Published 2020 by John Wiley & Sons, Inc.

that his financial situation at this time was grim, since he sought and received royal protection. Chaucer had received royal protections before, especially when he was away on the king's business (see Myth 16). And this protection might be seen as similar, as it specifically says that he was "going on the king's urgent business to divers parts of England," but there is no evidence that the poet was actually engaged in any royal business at this time.[4] In addition, this protection was different in that it "contains a specially worded statement to protect the recipient from lawsuits."[5]

It was around this time that Chaucer began to have difficulty in obtaining an annuity that had been granted by Richard II. This was, perhaps, understandable, since Richard was deposed on 30 September 1399 and his successor Henry IV probably had other things on his mind. The poet had already taken steps to prove his claim to the annuity shortly after Richard's deposition, but the money was not forthcoming and the poet composed the aforementioned begging poem known as "The Complaint of Chaucer to His Purse," a humorous and skillful, four-stanza work that contained an envoi (a short concluding stanza) that directly addressed Henry IV. Chaucer's financial circumstances might well be reflected in the line "For I am shave as nye as any frere" (l. 19), which might be rendered "as bare of money as the tonsure of a friar is of hair."[6] But this could simply be in line with the jocular exaggeration that Chaucer employs throughout the poem. In fact, it is hazardous to make too much of the poem's references to poverty, because begging poems were something of a convention. Poets as various as Guillaume de Machaut, Eustache Deschamps and even Chaucer's contemporary Thomas Hoccleve all wrote poems to their sovereigns begging for money (indeed, Chaucer's own poem was ascribed to Hoccleve in Thomas Speght's 1602 edition). At the same time, it is well to keep in mind that something must have motivated Chaucer to write to the king, and that something was most likely a need for his delayed annuity (which he would not receive until February 1400).[7]

While Chaucer had obtained royal protection from his creditors, it only extended until 4 May 1400, and the sum demanded by Buckholt was substantial, almost three-quarters of the entire annuity promised by Richard II. Additionally (though it is unclear whether Chaucer knew this ahead of time), he would have been hard pressed to pay the entire sum because he received only a partial payment on the annuity. Other gifts would come from Henry IV, but not until well after his royal protection had ended. It was around this time (24 December 1399) that Chaucer obtained a fifty-three-year lease on a house within the precincts of Westminster Abbey. This would be unremarkable if not for the fact that those residing within the walls of the Abbey received sanctuary.[8] Chaucer was, according to the terms of the lease, forbidden from "receiv[ing] and giv[ing] hospitality to anyone seeking the privileges and liberties and immunities of sanctuary of the aforementioned Westminster" without permission, but he himself could not be prosecuted for debt (or other crimes) as long as he remained within the precincts.[9]

Critics have traditionally been skeptical about the possibility that Chaucer sought sanctuary within the Abbey precincts.[10] But the timing of the lease is suspicious. Here was a man who depended on his annuity from his king. In the year leading up to the leasing of the property, the king who originally granted the annuity had been deposed. The new king had failed to pay the annuity and enough time had gone by that the poet felt the need to remind the king of his great need. In addition, the poet was engaged in defending himself against a series of actions for debt. The situation had gotten so bad that a sheriff had been sent to seek him out (ultimately, he was unable to find Chaucer). And finally, Chaucer's royal protection against lawsuits was about to run out, so it would seem prudent to prepare against the possibility that he would find himself in sufficiently straitened circumstances that he would need someplace he could remain safe.

There is one other intriguing, if entirely circumstantial, piece of evidence that might indicate a kind of communal or folk memory of Chaucer's reasons for taking the house at Westminster. In 1566, ten years after Chaucer was translated to the Purbeck marble tomb where he apparently now rests (see Myth 28), there is a "Decree of the Court of Requests as to the payment of money at Chaucer's tomb." There are at least two other mentions of payments of debts at Chaucer's tomb from the Court of Requests in the years 1566–1599.[11] It is possible that the tomb was simply a kind of mid-sixteenth-century landmark that provided a convenient meeting place, a bit like the great clock in the Waldorf Astoria Hotel in New York City, but it is interesting that this landmark was in a Chartered Sanctuary where the debtor could not be seized. And it is also interesting that this landmark was the tomb of a prominent man who had been in debt. Lacking some direct evidence of Chaucer's intent vis-à-vis the lease of the house in Westminster, we cannot prove that he prepared against being taken for debt. And it is true that the story fits neatly into a romance of the poet as one who is "a martyr to the world's forgetfulness of men of genius," but the historical and literary evidence is, at the very least, suggestive.[12]

Notes

1 Thomas Speght, ed., *The Workes of our Antient and Learned English Poet, Geffrey Chavcer, newly printed* (London, 1598), B.6v.

2 William Godwin, *Life of Geoffrey Chaucer*, 2 vols. (London: Printed by T. Davison for R. Phillips, 1804), 1:xxxv.

3 Martin M. Crow and Clair C. Olson, eds., *Chaucer Life-Records* (Oxford: Oxford University Press, 1966), 399. During the preparation of this manuscript, another life record was found that suggests that as late as the Easter term of 1400, the case was not resolved. For when the sheriff sought Chaucer, he could not be found. http://newchaucersociety.org/blog/entry/stones-left-unturned-psst-more-new-chaucer-life-records

4 Ibid., 399.

5 Ibid., 63.

6 The gloss is from Larry D. Benson, Robert Pratt and F.N. Robinson, eds., *The Riverside Chaucer*, 3rd edn. (Boston, MA: Houghton Mifflin, 1987), 656.

7 Sumner Ferris, "The Date of Chaucer's Final Annuity and of the 'Complaint to His Empty Purse,'" *Modern Philology* 65 (1967), 45–52, here 47.

8 Andrew J. Finnel was the first to suggest that Chaucer might have taken sanctuary within the Abbey precincts in order to avoid his creditors, in "The Poet as Sunday Man: 'The Complaint of Chaucer to His Purse,'" *Chaucer Review* 8 (1973), 147–58.

9 Crow and Olson, *Chaucer Life-Records*, 536.

10 See, for instance, Derek Pearsall, *The Life of Geoffrey Chaucer* (Oxford: Blackwell, 1992), 207.

11 Thomas A. Prendergast, *Poetical Dust: Poets' Corner and the Making of Britain* (Philadelphia, PA: University of Pennsylvania Press, 2015), 40.

12 James Lorimer, "Chaucer," *Eclectic Magazine of Foreign Literature, Science and Art* 17 (1849), 64–83, here 73.

Myth 27

CHAUCER RENOUNCED HIS WORKS ON HIS DEATHBED

Alongside Chaucer's dominant reputation as a cheerful poet with a wry and ironic sense of humor and an abiding love of humanity, there also persists a sense that he was writing somehow ahead of his time; that his apparent modernity was exceptional; and that sooner or later he would fall back under the "spell" of the medieval Church and its repressive institutions. We exaggerate, of course, but we do not underestimate the strength of this vision of the Middle Ages as overwhelmingly governed by religious feeling. That vision has fed the myth that Chaucer turned away from his life's work when he was dying, took on a more penitential mode and, as he faced death, sought to call back or "retract" some of his works.

We should first acknowledge that this myth is associated with a number of other writers and artists – from Virgil to Francis Bacon to Philip Larkin – who gave orders for their works or parts of their unfinished or unsatisfactory artworks or diaries to be destroyed. As a writer approaches death, perhaps the imperfections of their completed, or indeed their uncompleted, works seem magnified, and in a last attempt to shape their fame, or to ensure spiritual salvation, they recall or disown part or all of their works, or even ask that their books be burned.

At the end of the *Canterbury Tales*, Chaucer does indeed perform such an act. His "Retracciouns" begin awkwardly, however, as they are written in the same prose voice as the preceding and final tale, told by the Parson, so it takes a while to realize that Chaucer is performing a gradual segue from the voice of the Parson to the voice of the author of the *Tales*, and then, indeed, to the voice of Chaucer himself. In this voice, he begs those who are reading his "litel tretys" to thank God if there is anything in it

30 Great Myths About Chaucer, First Edition. Thomas A. Prendergast and Stephanie Trigg.
© 2020 John Wiley & Sons, Inc. Published 2020 by John Wiley & Sons, Inc.

they like; but says if there are things his readers do not like, then they should blame the author's own lack of knowledge and understanding.[1] He then specifically identifies his translations and poems of "worldly vanitees, the whiche I revoke in my retracciouns" (X.1085); and names *The Book of Troilus*, several of his dream visions and those of the *Canterbury Tales* "that sownen [lead, tend toward] into synne" (X.1085). He then makes a point of commending to us his translation of Boethius and the saints' lives he has written, as well as his other books of morality and devotion, though without naming any of them.

This Retraction has been a difficult text for many Chaucerians to read, as the author seems to call back, or at least disown, many of his most popular works. It has been argued, for example, that in the words used, Chaucer is merely "performing" the voice of a poet retracting his works, just as he performs enthusiastic admiration for most of the pilgrims, with all their evident human flaws, in the *General Prologue*. A number of critics and commentators note that Chaucer similarly turns to a mode of renunciation of "worldly vanyte" at the end of *Troilus and Criseyde* (V.1837), where he similarly diminishes that work, in his famous envoi, as his "litel bok" (V.1786).

Nevertheless, Chaucer also uses the Retraction as a means of naming and claiming all his works, so while in the literal sense he calls his writings back, he similarly ensures that they go forth accompanied by his own name as author. This text, then, serves as a kind of litmus test for broader patterns of Chaucerian interpretation: whether we regard him primarily (or ultimately, we might say) as an ironist and a pluralist, or whether we see him as fundamentally framed by Christian sentiments of piety and faith.

In the long history of Chaucerian reception and biography, there are a number of imaginative scenarios that depict Chaucer's death and speculate about the circumstances in which he may have written the Retraction.

The most famous dramatization of Chaucer's death was written by Thomas Gascoigne (1403–45), the Chancellor of Oxford University. In his *Dictionarium theologicum*, under the entrance for "Penitence," he discusses the situation of those who turn too late to penitence. Judas Iscariot, who repented of his act in betraying Christ for thirty pieces of silver, but too late to undo his deed, is his most notorious example. Gascoigne compares the case of Chaucer, as a more recent example:

> Thus Chaucer before his death often exclaimed "woe is me, because now I can not revoke nor destroy those things I evilly wrote concerning the evil and most filthy love of men for women and which even now continue to

pass from man to man. I wanted to. I could not." And thus complaining, he died. This Chaucer was the father of Thomas Chaucer, knight, the which Thomas is buried in Huhelm near Oxford.[2]

Gascoigne's conjunction of Chaucer with Judas is certainly confrontational. In 1893, J.W. Hales exclaimed in a note, "May Heaven forgive him for such an unkindly conjunction!"[3] D.J. Wurtele suggests that Gascoigne "very probably" knew Chaucer's son Thomas, and that this story "evidently" reached Gascoigne through Thomas, though Míceál Vaughan casts doubt on this association and finds no evidence that Gascoigne had any kind of acquaintance with the poet's son.[4] And indeed, the historical relation between Gascoigne's account and Chaucer's own Retraction is tenuous at best. Chaucer emphasizes sin, certainly, but the umbrella phrase he uses is "my translacions and enditynges of worldly vanitees" (X.1084) – his emphasis does not fall on sexuality as such – while in his works there are almost as many complaints about the destructiveness of male desire as there are celebrations of it.

We may also note the interesting act of critical ventriloquism in Gascoigne's account. Chaucer's poetry is full of a range of voices, but he can also be read as *performing* a wide range of voices and characters. This desire to hear the poet speaking directly, free from the constraints and demands of fiction, is a very persistent one in Chaucer criticism and reception.

But of course, what is most extraordinary here is that Gascoigne is actually dramatizing a Chaucer who has *not* retracted, who "often" (*saepe*) lamented his inability to call back his works: "I wanted to. I could not." (*Velim. Nolim.*) That is, Gascoigne's invocation of Chaucer's penitence may seem to stem from the text of the Retraction, but it is as if that speech act (or that act of writing) had never taken place or had been completely ineffectual. Moreover, Gascoigne's Chaucer is apparently most concerned about a very specific matter: the way his writings about masculine desire for women might continue to spread. Vaughan argues that Gascoigne was motivated by anti-Lancastrian sentiment, expressed elsewhere in his writings about John of Gaunt, and William de la Pole, who was to become the Duke of Suffolk and the third husband of Alice Chaucer, the daughter of Thomas.[5] Vaughan is adamant: "To [Gascoigne] Chaucer and Judas remained morally indistinguishable."[6]

Whatever his sources or his motivations, Gascoigne's passage set the tone for a number of similar fantasies about Chaucer's deathbed penitence, usually framed as critical or textual studies of the Retraction (still often read as a problematic text). A similar story was spread that he was influenced by the monks at Westminster Abbey, where he was living in the last year of his life. John Urry, Chaucer's editor in 1721, speculated that the entire Retraction was not written by Chaucer. He links it to the *Plowman's Tale* (the anti-Catholic piece is now regarded as "spurious" but at that time was attributed to Chaucer) and says, "I fancy the Scriveners were prohibited transcribing it, and injoyn'd to subscribe an Instrument at the end of the Canterbury Tales, call'd his Retraction."[7] Nevertheless, the Retraction appears in every manuscript that is complete at the end of the *Tales*, and there is little doubt now about their authenticity.

Chaucer's eighteenth-century editor Thomas Tyrwhitt, by contrast, accepted the Retraction as authentic, but found himself unable to give "any satisfactory account" of the text, and he did wonder whether part of it – the problematic middle section – might have been added later by someone else; or indeed, whether Chaucer might have been persuaded by "the Religious who attended him in his last illness, to revoke or retract, some of his works."[8]

Thus, in John Gardner's fictionalized biography, *The Life and Times of Chaucer*, the poet hears confession and eventually he

> gave them their desire, and understood that of course they were right in a way: .... No one living or ever to be born would escape this painful, slightly frightening, but above all humiliating thing that was happening even to him, Geoffrey Chaucer, his body wasted, his eyes half blind, his voice like an adder's, old grim Grisel Death shaming him like an old smell of catshit in the house (yes, yes, he should have written poetry to ease men through this, should have written holy saints' lives, fine, moving songs about the gentleness of Jesus ...).[9]

Having called for quill, ink and the "laste page" of the *Tales*, Chaucer then begins to scratch out the Retraction.

There is also the issue of whether the Retraction was the last thing Chaucer wrote. This brings us to the vexed issue of the date of composition of the *Canterbury Tales*. We simply do not have enough concrete evidence to confirm that the *Tales* were written in the order in which they appear; and indeed, there is some evidence to suggest the *Knight's Tale* and the *Shipman's Tale*, at least, belong to an earlier phase of writing. Derek Pearsall, moreover, follows Charles Owen to suggest that the *Parson's Tale* and the Retraction come from an earlier period. He suggests that in his last days Chaucer was working on the lively urban comedy promised by the *Cook's Tale*; he draws attention to the fifty-three-year lease Chaucer took out on his house in 1399, intending "to live forever" (though see Myth 26). There, Pearsall speculates, he started revising the *Tales* "so that it could accommodate everything that he had no chance or intention of writing."[10] This is an image of the anti-penitential, humanist Chaucer, still entranced with the human comedy and the delights of narrative.

As we see from this debate, the meaning of the Retraction and our views of Chaucer's last moments have tremendous capacity to shape the way we see his life unfolding and then drawing to a close. Was this life affected and shaped by medieval ideology? Can we read and speculate about the state of a man's soul by reading his last works (if indeed we could be sure we knew which they were)? We might also observe that the customary placement of the *Canterbury Tales* at the beginning of Chaucer's "Works" has the effect of burying the Retraction in the midst of editions like the *Riverside Chaucer*, for example. The customary sequence, fading away into works of "doubtful" authorship, actually obscures Chaucer's last moments.

This does not stop his biographers drawing their own conclusions. If Derek Pearsall imagines a resolutely cheerful and optimistic Chaucer, Donald Howard suggests Chaucer is practicing the medieval "'art of dying,' a conscious discipline on which hundreds of treatises were written."[11] Howard draws attention to the prayer with which the text ends:

> Here in these last words of his retraction, from that pious side of his mind, is his last effort to renounce the world. But from the side of him that viewed fame as the reward of endeavor, an earthly immortality in the stream of human lives, here is his effort to *surrender* his works to the world that will live on after him.[12]

This reading is characteristic of much Chaucer criticism in general, underlining the poet's capacity to see both sides of an argument, subtended by a strong spiritual disposition. Indeed, Howard concludes his biographical study by referring to the latter: "It was the personal slant of his religion, ... that he viewed extreme virtue, 'saintliness,' not as growth but as renunciation."[13] Peter Ackroyd claims that Chaucer's burial place in the Abbey was relatively obscure, accompanied by no great ceremonial: "He remained circumspect, and reticent, until the end."[14]

Our conclusion, then, is typically ambivalent. Once more, Chaucer has not left us any kind of unambiguous answer – just the traces of a text that can be read as performing a number of different selves.

Notes

1 Whether "litel tretys" means the *Tales* or more specifically the *Parson's Tale* remains under discussion. See Míceál Vaughan, "Creating Comfortable Boundaries: Scribes, Editors and the Invention of the *Parson's Tale*," in *Rewriting Chaucer: Cultural Authority and the Idea of the Authentic Text 1400–1602*, ed. Thomas A. Prendergast and Barbara Kline (Columbus, OH: Ohio State University Press, 1999), 45–90; and Charles A. Owen, "What the Manuscripts Tell Us About the *Parson's Tale*," *Medium Aevum* 63 (1994), 239–249.

2 This translation taken from Harvard University's Geoffrey Chaucer Website, https://chaucer.fas.harvard.edu/pages/chaucers-retraction, accessed 18 September 2018. For full Latin text and detailed discussion, see D.J. Wurtele, "The Penitence of Geoffrey Chaucer," *Viator* 11 (1980), 335–9. The "Huhelm" in this translation was spelled as "Nuhelm" (that is, modern Ewelme) in Wurtele's transcription of Gascoigne's Latin.

3 Wurtele, "The Penitence," 344.

4 Míceál F. Vaughan, "Personal Politics and Thomas Gascoigne's Account of Chaucer's Death," *Medium Aevum* 75.1 (2006), 103–22, here 105–6.

5 Ibid., 109–10.

6 Ibid., 112.

7 Quoted in William L. Alderson, "John Urry," in *Editing Chaucer: The Great Tradition*, ed. Paul G. Ruggiers (Norman, OK: Pilgrim Books, 1984), 93–115, here 107.

8 Thomas Tyrwhitt, ed. *The Canterbury tales of Chaucer: to which are added an essay on his language and versification; an introductory discourse; and notes*, 5 vols. (London: Payne, 1775–78), 3:311. Wurtele is also of this view.

9 John Gardner, *The Life and Times of Chaucer* (London: Jonathan Cape, 1977), 313.

10 Derek Pearsall, *The Life of Geoffrey Chaucer: A Critical Biography* (Oxford: Blackwell, 1992), 184.

11 Donald R. Howard, *Chaucer: His Life, His Works, His World* (New York: E.P. Dutton, 1987), 501.

12 Ibid., 502.

13 Ibid., 502.

14 Peter Ackroyd, *Chaucer*, Brief Lives (London: Chatto & Windus, 2004), 163. Though see Thomas A. Prendergast, *Poetical Dust: Poets' Corner and the Making of Britain* (Philadelphia, PA: University of Pennsylvania Press, 2015), 28–41.

Myth
28
CHAUCER IS BURIED IN HIS OWN TOMB

In the South Transept of Westminster Abbey (popularly known as Poets' Corner), the marshals generally point to an unprepossessing tomb against the east wall and say something to the effect that it all began when Geoffrey Chaucer was buried there in 1400. It is true that Chaucer was the first poet to be buried in the South Transept, but the tomb they point to is not the tomb in which Chaucer was originally buried. In fact, it is not completely certain that Chaucer's body (or what remains of it) currently resides in the Purbeck marble tomb that is popularly known as the last resting place of the father of English poetry. Even the traditional date of Chaucer's death (25 October 1400) is doubtful, as it is based on an illegible (though now retouched) inscription on this tomb.

All we really know of Chaucer's death is that he probably passed away some time between 28 September 1400 and 28 September 1401. And we only know this because the lease on his house within the Abbey precincts passed from Chaucer to a certain Master Paul on 28 September, also known as Michaelmas. Just as we have no contemporary reports of Chaucer's death, so we have no contemporary reports of how and where he was buried. The earliest mention of his tomb is by William Caxton, who some seventy-eight years after Chaucer's death called for prayers for him, writing:

> and therfore he ought eternelly to be remembrid of whom the body and corps lieth buried in the thabbay of westmestre beside london to fore the chapele of seynte benet. by whos sepulture is wreton on a table, hongying on a pylere his Epitaphye maad by a poete laureat.[1]

30 Great Myths About Chaucer, First Edition. Thomas A. Prendergast and Stephanie Trigg.
© 2020 John Wiley & Sons, Inc. Published 2020 by John Wiley & Sons, Inc.

It would seem that the original burial place of Chaucer was close to where the monument to John Dryden is presently located: in front of the chapel of St. Benedict, a little north of the current tomb. No trace of the epitaph remains, but Caxton, who apparently commissioned it, prints a version (originally in Latin verse), a portion of which reads: "Let these words as spoken on his own behalf, be inscribed on his marble tomb. Let this remain the crowning burden to his own praise. I, Geoffrey Chaucer, the bard, glory of my own native poesy am buried in this sacred ground."[2] The epitaph, by Stephen Surigonus, focuses on Chaucer's greatness as a poet. And Caxton's intent in reproducing it here would seem to be an attempt to link the greatness of Chaucer's poetry with the greatness of the royal burials in the Abbey (the last four kings had been buried there).[3]

The next time we hear anything about the tomb is over sixty years later, when the antiquary John Leland claims that Caxton had actually taken the last distich of the epitaph ("I, Geoffrey Chaucer…") and had it inscribed on his tomb.[4] But whether or not this is true would seem to be impossible to discover, because in 1556 Nicholas Brigham apparently decided to translate the bones of Chaucer into a new tomb. The first mention of the translation is by the physician William Bullein in a 1564 work that has Chaucer "commend his deare Brigham for the worthy entombing of his bones, worthy of memorie, in the long slepyng chamber of most famous kinges."[5] "Entombing" would seem to suggest that Brigham actually moved Chaucer's bones; and this would appear to be confirmed in the first "guidebook" to the Abbey, written by William Camden some forty-four years after the translation. But contemporary witnesses problematize this assumption. The martyrologist John Foxe, who was acquainted with Bullein, says some fourteen years after the purported translation that Brigham merely bestowed "more cost vpoon his tombe" and added some verses. The suggestion would then seem to be that Brigham did not translate Chaucer, but renovated his already existing burial place. Further, John Stow, in his 1561 edition of Chaucer (which would have placed it five years after Brigham supposedly translated Chaucer), confusingly makes no mention of Brigham's tomb, but instead reprints the epitaph that was near Chaucer's original grave at the end of his edition.[6]

Things become more confusing in 1700, when a number of sources claim that the poet John Dryden was buried in Chaucer's tomb. The rationale for his burial with Chaucer is clear, as Henry Hall puts it in an epitaph addressed to the recently deceased poet:

> Nor is thy latest Work, unworthy Thee
> New Cloath'd by You, How *Chaucer* we esteem;
> When You've new Polish'd it, how bright the Jem!
> And lo, the Sacred Shade for thee make's room,
> Tho' Souls so alike, should take but up one tomb.[7]

Dryden had earned the right to be buried with Chaucer because he and the medieval poet were kindred spirits – which was demonstrated by Dryden's "brilliant" (according to Hall and others) modernizations of Chaucer's works.

We would assume, then, that when sources like the diarist Samuel Pepys say that Dryden was buried "in Chaucer's grave," this would be the tomb that Brigham had raised in 1556. Yet in 1723, the antiquary John Dart says that Chaucer's "stone of broad Grey Marble, as I take it, was not long since remaining; but was taken up when Mr. *Dryden's* Monument was erected, and sawn to mend the pavement."[8] Dryden's monument was erected in 1720, very close if not actually on the spot that Caxton reported as Chaucer's original grave, so it would make sense that it would interfere with the original slab; but it remains unclear why, if Chaucer had been translated to the tomb, Dart would refer to the stone as Chaucer's, or why the stone would remain there at all, unless Dart is suggesting that Chaucer was not translated to the tomb.

In the middle part of the nineteenth century, it became apparent that the tomb apparently raised by Brigham was decaying and needed to be refurbished or restored. It was at this time that Dart's comments were revisited, leading to doubt whether the tomb actually contained Chaucer's bones or was merely an empty monument. One of the leaders of the restoration effort dismissed Dart's comments and returned to Foxe's claim that Brigham had renovated an already existing tomb. In other words, the original burial place of Chaucer and the original tomb *was* the tomb that Brigham refurbished. Caxton's location of the grave in front of the Chapel of St. Benedict was a mistake, and Dart's comment was nothing more than a supposition based on Caxton's inaccurate rendering of Chaucer's original grave. The doubts about Chaucer's resting place were so great that the nineteenth-century dean of the Abbey, Dean Stanley, decided to cut on the gravestone of Abraham Cowley the following words in 1880: "NEAR THIS STONE LIE BURIED Geoffrey Chaucer 1400, John Dryden 1700 ...." Where is Cowley's gravestone? It is located right in between Dryden's monument and the tomb apparently raised by Brigham.[9]

So, is Chaucer buried in Chaucer's tomb? It seems unlikely that Caxton, who actually worked in the Abbey precincts, would be so wrong about the location of Chaucer's original grave – especially as he claims to have raised the tablet near that grave. It also seems likely that if Brigham raised a tomb to the poet, he would have moved the bones to the tomb. There is nothing to keep Dart from being wrong about the interference of the stone that covered Chaucer's original gravesite – he never claims that the grave was violated, so it is likely that the original stone had remained and John Dryden was buried in what had been Chaucer's grave or, as some have styled it, at his feet. But what about Stow's relative ignorance of the tomb and John Foxe's strange statement that Brigham had merely bestowed more cost on the tomb? To understand these things, it is important to understand why Chaucer would have been translated to the new tomb.

First, the timing of Brigham's translation of Chaucer's bones is crucial. It occurred during the reign of the Catholic Queen Mary, who was in the midst of a furious attempt to undo the work of her brother and her father and return England to Catholicism. Derek Pearsall has suggested that the reburial of the father of English poetry was an attempt to counter the perception that Chaucer, being a keen critic of the Church, was actually a proto-Protestant (see Myth 14).[10] This reclamation of Chaucer as a Catholic poet would seem to be supported by the fact that Brigham achieved his highest office under Mary, had several Catholic friends and showed an interest in "old books" (like saints' lives) that might have been seen to have a papist cast.[11] Both Stow and Foxe are writing after Mary's death and after Elizabeth had begun to re-align the English Church with the beliefs of her father and brother. Stow may have had sympathies with the old religion (he was certainly seen as suspect, as he possessed "old, fantastical Popish books"),[12] but it may not have been safe for him to acknowledge an attempt to re-Catholicize Chaucer. Foxe, of course, was a firm advocate of reform, and might have been interested in a renewal of the tomb without acknowledging that the translation of the bones would have been occasioned by anything like what Pearsall would call a cultural "counter-reformation." What the controversy over Chaucer's tomb demonstrates is that bodies, especially dead ones, can be meaningful markers of cultural prestige. Where they are located and how they got there remain important to the living, even in a culture that resists the profoundly Catholic and medieval idea of the relic.

Notes

1 *The Prologues and Epilogues of William Caxton*, ed. W.J.B. Crotch, Early English Text Society original series 176 (London: Oxford University Press, 1928), 37.

2 Text and translation (by R.G.G. Coleman) can be found in Derek Brewer, *Chaucer: The Critical Heritage: 1386–1837*, 2 vols. (New York: Barnes and Noble, 1974), I:78–9.

3 The real reason that Chaucer was buried in the Abbey probably had more to do with the fact that he was living in its precincts than with his poetic status.

4 For the problems associated with Leland's report of the inscription as well as a detailed treatment of the writing on Chaucer's tomb, see Joseph A. Dane, *Who Is Buried in Chaucer's Tomb?* (East Lansing, MI: Michigan State University Press, 1998), 11–32.

5 William Bullein, *A Dialogue bothe plesaunte and pietifull, wherein is a goodly regimente against the feuer Pestilence*, ed. M.W. Bullen and A.H. Bullen, Early English Text Society extended series 52 (London: N. Trübner, 1888), 16.

6 Thomas A. Prendergast, *Chaucer's Dead Body: From Corpse to Corpus* (New York: Routledge, 2004), 52–3.

7 "To the Memory of John Dryden, Esq.," in *Luctus Britannici or the Tears of the British Muses for the Death of John Dryden, Esq ...written by the most Eminent Hands in the two Famous Universities, and by several Others* (London, 1700), 18.

8 John Dart, *Westmonasterium, or the History and Antiquities of the Abbey Church of St. Peter's, Westminster*, 2 vols. (London, 1723), 1:83.

9 Ultimately this inscription would cause some mischief, as the son of an Abbey canon and precentor would claim that he had uncovered and examined the bones of "Chaucer" when Robert Browning's grave was being dug. Browning's grave is distant from Chaucer's tomb, but close to Cowley's stone.

10 Derek Pearsall was following up on a suggestion made much earlier by W.R. Lethaby, the Abbey's Surveyor of the Fabric: "Chaucer's Tomb: The Politics of Reburial," *Medium Aevum* 64 (1995), 51–73, here 64.

11 Prendergast, *Chaucer's Dead Body*, 48.

12 John Strype, *The History of the Life and Acts of the most reverend father in God, Edmund Grindal* (Oxford: Clarendon Press, 1821), 184.

Myth 29

CHAUCER WAS THE FIRST POET LAUREATE

The term "poet laureate" conjures a pleasant image of mutual love and respect between poetry and the state, or more personally, between poet and ruler. The poet steps up to the dais on a ceremonial occasion; wears a vaguely old-fashioned outfit, perhaps a floppy velvet coat with a feather in his cap; smiles and bows to the monarch; and reads a poem to honor a coronation, the birth of a royal baby or, in older times, a great battle. The idea that a king or queen might appoint a court poet – much as they might appoint a jester – seems a deeply archaic one, and this is perhaps one of the reasons that the myth that Chaucer was England's first poet laureate has persisted since at least the seventeenth century.

Yet, the first "official" poet laureate for England was John Dryden, appointed in 1668 by Charles II just two years after the Restoration of the English monarchy after the Civil War.[1] Charles's court was a traditional one: the king was keen to revive the pomp and glory of the monarchy, an institution that barely survived the execution of his father, Charles I, in 1649. Charles II enthusiastically revived the traditional costumes and processions of the medieval Order of the Garter, for example, and the appointment of a poet laureate seems consonant with his other revivals of medieval court practice. Medieval rulers did indeed offer patronage to poets and musicians, though Dryden's laureateship represented a new, more formal model of appointment.

In poetic terms, as we have seen elsewhere, Dryden paid powerful homage to Chaucer as a foundational and generative poet in the English tradition. He certainly seems to have believed that Chaucer occupied the position of poet laureate. In 1700, in his Preface to his translations of Chaucer and

30 Great Myths About Chaucer, First Edition. Thomas A. Prendergast and Stephanie Trigg.
© 2020 John Wiley & Sons, Inc. Published 2020 by John Wiley & Sons, Inc.

other poets, he writes of Chaucer: "He was employ'd abroad, and favour'd by Edward the Third, Richard the Second, and Henry the Fourth, and was Poet, as I suppose, to all Three of them."[2] He also refers to him as "my Country-man, and Predecessor in the Laurel,"[3] so it seems that at least in the seventeenth century, the myth of Chaucer's laureate status was current, and that Dryden was only too keen to embrace the idea of such continuity between himself and Chaucer.

The myth of Chaucer as a court poet is at the heart of the medievalist imaginary in the nineteenth century, in, for example, the large painting by Ford Madox Brown of 1847–51, now in the Art Gallery of New South Wales, *Chaucer at the Court of Edward III*.[4] It also passed into general acceptance: it is the subject of an article in *Look and Learn*, a popular educational magazine for children published in England between 1962 and 1982 that presents short articles on topics of general interest. The article from 1968 is titled "Geoffrey Chaucer Was the First 'Versificator Regis' or Poet Laureate."[5] It comments that the Latin phrase was apparently used first by Henry III referring to Henri d'Avranches.

Chaucer's association with the role of poet laureate is closely linked with Myth 2 about Chaucer as the first major poet to write in English; and Myth 1 that Chaucer, as the father of English poetry, also inaugurated a poetic tradition. One of the reasons for the appeal of this myth is the evidence it seems to offer that Chaucer's genius might have been recognized in his own time by those in positions of public power. Yet, as we have seen elsewhere in this book, there is not much concrete evidence that Chaucer's work was praised by the royal court. In these circles, French was still the language of choice for vernacular poetry; and while Chaucer seems to have found readers among his social equals at court, the most elaborate manuscripts were reserved for Latin and French texts, while English poetry was rarely performed or read aloud in a court setting.

Before we turn to the further implications and resonances of this myth, there is a germ of evidence in Chaucer's laureate history that we must consider: the grant of a pitcher of wine to Chaucer from all three kings, Edward III, Richard II and Henry IV, in 1374, 1378, 1398 and 1399.[6] The first grant was made at Windsor by Edward III, on 23 April 1374, while the King was at Windsor for the celebration of the feast of the new Order of the Garter.[7]

But was Chaucer given this grant of wine as recognition of his poetic accomplishments? Almost certainly not. And while it may be pleasant to speculate about his role in the Garter festivities, as these were conducted in Latin and French, not English, it would seem unlikely that Edward was celebrating English poetry on this occasion, so early in Chaucer's career. Nor is there any evidence that Chaucer held any kind of court position as official poet. The surviving evidence points in the opposite direction: none of the records about Chaucer in the six-hundred-page *Chaucer Life-Records* mentions his poetry; and there is very little evidence that he was prized for it. In fact, this grant of wine (later commuted to a financial payment) was made to Chaucer both as an "esquire of the king's chamber" and as part payment for his work as Controller of Customs, and has nothing to do with his work as a poet.[8] Nevertheless, the cultural associations of poetry and the drinking of wine have had the effect of naturalizing this association.

We may even speculate that this gift of wine appears attractively quaint to modernity, and thus bolsters the *mythic* component of this idea. So yes, we want Chaucer to have been recognized, but we also want our institutions to have long histories, especially if they can be marked by arcane customs, or some kind of mythic originary moment that might ground the first instance of a tradition in a distant past beyond the certainty of the written record.

This aspect of Chaucer's laureate myth was given material and symbolic form in the creation, in 1963–64, of a Wedgwood china tankard illustrated with Blake's engravings of the Canterbury pilgrimage. The base of the tankard reads "Geoffrey Chaucer (Author of the Canterbury Tales) 1328–1400, Poet-Laureat [sic], in the twelfth year of Richard II. 1389, obtained a grant of an annual allowance of wine."[9] The form of this object, a tankard that could be described as a "pitcher," as in the *Life-Records*, brings together the concept of drinking with the very English institution or brand name Wedgwood. The idea of Chaucer's grant of wine is here associated with the idea of Chaucer as the ideal drinking companion (see Myth 9).

Appointing a poet laureate is an important act in the symbolic economy of the state: it declares that governments make space for and recognize the arts, even if this is not backed up by more financial support. It is also how our governments affirm their links to tradition. Far from dying out, indeed, this practice has enjoyed a kind of revival in the last hundred years. Many governments such as the USA (federal and state) instituted the office only relatively recently.[10] In the UK, the tradition is of longer standing and is linked to royal, not parliamentary, appointments. Recent laureates include Andrew Motion and Carol Ann Duffy, Britain's first female poet laureate, appointed in 2009 and most recently, Simon Armitage, also well known as a translator of poetry in Middle English, in 2019.[11]

In 2000, when the New Chaucer Society Congress was held in London, in the year of the six-hundredth anniversary of Chaucer's death, it seemed specially fitting that Andrew Motion, then the poet laureate, read some selections from Chaucer's poetry in a commemorative service at Westminster Abbey, not far from the area known as Poets' Corner, where Chaucer and so many later English poets were buried (see Myth 28). Chaucerians themselves, though skeptical about Chaucer's own status as laureate, were thrilled at this semblance of continuity and this recognition of Chaucer's contemporary significance.[12]

As an idea, the laureateship is a mixed blessing for poetry, though. It seems to imply that poetry is for special occasions only, and that its most rewarded function is to celebrate and commemorate, not to critique. The idea of poetry as a commission also runs counter to the Romantic notion of poetry as stemming from the "spontaneous overflow of powerful feelings … recollected in tranquillity," in Wordsworth's expression.[13] Poems produced by laureates are often despised, receiving a hostile response (probably a greater amount of criticism than any other poem), while there persists a general and related suspicion that any poet who *accepts* a commission has probably sold his or her soul. Laureates sometimes take on the role as advocates for the study of poetry in schools and the broader community, but some poets have been reluctant to be named as laureate, and Andrew Motion, indeed, was the first laureate to resign his position. In the UK, the honor is now given only as a ten-year appointment.

When Chaucer is claimed as a poet laureate, however, it seems to represent an emotional investment in wanting to see his work recognized at a high level. There *is* the famous illustration of Chaucer reading to the court that appears in the Corpus Christi manuscript of *Troilus and Criseyde*.[14] This image shows a crowd of elegant courtiers descending from a pink stone castle to settle in elegant attitudes of attention around the poet, who stands behind a lectern to read from his works. For many decades this image was thought to document Chaucer reading at the royal court of Edward (1327–77) or Richard (1377–99), while attempts were also made to identify particular courtiers. But more recent scholarship prefers to see this image rather as an idealized representation of Chaucer reading to the court, or perhaps even an illustration of the poem's opening narrative frame, in which Chaucer addresses a mixed company of young lovers.[15]

In fact, it is actually Chaucer's contemporary John Gower who was given royal poetic commissions. Gower and later poets such as Thomas Hoccleve and John Lydgate, and in France women writers like Christine de Pizan, also appear in "presentation manuscripts": books addressed to rulers that feature a frontispiece portraying the author kneeling to offer the book to the king.[16] By contrast, we have no such image of Chaucer.

There is also another sense in which Chaucer was described as "laureate" in the fifteenth century that indirectly feeds this myth. Many of Chaucer's followers portrayed him in this way to acknowledge and praise the "golden" or "illuminated" quality of his English writing. He is regularly praised as such by his followers in the fifteenth and sixteenth centuries, and there seems to be a curious conflation between "aureate" or "golden" high style and the "laureate" ethos. The tradition of the laureate poet goes back to the fourteenth-century example of Francesco Petrarch, who had himself "crowned" as laureate poet in Rome in 1341. The laurel wreath is associated with the god Apollo and was the sign of martial or athletic prowess and victory. Petrarch was deliberately invoking a classical revival – he wrote mostly in Latin – but the idea also combined with the "medieval" idea of his courtly devotion to the beautiful "Laura." For Chaucer's followers, a "laureate" style was a high style, the language of *Troilus and Criseyde*, rather than most of the *Canterbury Tales*, for example; although in his second edition of the *Tales* in 1483, Caxton offered this praise of Chaucer, who "for his ornate wrytyng in our tongue maye wel have the name of a laureate poete. For tofore that he by hys labour enbelysshyd, ornated, and made faire our Englisshe ...."[17]

This is one of those myths that is also like a tradition. There is a slim kernel of truth (Chaucer *was* given a grant of wine), but the tradition tells us more about our desire to find a point of origin for our own love of the poet.

Notes

1 Ben Jonson is often named the first Poet Laureate, but the position was not formalized until Dryden's appointment.

2 John Dryden, *The Poems of John Dryden, Volume IV*, ed. James Kinsley (Oxford: Clarendon Press, 1958), 1453.

3 Ibid., 1445.

4 Ford Madox Brown, *Chaucer at the Court of Edward III*, 1847–1851, oil on canvas, 372 × 296 cm, Art Gallery of New South Wales, Sydney, http://www.artgallery.nsw.gov.au/collection/works/703, accessed 19 November 2018.

5 Anon., "Geoffrey Chaucer was the first 'Versificator Regis' or Poet Laureate," *Look and Learn* 349 (21 September 1968), https://www.lookandlearn.com/blog/26122/geoffrey-chaucer-was-the-first-versificator-regis-or-poet-laureate, accessed 19 November 2018.

6 Martin M. Crow and Clair C. Olson, eds., *Chaucer Life-Records* (Oxford: Clarendon Press, 1966), 554, 561, 595, 596.

7 J.M. Manly, *Some New Light on Chaucer* (Gloucester, MA: Peter Smith, 1959), 68–9.

8 Derek Pearsall, *The Life of Geoffrey Chaucer: A Critical Biography* (Oxford: Blackwell, 1992), 95.

9 *Collectors Mug: Geoffrey Chaucer's Canterbury Pilgrims*, designed by Victor Skellern for Wedgwood, 1963–64, http://www.wedgwoodmuseum.org.uk/collections/collections-online/object/collectors-mug-geoffrey-chaucer-canterbury-pilgrims, accessed 13 August 2018.

10 The first "Consultant in Poetry to the Library of Congress" was appointed in 1937. The title was changed to "Poet Laureate Consultant in Poetry" in 1986 by an act of Congress that described the role as "equivalent to that of Poet Laureate of the United States," https://loc.gov/poetry/about_laureate.html, accessed 13 August 2018.

11 The Editors of Encyclopaedia Britannica, "List of Poets Laureate of Britain," *Encyclopaedia Britannica*, 9 September 2014, https://www.britannica.com/topic/list-of-poets-laureate-of-Britain-1789231, accessed 19 November 2018.

12 Both of us attended this event.

13 William Wordsworth, "Preface to the Lyrical Ballads," in *Wordsworth & Coleridge: Lyrical Ballads & Other Poems*, ed. Martin Scofield (Ware: Wordsworth Editions, 2003), 5–25, here 21.

14 Cambridge, Corpus Christi College, MS 61: Geoffrey Chaucer, *Troilus and Criseyde*, https://parker.stanford.edu/parker/catalog/dh967mz5785, accessed 19 November 2018.

15 Derek Pearsall discusses this and a number of other Chaucer portraits in *The Life of Geoffrey Chaucer*, 285–305, especially 291.

16 See, for example, Hoccleve presenting his *Regiment of Princes* to Prince Henry (the future Henry V) in British Library, Royal 17.D.vi, f. 40r.; John Lydgate presenting his *Siege of Troy* to Henry V in the University of Manchester, English MS 1, f. 1r.; and John M. Bowers, "Thomas Hoccleve and the Politics of Tradition," *Chaucer Review* 36, no. 4 (2002), 353–69.

17 William Caxton, *Caxton's Own Prose*, ed. N.F. Blake (London: Andre Deutsch, 1973), 61.

Myth

30

CONTEMPORARY LITERARY THEORY IS IRRELEVANT TO CHAUCER

It is a common myth about older canonical authors – well, to be more specific, about Chaucer and Shakespeare – that their works will outlast and render redundant all the interpretive varieties and changing fashions of modern literary criticism. Critics and their fancy interpretive fashions may come and go, but literary works remain changeless and pristine, untouched by the vagaries and excesses of critical theory. This is an important aspect of the way these writers are said to partake in the unchanging, "common-sense" conventions of good literature and its timeless wisdom, or at least the imaginative experience it seems to offer: the delight of imagining ourselves in other people's lives.[1] In its rejection of academic discourse, this myth grants a significant role to the amateur or general reader of Chaucer who has no need of highfalutin critical theory; it also protects the first encounters of student readers with medieval poetry, as it encourages them to feel they may approach the poetry directly, without too much specialist or arcane knowledge or training. Implicit here, too, is the persistent idea that poets, novelists and playwrights are all more creative and original than professional literary critics, who invent ever more fanciful theories to account for what is blatantly obvious, who twist and contort the meaning of Chaucer's poetry to suit overly sophisticated reading methods, or who condemn Chaucer with the bluntest of blunt critical instruments for not being "politically correct." Indeed, it is sometimes suggested that Chaucer would find the changing critical fashions of the twentieth and twenty-first centuries amusing if not downright ridiculous or offensive.

---

30 Great Myths About Chaucer, First Edition. Thomas A. Prendergast and Stephanie Trigg.
© 2020 John Wiley & Sons, Inc. Published 2020 by John Wiley & Sons, Inc.

Naturally, as fully fledged professional literary critics, we argue that on the contrary, literary criticism is capable of deepening our encounters with literary texts in productive and engaging ways. Criticism in the form of source study helps us fill in the background to Chaucer's poetry; the study of the manuscripts in which his work appears helps to illuminate the contexts of textual production, circulation and contemporary reception of his work; and, indeed, it makes possible the edited, punctuated and variously modernized texts by which the general reader can seem to encounter Chaucer in an unmediated way. It is hard to underestimate the significance of all the micro editorial and scholarly decisions that sit behind every punctuation mark; every interpretive gloss that explains unfamiliar words, difficult syntax and puzzling historical allusions; and every decision about ordering the works in every scholarly edition of Chaucer's poetry; to say nothing of the biographical research that sits behind every introductory "life" of the poet.

In addition to emphasizing the importance of this extensive scholarly apparatus, we would also argue that the intellectual exercise of testing out different theories of reading and interpretation – the work of literary theory and criticism – certainly deepens our appreciation and understanding of Chaucer's aesthetic, ethical, political and intellectual accomplishment. For literary critics and theorists, the fact that different generations of critics have found different things to admire – and to lament – in Chaucer's poetry is testimony not to our own inconsistencies or failures, but rather to the welcome and lively sense that our relationship to the past is dynamic and, at best, interrogative and critical. Different Chaucerian texts, genres and styles have certainly gone in and out of fashion over the centuries, while the significance, meaning and value of the "Middle Ages" are similarly variable and changeable. It is an important aspect of the work of literary criticism to chart these changes, since they affect our choices of what works we read and the way we respond to them.

The critical forms of Chaucer studies may perhaps, though somewhat arbitrarily, be grouped into four kinds or patterns. First, there are the scholarly modes of criticism that are specifically developed in relation to medieval English literature. These would include, for example, the distinctive forms of exegetical criticism developed by D.W. Robertson and others that are based on the interpretive allegorical models of St. Augustine and early Church fathers, and other medieval reading and interpretive practices.[2] This category would also include the various forms of manuscript and codicological study that analyze the transmission and first editions of Chaucer's texts and that trace the transition from manuscript to print culture in the fifteenth and sixteenth centuries. It would incorporate too the more recent contemporary interest in seeing the culture of fourteenth-century England as a distinctively multicultural and multilingual one.[3] Second, there are the critical modes that were first developed in relation to later literature. These would include the mid-twentieth-century models of "new criticism" or formalism, which showed little interest in the relationship between literary texts and their historical context and have played an important role in insisting that Chaucer's works can be read alongside and compared with the work of later novelists and poets; "new historicism" as a development primarily originating in the study of Renaissance literature; and deconstruction, which was initially taken up in English literary studies mostly by critics of Romantic literature. Third, there are the broader movements in cultural criticism (for example Marxism, psychoanalysis, feminism, queer theory), whose insights are put to work in studying literature from all periods, not just medieval literature. Fourth, there are the critical modes that can be loosely clustered under the banner of medievalism: reading Chaucerian texts through the history of their critical reception, or their long histories of adaptation and translation, in both literary and popular culture (either faithfully or inventively), in English or in other languages, in poetry, prose, cinema, television or other media. We might also mention the newer forms of Chaucer and medieval criticism that are played out in social media. These are accessible to anyone inside or outside the academy; and thanks to the inventive work of Brantley Bryant and others, even give us the chance to "play" by hearing and speaking in the voice of Chaucer himself, in a forum that, for all its weaknesses, nevertheless breaks down the opposition between professional and amateur readers, making the enthusiastic appreciation of Chaucer's voice available to all.[4]

Among all these varieties and critical movements, which have all had interesting things to say about Chaucer's texts, it is probably fair to say that the 1980s and 1990s were the periods of greatest enthusiasm for critical experimentation. And while it would be invidious to single out particular examples, there may well have been some who "read too much" into the text; or tried too hard to make Chaucer's works fit a preordained interpretive model; or, indeed, who argued against the teaching and reading of Chaucer at all, given that, as we have seen at various points in this book, he seems to represent traditional, conservative, white, colonial, heterosexist and patriarchal culture so comprehensively.

Against some of these critical excesses, the idea of a common-sense appreciation of Chaucer starts to seem more attractive, but as we hope to have shown in this book, nearly all of our "obvious" or "natural" ideas about Chaucer have long and complicated histories. We do not think that there is anything much that is obvious or natural about the practice of criticism at all. Indeed, we think that one of the best ways to approach a literary text is fully armed with a sense of how it might surprise you.

But what did Chaucer have to say about literary criticism? As we saw in Myth 9, Chaucer relished the dramatization of a diversity of opinion, whether it was people discussing the nature of a magic horse in the *Squire's Tale*, or the comic tale told by the Miller, or birds debating the nature of love in *The Parliament of Foules*. Indeed, this interest in diversity has often been taken as a kind of guiding principle for Chaucerian studies, as if the community of Canterbury pilgrims, for example, might serve as a model for modern Chaucer critics, tolerant of difference and diversity (though at times, critical disputes have certainly been rather more acrimonious than this image suggests, just as the pilgrims also strive and argue with each other).[5] When it comes to interpreting texts, Chaucer also often seems unwilling to make a definitive judgment.

The fable of the cock and the fox in the *Nun's Priest's Tale*, for example, produces several different proverbial "moralitees" or conclusions, both from the two protagonists and from the narrator, who then addresses the company more directly and encourages them to see this tale as more than a "folye":

> But ye that holden this tale a folye,
> As of a fox, or of a cok and hen,
> Taketh the moralite, goode men.
> For Seint Paul seith that al that writen is,
> To oure doctrine it is ywrite, ywis;
> Taketh the fruyt, and lat the chaf be stille.
>
> (VII.3438–43)

This speech is frequently cited in support of Chaucer's deep sympathy for allegorical and ethical patterns of interpretation, but the same tale also offers a number of different readerly positions. For example, the rooster Chauntecleer and the hen Pertelote have engaged in a learned but famously inconclusive and deferred debate about the interpretation of dreams, while the narrator opens up but fails to resolve the question of predestination and insists (contrary to the lines just quoted) that his tale is simply that of a cock. Like several other Chaucerian narrators, the Nun's Priest seems to want to spark a gendered debate among his readers, as he appeals to women's love of romance and the biblical tradition that blames Eve for the expulsion from Paradise.

Chaucer himself seems often to refuse to make a determination, though he appears comfortable enough rehearsing other people's opinions and deferring judgment. There are a number of occasions where this pattern can be discerned. When the narrator of *The Parliament of Foules* hesitates indecisively before the two contradictory inscriptions over the gate of the park in the dream landscape, his dream guide Scipio takes his hand and walks him into the garden, saying these two texts (one promising misery; one promising bliss) concern only lovers. These are indeed two texts, but this scene is frequently read as a kind of critical allegory for interpretive ambiguity: the difference between two readings; and the power of bypassing the obvious reading.

But perhaps the most typically complex example comes from the Wife of Bath. We will bring the discussion of this myth – and this volume – to an end with a consideration of Alisoun's understanding of the relationship between text and commentary in her *Prologue*. She famously opens her discourse by claiming she does not need to read the works of written authority to know that marriage can offer its own form of misery, and she is able to read selectively the "gentil text" of the Bible that commands humans to wax and multiply. But the remainder of her *Prologue* is a series of close engagements with biblical and antifeminist texts that show her awareness of the power of "glossing," and her delight in arguing against St. Paul's and St. Jerome's views of women. As she says, clerks have written many books against women, but this textual history is wildly unbalanced because it has been written by men; if women had written as many books the representation of gendered activity would appear very different:

> "By God, if wommen hadde writen stories,
> As clerkes han withinne hire oratories,
> They wolde han writen of men moore wikkednesse
> Than al the mark of Adam may redresse."
>
> (III.693–6)

The episode of domestic violence that brings the Wife's *Prologue* to an end – after she tears three leaves out of her fifth husband's "cursed book" of women and wives who have behaved badly – leaves us in no doubt that Chaucer was aware of the contentiousness of literary interpretation. Throughout his works he consistently demonstrates the power of narrative and language to shape social meaning in the world: the world of literature is intimately bound up with the world of literary criticism and the act of reading.

What would Chaucer have made of our contemporary literary enterprises? It is easy to imagine he might indeed have found some of our debates and quarrels laughable or incomprehensible; or wondered at some of the more arcane institutional practices that structure our work.

But it is worth remembering that his characters were no strangers to debate – often over institutional concerns. And if we learn anything from reading Chaucer, it is that *he* embraces the complexity and importance of *his* literary enterprise, even if he winkingly skewers the critic who would "studie ... upon a book in cloystre ... and make hymselven wood" (I.184–185).

Notes

1 See, for example, Lisa Zunshine, *Why We Read Fiction: Theory of Mind and the Novel* (Columbus, OH: Ohio State University Press, 2006).

2 D.W. Robertson, *A Preface to Chaucer: Studies in Medieval Perspectives* (Princeton, NJ: Princeton University Press, 1962). See also Lee Patterson, *Negotiating the Past: The Historical Understanding of Medieval Literature* (Madison, WI: University of Wisconsin Press, 1987).

3 For example, Ardis Butterfield, *The Familiar Enemy: Chaucer, Language, and Nation in the Hundred Years War* (Oxford: Oxford University Press, 2009); and the collection edited by Jeffrey Jerome Cohen, *Cultural Diversity in the British Middle Ages* (New York: Palgrave, 2008).

4 See Brantley Bryant, *Geoffrey Chaucer Hath a Blog: Medieval Studies and New Media* (New York: Palgrave Macmillan, 2010); and Bryant's Twitter feed @LeVostreGC, which currently has over 86,000 followers.

5 Stephanie Trigg, *Congenial Souls: Reading Chaucer from Medieval to Postmodern* (Minneapolis, MN: Minnesota University Press, 2002).

CODA

Much of this book has been dedicated to what can only be called "mythbusting." The method that we use is pretty straightforward: return to the origin of the story that gave rise to the myth and weigh the evidence as to whether the source of the story can be trusted, or whether it squares with what we know of Chaucer's life and works. It seems simple enough, but as is clear, there have been many times when Chaucerian "myths" do not offer themselves up so easily to be proven true or false. Part of the reason for this is that some of the myths have been transmitted by what can only be called gossip; a discourse with which Chaucer was very familiar. Famously, at the end of *The House of Fame*, the narrator is taken up to look inside the "House of Tidings" where "alle the ... angles / Ys ful of rounynges and of jangles" (1959–60). These "rounynges and ... jangles" (whispers and gossip) consist of truths and falsehoods, but as the narrator discovers, it is not so easy to separate one from the other, for they often "medle [mingle] us ech with other" (2102). The result is "That no man, ... , / Shal han on ... , but bothe / At ones, ..." (2103–5). So what good is this gossip if we cannot separate truth from falsehood?

Certainly there is a lot of "gossip" about Chaucer that is dubious if not downright fictional. And this gossip about the poet often tells us more about the historical moments in which the myths were constructed than they do about Chaucer himself (for example, Chaucer had an unhappy marriage or Chaucer was cuckolded). But we cannot simply abject gossip as a means of transmitting something that might be valuable. To value gossip is to understand that the world is not governed by a simple binary

30 Great Myths About Chaucer, First Edition. Thomas A. Prendergast and Stephanie Trigg.
© 2020 John Wiley & Sons, Inc. Published 2020 by John Wiley & Sons, Inc.

of true/false. A cautionary tale involves one of the more spectacular recent discoveries about Chaucer: the identity of his scribe.

In July 2004, an article appeared in *The Guardian* entitled "The Scrivener's Tale: How Chaucer's Sloppy Copyist Was Unmasked after 600 Years."[1] The article reported how Linne Mooney had uncovered the identity of Chaucer's scribe, who had been immortalized in a poem with the title "Chauciers wordes . a Geffrey vn to Adame his owen scryveyne /":

> Adam . scryveyne / if euer it thee byfalle
> Boece or Troylus / for to wryten nuwe /
> Vnder thy long lokkes / thowe most haue the scalle
> But affter my makyng / thowe wryte more truwe
> So offt adaye . I mot thy werk renuwe /
> It to . corect / and eke to rubbe and scrape /
> And al is thorugh . thy necglygence and rape /[2]

The existence of the poem is a kind of miracle, because it is seemingly at once a product of the poet and a meditation on the means by which the productions of the poet come to be transmitted. It is also, of course, a complaint about the very person who might well be copying the poem. Further, it seems to offer the reader a peek at the personal relationship between Geoffrey and Adam that might illuminate "the unfamiliarity of Chaucer's world ... [and] the alterities of manuscript production in an age of print."[3]

Mooney's discovery of the actual Adam (whose last name was "Pynkhurst") "rocked ... the world of medieval studies."[4] We could now ostensibly trace the historical figure who was, as Mooney argued, the copyist of the two earliest manuscripts of the *Canterbury Tales*. Most scholars accepted the attribution and, as Lawrence Warner puts it, "its biggest impact was surely in the classroom, but a vibrant Pynkhurst scholarly industry, too, quickly materialized."[5] Yet there remained doubts among certain scholars.[6] After the formal publication of Mooney's research,[7] some critics turned back to the poem and began to question its attribution to Chaucer.[8] They expressed concern that the poem only exists in one manuscript (Trinity College Cambridge MS R.3.20) in the hand of John Shirley – who was perhaps not the most accurate of copyists, and this reputation for inaccuracy was extended by some to his attributions.[9]

Much of this distrust focused on the heading (or "title") to the poem. As Alexandra Gillespie put it, "My point is that 'Chauciers wordes . a Geffrey vn to Adame his owen scyveyne' is an unlikely choice of title for Chaucer. But it is very like one of John Shirley's characteristically 'gossipy' headnotes." And what does this gossip do? It enables Shirley to "construct his own Chaucer from Chaucer's words" and thus "ensures that his readers can make their Chaucer from the same words, and, by that process, assign Shirley a fêted role in Chaucerian tradition."[10] This invocation of gossip would be unremarkable, except that Gillespie later claims that this medieval gossip mirrors the way that Mooney's discovery of the identity of Chaucer's scribe was announced and reported: "Mooney's work was presented to a wider public in the same way Shirley presents his work: some gossipy remarks about Chaucer were used to make the Pinkhurst discovery interesting to readers."[11] The transmission of the story of Chaucer's scribe is thus, apparently, less dependent on whether it is true and more dependent on the irresistible nature of gossip, a reference that is repeated by Mooney's most recent critic, Lawrence Warner.[12]

But where did this idea of the gossipy copyist, John Shirley, come from? It appears to have started in 1866 when the textual scholar, Henry Bradshaw, in an offhand comment in a private letter, referred to the "gossiping rubrics" of Shirley.[13] Eleanor Prescott Hammond, referencing Bradshaw, describes the "gossiping headings" as in the "tone of a modern publisher's jacket."[14] This then was repeated by Derek Pearsall and commented upon by David Burnley.[15] As Margaret Connelly notes in her defense of Shirley's attribution, "'Gossip'" in these formulations could be read as neutral, but, in fact (and as Chaucer himself suggested), it "carries a whole range of negative associations: gossip is unauthorised, unofficial, and liable to be untrue, or at best a mixture of truth and lies in which the two cannot reliably be separated."[16] If it is not too obvious, the idea of Shirley's "gossipy headings" is really itself a piece of academic gossip that, having been amplified and repeated so many times, has gained the currency of truth. As we have suggested, its status as gossip is not enough to dismiss doubts about the authenticity of Chaucer's poem or the identity of Chaucer's scribe (and there might well be other reasons to doubt both), but, as with so many of the "myths" about Chaucer, the myth of Chaucer's scribe cannot be dismissed simply because it is generated by gossip.[17]

As Susan E. Phillips has noted, one of Chaucer's greatest creations, the Wife of Bath, is a testament to the potentially positive generative nature of gossip. She points out that Alisoun famously shares with her "gossyb Dame Alys" (III.548) all of her husband's secrets, "For hadde myn housbonde pissed on a wal, / Or doon a thyng that sholde han cost his lyf / To hire … / I wolde han told his conseil every deel" (III.534–6, 538).[18] Chaucer communicates the wide range of gossipy talk – from the insignificant, if embarrassing (public urination), to something that was so scandalous that it was dangerous. But if gossip was sometimes characterized as small talk (the term "small things" was often a euphemism for salacious matters), Chaucer also uses it to talk about the kinds of tales that he himself tells.[19] The fictional intimacy that this produces between author and reader is one of the great pleasures of Chaucer's works and may, in itself, tell us why we care about whether these Chaucerian myths are true or false.

Notes

1 John Ezard, "The Scrivener's Tale: How Chaucer's Sloppy Copyist Was Unmasked after 600 Years," *The Guardian* (20 July 2004), https://www.theguardian.com/uk/2004/jul/20/highereducation.books, accessed 8 July 2019.
2 As A.S.G. Edwards notes, the *Riverside Chaucer*'s version of this poem (as well as the title) is not quite what appears in the manuscript: "Chaucer and 'Adam Scriveyn,'" *Medium Aevum* 81, no. 1 (2012), 137. We have used the version that appears in *A Variorum Edition of the Works of Geoffrey Chaucer, 5: The Minor Poems, Part One*, ed. George B. Pace and Alfred David (Norman, OK: University of Oklahoma Press, 1982), 136–7. We have replaced the thorns with their modern equivalents.
3 Seth Lerer, *Chaucer and His Readers* (Princeton, NJ: Princeton University Press, 1993), 143.
4 Mary C. Flannery, "Rubbing and Scraping: Who *wrote* Chaucer's poetry?" *Times Literary Supplement* (5 February 2019), 36. It should be noted that Bernard Wagner had first suggested Pinkhurst as a candidate for "Adam," in "Chaucer's Scrivener," *Times Literary Supplement* (13 June 1929), 474.
5 Lawrence Warner, *Chaucer's Scribes: London Textual Production, 1384–1432* (Cambridge: Cambridge University Press, 2018), 6.
6 Many of these doubts were initially expressed informally or only in orally delivered addresses. It remains unclear how widespread initial resistance was. See ibid., 6–8.
7 Mooney, Linne R., "Chaucer's Scribe," *Speculum* 81 (2006), 97–138.
8 Though Seth Lerer had suggested that the copyist of the poem John "Shirley may have responded to many familiar things in *Adam Scriveyn*; but he just might have created them, as well" (*Chaucer and His Readers*, 121).
9 Edwards points out that several of the poems he attributes to Chaucer are not widely accepted by critics as the poet's.
10 Alexandra Gillespie, "Reading Chaucer's Words to Adam," *Chaucer Review* 42, no. 3 (2008), 276.
11 Ibid., 276.
12 He suggests, along with Edwards, that the poem seems to be less about how an author would treat a text than how a supervisor might treat the work of a careless scribe, and thus may not be by Chaucer. Warner, *Chaucer's Scribes*, 17, 21; Edwards, "Chaucer and 'Adam Scriveyn,'" 136–7.

13 The letter is quoted by F.N. Robinson in "On Two Manuscripts of Lydgate's Guy of Warwick," in *Studies and Notes in Philology and Literature 5* (Boston, MA: Published under the direction of the Modern Language Depts. of Harvard University by Ginn & Co., 1896), 179.

14 Eleanor Prescott Hammond, *English verse between Chaucer and Surrey: being examples of conventional secular poetry, exclusive of romance, ballad, lyric, and drama, in the period from Henry the Fourth to Henry the Eighth* (Durham, NC: Duke University Press, 1927), 191.

15 Derek Pearsall, *John Lydgate* (Charlottesville, VA: University of Virginia Press, 1970), 74. David Burnley, "Scogan, Shirley's Reputation and Chaucerian Occasional Verse," in *Chaucer in Perspective*, ed. Geoffrey Lester (Sheffield: Sheffield Academic Press, 1999), 31. Burnley acknowledges that not all gossip is false, but concedes that it is often vain.

16 Margaret Connelly, "What John Shirley Said about Adam: Authorship and Attribution in Cambridge, Trinity College, MS R.3.20," in *The Dynamics of the Medieval Manuscript: Text Collections from a European Perspective*, ed. Bart Besamusca, Matthias Meyer, Karen Pratt, et al. (Göttingen: V & R Unipress, 2017), 86.

17 See, for instance, Warner, *Chaucer's Scribes*.

18 Susan E. Phillips, *Transforming Talk: The Problem with Gossip in Late Medieval England* (University Park, PA: Pennsylvania State University Press, 2007). The word "gossip" originally meant one who was a sponsor or godparent, from *God* and *sibb*, "relative." In Middle English it was extended to mean a familiar acquaintance, and in the sixteenth century was used to identify the kind of talk in which you would engage with your "gossip."

19 Ibid., 112–13.

FURTHER READING

Chaucer's Works

For all our citations from Chaucer's works, we have used the text that has been for many years the "standard edition": *Geoffrey Chaucer, The Riverside Chaucer*, edited by Larry Benson, with a new foreword by Christopher Cannon (2008). This is the third, revised and updated edition of the volume first edited by F.N. Robinson in 1933. It includes all Chaucer's works and translations, with a substantial introduction, glosses at the foot of the page and two sets of commentaries (one historical and literary, one textual). It remains the text cited by most scholars. But there are many other editions available, of both the complete works and individual texts, which are perhaps more accessible for students and readers who may not want or need such a comprehensive edition. There are too many to mention them all here, but let us begin by drawing attention to a selection of alternatives. David Lawton has recently produced a new edition of Chaucer's works for the Norton series (2019), which is available both in print and in a digital edition. Scholars are perhaps less bound these days to the idea of a single "standard" edition, but Lawton's new text may come to occupy this position. Norton has also published a separate volume containing just Lawton's edition of the *Canterbury Tales* (2019). Other works include Barry Windeatt's text of *Troilus and Criseyde: A New Edition of 'The Book of Troilus'* (1984) with the corresponding text of Boccaccio's *Il Filostrato* on opposite pages; or Stephen A. Barney's edition for Norton, *Troilus and Criseyde* (2006), which translates these

30 Great Myths About Chaucer, First Edition. Thomas A. Prendergast and Stephanie Trigg.
© 2020 John Wiley & Sons, Inc. Published 2020 by John Wiley & Sons, Inc.

passages from Boccaccio's Italian into English. For Chaucer's dream poems, see the editions by Helen Phillips and Nick Havely, *Chaucer's Dream Poetry* (1997), or by Kathryn L. Lynch, *Dream Visions and Other Poems: Authoritative Texts, Contexts, Criticism* (2007).

There are currently two new projects for editing all of Chaucer's works to watch out for in the future. Christopher Cannon and James Simpson are editing all of Chaucer's works for an online edition from Oxford University Press, while Julia Boffey and A.S.G. Edwards are compiling the *Cambridge Complete Works of Geoffrey Chaucer* (forthcoming in 2020). This rush of activity tells us that many of the complex issues of finalizing and determining the text of what Chaucer wrote (given that nearly all the surviving manuscripts were written after his death) remain unresolved and contested, especially for the *Canterbury Tales*.

If you prefer to read Chaucer in modern translation, there are a number of excellent versions available, such as David Wright's edition with Christopher Cannon, *Geoffrey Chaucer: Canterbury Tales* (2011), Barry Windeatt's *Troilus and Criseyde* (2003) and Brian Stone's *Love Visions* (1983). For a more experimental, less literal and emphatically lyrical version of *Troilus and Criseyde*, you might like Lavinia Greenlaw's *A Double Sorrow: Troilus and Criseyde* (2014).

And if you would like to work with a more literal translation, the Harvard's Geoffrey Chaucer Website includes interlinear translations of the *Canterbury Tales*: https://chaucer.fas.harvard.edu.

Conversely, if you would like to view the manuscripts and printed editions, many libraries and archives have digitized volumes in their collection. A comprehensive list of Chaucerian texts available online is maintained by Siân Echard of the University of British Columbia: http://faculty.arts.ubc.ca/sechard/346mss.htm.

Backgrounds and Contexts

Throughout this book we have mentioned a number of modern biographical studies, and for further discussion of Chaucer's life we recommend especially the biographies by Derek Pearsall (*The Life of Geoffrey Chaucer*, 1992), Paul Strohm (*Chaucer's Tale: 1386 and the Road to Canterbury*, 2014) and the most recent by Marion Turner (*Chaucer: A European Life*, 2019). There is also a short and very readable study by David Wallace, *Geoffrey Chaucer: A New Introduction* (2017), and there are many other short introductions to Chaucer and his poetry available, often written for a secondary school or undergraduate audience.

If you would like to immerse yourself more thoroughly in the literary contexts familiar to Chaucer, try Robert M. Correale and Mary Hamel's collection, *Sources and Analogues of the* Canterbury Tales, 2 vols. (2002, 2005). Another excellent compilation of literary and historical source material for medieval England (not just Chaucer's literary sources) is assembled by Matthew Boyd Goldie in *Middle English Literature: A Historical Sourcebook* (2003). For a comprehensive account of medieval English literature, we have cited the *Cambridge History of Medieval English Literature*, edited by David Wallace (1999), an authoritative collection of essays by a diverse group of scholars; and we have already mentioned James Simpson's revolutionary *Reform and Cultural Revolution* (2002), volume two of the Oxford English Literary History, 1350–1547.

For more focused and detailed discussions of Chaucer's works, there are a number of fine guides and companions to Chaucer and his works that we recommend as excellent places to begin, such as Helen Cooper's *Oxford Guides to Chaucer: The Canterbury Tales* (1996) and Barry Windeatt's *Oxford Guides to Chaucer: Troilus and Criseyde* (1995). More recent studies and collections include the *Yale Companion to Chaucer*, edited by Seth Lerer (2006); *Chaucer: An Oxford Guide*, edited by Steve Ellis (2005); *The Cambridge Introduction to Chaucer*, edited by Alastair Minnis (2014); and *A New Companion to Chaucer*, edited by Peter Brown (2019). For a reading guide to *The Canterbury Tales*, there is Elizabeth Scala's *Canterbury Tales Handbook* (2019); and for your first encounter with Chaucer's absorbing but difficult Trojan epic poem, Jenni Nuttall's *Troilus and Criseyde: A Reader's Guide* (2012) offers an intelligent and well-informed commentary on the story as it unfolds.

The major resource for Chaucer's language is the Middle English Dictionary, hosted by the University of Michigan: https://quod.lib.umich.edu/m/middle-english-dictionary/dictionary.

Further Criticism

Again, while noting that some of our favorite essays, books and chapters on Chaucer are already mentioned in the works cited, we focus on relatively recent publications to suggest some studies that explore a range of theoretical and critical perspectives on Chaucer's works. The essay collection edited by Thomas A. Prendergast and Jessica Rosenfeld, *Chaucer and the Subversion of Form* (2018), draws inspiration from a revival of interest in formalist criticism. Elizabeth Scala's *Desire in the Canterbury Tales* (2015) explores the implications of psychoanalytic criticism and theory for new readings of the *Canterbury Tales*; the most recent study of the scribal production of Chaucer's works is Lawrence Warner, *Chaucer's Scribes: Medieval Textual Production 1384–1432* (2018); and Megan L.

Cook's *The Poet and the Antiquaries* (2019) focuses on the printed editions of Chaucer produced between 1532 and 1602. The collection edited by Isabel Davis and Catherine Nall, *Chaucer and Fame: Reputation and Reception* (2015), includes essays that study the concept of fame in Chaucer's works, but also engage with some of the questions of reputation and celebrity we have been concerned with in this book. A number of recent studies focus on Chaucer's life in the economic and social contexts of medieval London, such as Ardis Butterfield's edited collection, *Chaucer and the City* (2006) and Marion Turner's *Chaucerian Conflict: Languages of Antagonism in Late Fourteenth-Century London* (2006). Another collection, edited by Helen M. Hickey, Anne McKendry and Melissa Raine, brings medieval and medievalism studies together to study Chaucer's poetry and his reception from medieval through to contemporary culture: *Contemporary Chaucer across the Centuries* (2018).

Other Resources

The key academic journals for Chaucer studies are *Studies in the Age of Chaucer*, published by the New Chaucer Society (which you can join), and which also sponsors the publication of the Online Chaucer Bibliography (http://newchaucersociety.org/pages/entry/chaucer-bibliography); and the *Chaucer Review*. If you are interested in the way Chaucer's works have traversed global culture, the Global Chaucers blog (https://globalchaucers.wordpress.com), maintained by Candace Barrington and Jonathan Hsy, collects and features translations and adaptations of Chaucer's work in other languages and cultures.

The Open Access Companion to the *Canterbury Tales* (https://opencanterburytales.dsl.lsu.edu) is a freely available and authoritative interactive guide for readers; and *Visualizing Chaucer* (https://d.lib.rochester.edu/chaucer), from the University of Rochester, collects illustrations of Chaucer's works.

WORKS CITED

Chaucer Editions (All Works by Chaucer, Listed by Editor)

Andrew, Malcolm, Charles Moorman, and Daniel J. Ransom, eds. *A Variorum Edition of the Works of Geoffrey Chaucer, 2: The Canterbury Tales, The General Prologue*. Norman, OK: University of Oklahoma Press, 1993.

Barney, Stephen, ed. *Geoffrey Chaucer: Troilus and Criseyde*. Norton Critical Editions. New York: W.W. Norton, 2006.

Benson, Larry D., gen. ed. *The Riverside Chaucer*. Boston, MA: Houghton Mifflin, 1987.

Boenig, Robert, and Andrew Taylor, eds. *The Canterbury Tales*. 2nd edn. Peterborough: Broadview, 2012.

Boyd, Beverly, ed. *A Variorum Edition of the Works of Geoffrey Chaucer, 2: The Prioress's Tale*. Norman, OK: University of Oklahoma Press, 1987.

Lawton, David, ed. *The Norton Chaucer*. Prose texts edited by Jennifer Arch, and dream poems edited by Kathryn Lynch. New York: W.W. Norton, 2019.

Lawton, David, ed. *The Norton Chaucer: The Canterbury Tales*. New York: W.W. Norton, 2019.

Lipscomb, William, ed. *The Canterbury Tales of Chaucer; Completed in a Modern Version*, 3 vols. Oxford: J. Cooke, 1795.

Lumiansky, R.M., ed. and trans. *The Canterbury Tales of Geoffrey Chaucer*. New York: Simon and Schuster, 1948.

Lynch, Kathryn L., ed. *Dream Visions and Other Poetry: Authoritative Texts, Contexts, Criticism*. Norton Critical Editions. New York: W.W. Norton, 2007.

Pace, George B., and Alfred David, eds. *The Chaucer Variorum, 5: The Minor Poems, Part One*. Norman, OK: University of Oklahoma Press, 1982.

30 Great Myths About Chaucer, First Edition. Thomas A. Prendergast and Stephanie Trigg.
© 2020 John Wiley & Sons, Inc. Published 2020 by John Wiley & Sons, Inc.

Phillips, Helen, and Nick Havely, eds. *Chaucer's Dream Poetry*. New York: Longman, 1997.

Speght, Thomas, ed. *The Workes of our Antient and Learned English Poet, Geffrey Chaucer, newly printed*. London: Adam Islip, at the charges of Thomas Wight, 1598.

Stone, Brian, trans. *Love Visions*. Harmondsworth: Penguin, 1983.

Thynne, William, ed. *The Workes of Geffray Chaucer newly imprinted*. London: Thomas Godfray, 1532.

Tyrwhitt, Thomas, ed. *The Canterbury tales of Chaucer to which are added, an essay upon his language and versification; an introductory discourse; and notes*. 5 vols. London: T. Payne, 1775–78.

Urry, John, ed. *The Works of Geoffrey Chaucer*. London: B. Lintot, 1721.

Windeatt, Barry, ed. *Troilus and Criseyde: A New Edition of "The Book of Troilus."* London: Longman, 1984.

Windeatt, Barry, ed. *Troilus and Criseyde. Oxford World's Classics*. Oxford: Oxford University Press, 2009.

Wright, David, and Christopher Cannon, eds. *Chaucer: Canterbury Tales*. Oxford World Classics. Oxford: Oxford University Press, 2011.

Manuscripts

Aberystwyth, National Library of Wales, Peniarth MS 392D: Hengwrt Chaucer. https://www.llyfrgell.cymru/?id=257.

Alnwick, Alnwick Castle, Collection of the Duke of Northumberland, MS 455: The Prologue to the Tale of Beryn.

Cambridge, Corpus Christi College, MS 61: Geoffrey Chaucer, *Troilus and Criseyde*. https://parker.stanford.edu/parker/catalog/dh967mz5785.

Cambridge, University Library, MS Dd.4.24 (Dd): Chaucer's *Canterbury Tales*.

Edinburgh, National Library of Scotland, Advocates MS.19.2.1: Auchinleck Manuscript.

London, British Library, MS Royal 17.D.vi, f. 40r: Hoccleve presenting his *Regiment of Princes* to the future Henry. http://www.bl.uk/manuscripts/Viewer.aspx?ref=royal_ms_17_d_vi_fs001r.

Manchester, University of Manchester, English MS 1, f. 1r: Lydgate presenting his *Siege of Troy* to Henry V. https://www.library.manchester.ac.uk/inthebigynnyng/manuscript/ms1.

Other Primary Texts

Baker, Richard. *A Chronicle of the Kings of England*. 8th edn. London: H. Sawbridge, B. Tooke, T. Sawbridge, 1684.

Bede. *An Ecclesiastical History of the English People*. In *The Norton Anthology of English Literature, Vol. A: The Middle Ages*, 9th edn., eds. James Simpson and Alfred David, 30–31. New York: W.W. Norton, 2012.

Blake, William. *Blake: Complete Writings*, ed. Geoffrey Keynes. Oxford: Oxford University Press, 1969.

Bowers, John, ed. *The Canterbury Tales: Fifteenth-Century Continuations and Additions*. Kalamazoo, MI: Medieval Institute Publications, 1992.

Brown, Ford Madox. *Chaucer at the Court of Edward III*. 1847–51. Oil on Canvas, 372 × 296 cm. Art Gallery of New South Wales, http://www.artgallery. nsw.gov.au/collection/works/703.

Bullein, William. *A Dialogue bothe plesaunte and pietifull, wherein is a goodly regimente against the feuer Pestilence*, eds., M.W. Bullen and A.H. Bullen. Early English Text Society extended series 52. London: N. Trübner, 1888.

Burrow, J.A., ed. *Geoffrey Chaucer: A Critical Anthology*. Harmondsworth: Penguin, 1969.

Caxton, William. *Caxton's Own Prose*, ed. N.F. Blake. London: Andre Deutsch, 1973.

Christine de Pizan. *The Book of Arms and of Chivalry*, ed. Charity Cannon Willard, trans. Sumner Willard. University Park, PA: Pennsylvania State University Press, 1999.

Douglas, Gavin. *The Poetical Works of Gavin Douglas, Bishop of Dunkeld*, Vol II. Notes and glossary by John Small. Edinburgh: William Paterson, 1874.

Dryden, John. *The Poems of John Dryden*, Vol. IV, ed. James Kinsley. Oxford: Clarendon Press, 1958.

Foxe, John. *The Acts and Monuments of the Christian Martyrs*, 4th edn, ed. Josiah Pratt. 8 vols. London: Religious Tract Society, 1877.

Froissart, Jean. *Les chroniques de Sire Jean Froissart, Vol. II*, ed. J.A.C. Buchon. Paris: Wattelier, 1867.

Gower, John. *Confessio Amantis*. In *The English Works of John Gower*, Vol. II, ed. G.C. Macaulay. Early English Text Society extended series 82. Oxford: Clarendon Press, 1900–2, 1–480. Repr. Oxford: Oxford University Press, 1971.

Gower, John. *Mirour de l'omme*. In *The Complete Works of John Gower*, ed. G.C. Macaulay. 4 vols. Oxford: Clarendon Press, 1899.

Hoccleve, Thomas. *The Regiment of Princes*, ed. Charles R. Blyth. Kalamazoo, MI: Medieval Institute Publications, 1999.

Iack vp Lande Compyled by the famous Geoffrey Chaucer. Southwark: Prynted by J. Nicolson for Ihon Gough, 1536.

Jonson, Ben. "Preface to the First Folio." In *Mr. William Shakespeare's Comedies, Histories, & Tragedies*. London: E. Blount and Isaac Jaggard, 1623, sig. A4.

Kurath, Hans, Sherman M. Kuhn and Robert E. Lewis. *Middle English Dictionary*. Ann Arbor, MI: University of Michigan Press, 1952. https://quod.lib.umich. edu/m/middle-english-dictionary/dictionary.

Langland, William. *The Vision of Piers Plowman: A Critical Edition of the B-Text based on Trinity College Cambridge MS B.15.17*, ed. A.V.C. Schmidt. London: Dent, 1987.

Le prince noir poème du héraut d'armes Chandos: texte critique suivi de notes par Francisque-michel. London: J.G. Fotheringham, 1883.

Percy, Thomas. *Reliques of ancient English poetry: consisting of old heroic ballads, songs, and other pieces of our earlier poets, (chiefly of the lyric kind.) Together with some few of later date*. 3 vols. London: J. Dodsley, 1765.

"Peres the Ploughmans Crede." In *Specimens of English Literature*. Introduction and notes by Walter W. Skeat. Oxford: Clarendon Press, 1871, 1–12.

The Prologues and Epilogues of William Caxton, ed. W.J.B. Crotch. Early English Text Society original series 176. London: Oxford University Press, 1928.

Spenser, Edmund. *Shepheardes Calendar; the original edition of 1579 in photographic facsimile*, ed. H. Oskar Sommer. Manchester: Spenser Society, 1890.

Spenser, Edmund. *The Faerie Queene*, ed. Thomas P. Roche, Jr. London: Penguin, 1978.

The St Albans Chronicle: The "Chronica maiora" of Thomas Walsingham I: 1376–1394, eds. John Taylor, Wendy R. Childs and Leslie Watkiss. Oxford: Oxford University Press, 2003.

Statutes of the Realm. London: Dawsons of Pall Mall, 1810–28.

Trevisa, John, trans. *Polychronicon Ranulphi Higden, Monachi Cestrensis*, ed. Joseph Rawson Lumby. 9 vols. Cambridge: Cambridge University Press, 1874.

Wordsworth, William. "Preface to the Lyrical Ballads." In *Wordsworth & Coleridge: Lyrical Ballads & Other Poems*, ed. Martin Scofield. Ware: Wordsworth Editions Limited, 2003, 1–25.

Secondary Texts

Ackroyd, Peter. *Chaucer. Brief Lives*. London: Chatto & Windus, 2004.

Addison, Joseph. "An Account of the Greatest English Poets, 1694." In *The Works of the Right Honourable Joseph Addison*, notes by Richard Hunt, ed. Henry G. Bohn. Bohn's Standard Library. London: H.G. Bohn 1854–56, 22–7.

Aers, David. "Review of Terry Jones' *Chaucer's Knight: The Portrait of a Medieval Mercenary*." *Studies in the Age of Chaucer* 4 (1982), 169–75.

Alderson, William L. "John Urry." In *Editing Chaucer: The Great Tradition*, ed. Paul G. Ruggiers. Norman, OK: Pilgrim Books, 1984, 93–115.

Allen, Elizabeth. "The Pardoner in the 'Dogges Boure': Early Reception of the *Canterbury Tales*." *Chaucer Review* 56, no. 2 (2001), 91–127.

Anon. "Geoffrey Chaucer was the first 'Versificator Regis' or Poet Laureate." *Look and Learn* 349 (21 September 1968), n.p. https://www.lookandlearn.com/blog/26122/geoffrey-chaucer-was-the-first-versificator-regis-or-poet-laureate.

Anon. "John Gower and his Works." *British Quarterly Review* 27, no. 53 (1858), 3–36.

Anon. "Literary Gossip." *The Athenaeum* 2405 (29 November 1873), 698.

Anon. "Poet Laureate of the United States." https://loc.gov/poetry/about_laureate.html.

Arthurson, Ian. "Espionage and Intelligence from the Wars of the Roses to the Reformation." *Nottingham Medieval Studies* 35 (1991), 134–54.

Bailey, Mark. "The Ploughman." In *Historians on Chaucer: The "General Prologue" to the* Canterbury Tales, ed. Stephen H. Rigby. Oxford: Oxford University Press, 2014, 352–67.

Baum, Paull F. "Chaucer's Puns." *Publications of the Modern Language Association* 71, no. 1 (March 1956), 225–46.

Benson, C. David. "Chaucer's Pardoner: His Sexuality and Modern Critics." *Mediaevalia* 8 (1982), 337–46.

Blamires, Alcuin. "Chaucer's Revaluation of Chivalric Honor." *Mediaevalia* 5 (1979), 245–69.

Bloch, R. Howard. *Medieval Misogyny and the Invention of Western Romantic Love*. Chicago, IL: University of Chicago Press, 1991.

Bloom, Harold. *The Anxiety of Influence: A Theory of Poetry*. 1973. 2nd edn. Oxford: Oxford University Press, 1997.

Blurton, Heather, and Hannah Johnson. *The Critics and the Prioress: Antisemitism, Criticism, and Chaucer's* Prioress's Tale. Ann Arbor, MI: University of Michigan, 2017.

Bowden, Muriel. *A Commentary on the General Prologue to the Canterbury Tales*. New York: Macmillan, 1948.

Bowers, John M. "Thomas Hoccleve and the Politics of Tradition." *Chaucer Review* 36, no. 4 (2002), 353–69.

Braswell, Mary Flowers. *The Forgotten Chaucer Scholarship of Mary Eliza Haweis*. New York: Routledge, 2016.

Brewer, Derek, ed. *Chaucer: The Critical Heritage, Vol. I: 1385–1837*. London: Routledge & Kegan Paul, 1978.

Brewer, Derek, ed. *A New Introduction to Chaucer*. 2nd edn. London: Longman, 1998.

Brinkman, Baba. "The Rap *Canterbury Tales*." https://music.bababrinkman.com/album/the-rap-canterbury-tales.

Bryant, Brantley. *Geoffrey Chaucer Hath a Blog: Medieval Studies and New Media*. New York: Palgrave Macmillan, 2010.

Bryant, Brantley. Twitter handle: Chaucer Doth Tweet @LeVostreGC.

Burger, Glenn. *Chaucer's Queer Nation*. Minneapolis, MN: University of Minnesota Press, 2003.

Burger, Glenn. "Kissing the Pardoner." *Publications of the Modern Language Association* 107, no. 5 (1992), 1143–56.

Burnley, David. *A Guide to Chaucer's Language*. Houndmills: Macmillan, 1983.

Burnley, David. "Scogan, Shirley's Reputation and Chaucerian Occasional Verse." In *Chaucer in Perspective*, ed. Geoffrey Lester. Sheffield: Sheffield Academic Press, 1999, 28–46.

Burrow, J.A. "Sir Thopas in the Sixteenth Century." In *Middle English Studies Presented to Norman Davis in Honour of his Seventieth Birthday*, eds. Douglas Gray and E. G. Stanley. Oxford: Clarendon Press, 1983, 69–91.

Burton, T.L. "The Wife of Bath's Fourth and Fifth Husbands and Her Ideal Sixth: The Growth of a Marital Philosophy." *Chaucer Review* 13 (1978), 34–50.

Butterfield, Ardis. *The Familiar Enemy: Chaucer, Language, and Nation in The Hundred Years War*. Oxford: Oxford University Press, 2009.

Calabrese, Michael. "Performing the Prioress: 'Conscience' and Responsibility in Studies of Chaucer's *Prioress's Tale*." *Studies in Literature and Language* 44, no. 1 (2002), 66–91.

Cannon, Christopher. "Chaucer and Rape: Uncertainty's Certainties." In *Representing Rape in Medieval and Early Modern Literature*, eds. Christine Rose and Elizabeth Robertson. New York: Palgrave, 2001, 255–79.

Cannon, Christopher. *Middle English Literature: A Cultural History*. Cambridge: Polity Press, 2008.

Cannon, Christopher. "*Raptus* in the Chaumpaigne Release and a Newly Discovered Document Concerning the Life of Geoffrey Chaucer." *Speculum* 68 (1993), 74–94.

Carlson, David. *Chaucer's Jobs*. New York: Palgrave, 2004.

Carruthers, Leo. "'Honi soit qui mal y pense': The Countess of Salisbury and the 'Slipt Garter.'" In *Surface et Profondeur: Mélanges offert à Guy Bourquin*, edited by Colette Stévanovitch, and René Tixier. Grendel 7. Nancy: AMAES, 2003, 221–34.

Carruthers, Mary. *The Experience of Beauty in the Middle Ages*. Oxford: Oxford University Press, 2013.

Chesterton, G.K. *Chaucer*. London: Faber and Faber, 1932.

Classen, Albrecht. *The Medieval Chastity Belt: A Myth-Making Process*. New York: Palgrave, 2007.

Coghill, Nevill. *Chaucer's Idea of What Is Noble*. London: English Association, 1971.

Cole, Andrew. *Literature and Heresy in the Age of Chaucer*. Cambridge: Cambridge University Press, 2008.

Condren, Edward. "The Historical Context of the *Book of the Duchess*: A New Hypothesis." *Chaucer Review* 5, no. 3 (1971), 195–212.

Connolly, Margaret. "What John Shirley Said About Adam: Authorship and Attribution in Cambridge, Trinity College, MS R.3.20." In *The Dynamics of the Medieval Manuscript: Text Collections from a European Perspective*, edited by Bart Besamusca, Matthias Meyer, Karen Pratt, et al. Göttingen: Vandenhoeck & Ruprecht Unipress, 2017, 81–100.

Cooper, Helen. *Oxford Guides to Chaucer: The Canterbury Tales*. Oxford: Oxford University Press, 1991.

Crane, Susan. "Alison of Bath Accused of Murder: Case Dismissed." *English Language Notes* 25, no. 3 (1988), 10–15.

Crow, Martin M. and Clare C. Olson, eds. *Chaucer Life-Records*. Oxford: Clarendon Press, 1966.

Crowley, Duane. *Riddle Me a Murder*. Manchaca, TX: Blue Boar Press, 1986.

Curry, Walter Clyde. *Chaucer and the Mediaeval Sciences*. New York: Oxford University Press, 1926.

Dane, Joseph A. "Genre and Authority: The Eighteenth-Century Creation of Chaucerian Burlesque." *Huntington Library Quarterly* 48 (1985), 345–62.

Dane, Joseph A. *Who Is Buried in Chaucer's Tomb?* East Lansing, MI: Michigan State University Press, 1998.

Dart, John. *Westmonasterium, or the History and Antiquities of the Abbey Church of St. Peter's, Westminster*. 2 vols. London: 1723.

Dart, John and Rev. Timothy Thomas. *Life of Geoffrey Chaucer*. In *Geoffrey Chaucer, The Canterbury Tales of Chaucer*, ed. John Urry. London: Bernard Lintot, 1721.

de Selincourt, E. *Oxford Lectures on Poetry*. Oxford: Oxford University Press, 1934.

Delany, Sheila. *Writing Woman: Women Writers and Women in Literature Medieval to Modern*. New York: Schocken Books, 1983.

Diamond, Arlyn. "Chaucer's Women and Women's Chaucer." In *The Authority of Experience*, eds. Arlyn Diamond and Lee R. Edwards. Amherst, MA: University of Massachusetts Press, 1977, 60–83.

Dinshaw, Carolyn. *Chaucer's Sexual Poetics*. Madison, WI: University of Wisconsin Press, 1989.

Dinshaw, Carolyn. "Eunuch Hermeneutics." *ELH* 55, no. 1 (1988), 27–51.

Dinshaw, Carolyn. "Rivalry, Rape and Manhood: Gower and Chaucer." In *Chaucer and Gower: Difference, Mutuality, Exchange*, ed. Robert F. Yeager. Victoria, BC: University of Victoria, 1991, 130–52.

Ebin, Lois. "Chaucer, Lydgate and the 'Myrie Tale.'" *Chaucer Review* 13, no. 4 (1979), 316–36.

Editors of Encyclopaedia Britannica, "List of Poets Laureate of Britain," *Encyclopaedia Britannica*, https://www.britannica.com/topic/list-of-poets-laureate-of-Britain-1789231.

Edwards, A.S.G. "Chaucer and 'Adam Scriveyn.'" *Medium Aevum* 81, no. 1 (2012), 135–38.

Ezard, John. "The Scrivener's Tale: How Chaucer's Sloppy Copyist Was Unmasked After 600 Years." *The Guardian*, 20 July 2004, https://www.theguardian.com/uk/2004/jul/20/highereducation.books.

Fernholz, Jacquelyn and Jenni Nuttall. "Lydgate's Poem to Thomas Chaucer: A Reassessment of its Diplomatic and Literary Contexts." In *Identity and Insurgency in the Late Middle Ages*, ed. Linda Clark. The Fifteenth Century 6. Woodbridge: Boydell Press, 2006, 123–44.

Ferris, Sumner. "The Date of Chaucer's Final Annuity and of the 'Complaint to his Empty Purse'." *Modern Philology* 65, no. 1 (1967), 45–52.

Finnel, Andrew J. "The Poet as Sunday Man: 'The Complaint of Chaucer to His Purse.'" *Chaucer Review* 8 (1973), 147–58.

Fisher, John H. *The Importance of Chaucer*. Carbondale, IL: Southern Illinois Press, 1992.

Fisher, John H. *John Gower: Moral Philosopher and Friend of Chaucer*. New York: New York University Press, 1964.

Fisher, John H. "A Language Policy for Lancastrian England." *Publications of the Modern Language Association* 107, no. 5 (1992), 1168–80.

Flannery, Mary C. "Rubbing and Scraping: Who *Wrote* Chaucer's Poetry?" *Times Literary Supplement* (5 February 2019), 36–7.

Forni, Kathleen. *A Chaucerian Apocrypha: A Counterfeit Canon*. Tallahassee, FL: University Press of Florida, 2001.

Frank, R.W. *Chaucer and the Legend of Good Women*. Cambridge, MA: Harvard University Press, 1972.

Furnivall, F.J. "Thomas Chaucer, Not the Poet Geoffrey's Son." *Notes and Queries*, 4th Series, 9 (1872), 381–3.

Furnivall, F.J. *Trial-Forewords to my "Parallel-Text Edition of Chaucer's Minor Poems."* London: N. Trübner, 1871.

Galway, Margaret. "Chaucer's Hopeless Love." *MLN* 60, no. 7 (1945), 431–9.

Galway, Margaret. "Chaucer's Sovereign Lady: A Study of the Prologue to the 'Legend' and Related Poems." *MLR* 33, no. 2 (1938), 145–99.

Gardner, John. *The Life and Times of Chaucer*. London: Jonathan Cape, 1977.

Gaylord, Alan. "Chaucer's Dainty 'Dogerel': The 'Elvyssh' Prosody of *Sir Thopas*." *Studies in the Age of Chaucer* 1 (1979), 83–104.

Georgianna, Linda. "The Protestant Chaucer." In *Chaucer's Religious Tales*, eds. C. David Benson and Elizabeth Robertson. Woodbridge: D.S. Brewer, 1990, 55–69.

Gillespie, Alexandra. "Reading Chaucer's Words to Adam." *Chaucer Review* 42, no. 3 (2008), 269–83.

Godfrey, Mary F. "The Fifteenth-Century *Prioress's Tale* and the Problem of Anti-Semitism." In *Rewriting Chaucer: Culture, Authority and the Idea of the Authentic Text, 1400–1602*, eds. Thomas A. Prendergast and Barbara Kline. Columbus, OH: Ohio State University Press, 1999, 93–115.

Godwin, William. *Life of Geoffrey Chaucer, the Early English Poet*. 4 vols. London: Printed by T. Davison for R. Phillips, 1804.

Greenblatt, Stephen. *The Swerve: How the World Became Modern*. New York: W.W. Norton, 2011.

Greenlaw, Lavinia. *A Double Sorrow: Troilus and Criseyde*. London: Faber and Faber, 2014.

Hales, J.W. *Dictionary of National Biography*. Oxford: Oxford University Press, 1885–1900.

Hall, Vernon, Jr. "Sherlock Holmes and the Wife of Bath." *Baker Street Journal* 3 (1948), 84–93.

Hamel, Mary. "The Wife of Bath and a Contemporary Murder." *Chaucer Review* 14 (1979), 132–9.

Hammond, Eleanor Prescott. *English verse between Chaucer and Surrey: being examples of conventional secular poetry, exclusive of romance, ballad, lyric, and drama, in the period from Henry the Fourth to Henry the Eighth*. Durham, NC: Duke University Press, 1927.

Hansen, Elaine Tuttle. *Chaucer and the Fictions of Gender*. Berkeley, CA: University of California Press, 1992.

Hardyment, Christina. *Malory: The Knight Who Became King Arthur's Chronicler*. New York: Harper, 2006.

Harvard University's Geoffrey Chaucer Website. https://chaucer.fas.harvard.edu.

Hatts, Leigh. "Terry Jones Unveils Chaucer Plaque at Copyprints." *London SE1: Community Website*, 23 November 2003, http://www.london-se1.co.uk/news/view/737.

Haweis, Mary Elizabeth. "More News of Chaucer, Part I." *Belgravia: A London Magazine* 48 (1882), 34–46.

Helgeland, Brian, dir. *A Knight's Tale*. Columbia Pictures and Escape Artists, 2001.

Helgerson, Richard. *Self-Crowned Laureates: Spenser, Jonson, Milton, and the Literary System*. Berkeley, CA: University of California Press, 1983.

Higgins, Ann. "*Sir Tristrem*, a Few Fragments, and the Northern Identity of the Auchinleck Manuscript." In *The Auchinleck Manuscript: New Perspectives*, ed. Susanna Fein. York: York Medieval Press, 2016, 108–26.

Hinch, Jim. "Why Stephen Greenblatt Is Wrong—and Why It Matters." *Los Angeles Review of Books*, 1 December 2012, https://lareviewofbooks.org/article/why-stephen-greenblatt-is-wrong-and-why-it-matters.

Horobin, Simon. *Chaucer's Language*. 2nd edn. Houndmills: Palgrave Macmillan, 2013.

Howard, Donald R. *Chaucer: His Life, His Works, His World*. New York: E. P. Dutton, 1987.

Howard, Donald R. *Writers and Pilgrims: Medieval Pilgrimage Narratives and Their Posterity*. Berkeley, CA: University of California Press, 1980.

Hudson, Anne. *Lollards and Their Books*. London: Hambledon Press, 1985.

Hulbert, J.R. "Chaucer's Pilgrims." *Publications of the Modern Language Association* 64, no. 4 (1949), 823–28.

Ingham, Patricia Clare. *The Medieval New: Ambivalence in an Age of Innovation*. Philadelphia, PA: University of Pennsylvania Press, 2015.

John Lane's Continuation of Chaucer's Squire's Tale, ed. F.J. Furnivall, from the original ms. version of 1616, Douce 170, collated with its ms. revision of 1630, Ashmole 53; with notes "On the magical elements in Chaucer's 'Squire's tale,'" and analogues by W.A. Clouston. London: Kegan Paul, Trench, Trübner, 1888, 1890.

Jones, Terry. *Chaucer's Knight: The Portrait of a Medieval Mercenary*. Baton Rouge, LA: Louisiana State University Press, 1980.

Jones, Terry, Juliette Dor, Alan Fletcher et al. *Who Murdered Chaucer? A Medieval Mystery*. New York: St. Martin's Press, 2003.

Kelly, H. Ansgar. "Shades of Incest and Cuckoldry: Pandarus and John of Gaunt." *Studies in the Age of Chaucer* 13 (1991), 121–40.

Ker, W.P. *Epic and Romance*. London: Macmillan, 1926.

Ker, W.P. *Form and Style in Poetry*. London: Macmillan, 1929.

Kittredge, George Lyman. "Chaucer's *Envoy to Bukton*." *Modern Language Notes* 24, no. 1 (January 1909), 14–15.

Kittredge, George Lyman. *Chaucer and his Poetry, Lectures delivered in 1914 on the Percy Turnbull Memorial Foundation in the Johns Hopkins University, by George Lyman Kittredge*. Cambridge, MA: Harvard University Press, 1915.

Knight, Stephen. *Geoffrey Chaucer*. Oxford: Blackwell, 1986.

Kolve, V.A. and Glending Olson, eds. *Geoffrey Chaucer: The Canterbury Tales*. 2nd edn. New York: W.W. Norton, 2005.

Krauss, Russell, Haldeen Braddy and C. Robert Kase. *Three Chaucer Studies*. New York: Oxford University Press, 1932.

Kruger, Stephen F. "Claiming the Pardoner: Toward a Gay Reading of Chaucer's *Pardoner's Tale*." *Exemplaria* 6 (1994), 113–39.

Lambdin, Laura C. and Robert T. Lambdin, eds. *Chaucer's Pilgrims: An Historical Guide to the Pilgrims in* The Canterbury Tales. Westport, CT: Greenwood Press, 1996.

Lawton, David. *Voice in Later Medieval Literature: Public Interiorities*. Oxford: Oxford University Press, 2016.

Leicester, Marshall. *The Disenchanted Self: Representing the Subject in the* Canterbury Tales. Berkeley, CA: University of California Press, 1990.

León Sendra, Antonio R. and Jesús L. Serrano Reyes, "Chaucer and Montserrat." *Selim* 9 (1999), 121–43.

Lerer, Seth. *Chaucer and His Readers: Imagining the Author in Late-Medieval England*. Princeton, NJ: Princeton University Press, 1993.

Lightsey, Scott. "Chaucer's Return from Lombardy, the Shrine of St. Leonard at Hythe, and the 'corseynt Leonard' in the *House of Fame*, lines 112–18." *Chaucer Review* 52 (2017), 188–201.

Lipking, Virgil. L. *The Life of the Poet: Beginning and Ending Poetic Careers*. Chicago, IL: University of Chicago Press, 1981.

Loomis, Laura Hibbard. "Chaucer and the Auchinleck MS: 'Thopas' and 'Guy of Warwick.'" In *Essays and Studies in Honor of Carleton Brown*, ed. Percy Waldron Long. New York: New York University Press, 1940, 111–28.

Lorimer, James. "Chaucer." *Eclectic Magazine of Foreign Literature, Science and Art* 17 (1849), 64–83.

Lounsbury, Thomas R. *Studies in Chaucer*. 3 vols. New York: Russell & Russell, 1892.

Luctus Britannici or the Tears of the British Muses for the Death of John Dryden, Esq ... written by the most Eminent Hands in the two Famous Universities, and by several Others. London: Printed for H. Playford and sold by J. Nutt, 1700.

Lumiansky, R.M. *Of Sondry Folk: The Dramatic Principle of the Canterbury Tales*. Austin, TX: University of Texas Press, 1955.

Lyon, E.D. "Roger of Ware, Cook." *Modern Language Notes* 52 (1937), 491–4.

Maddern, Philippa. "'It Is Full Merry in Heaven': The Pleasurable Connotations of 'Merriment' in Late Medieval England." In *Pleasure in the Middle Ages*, eds. Naama Cohen-Hanegbi and Piroska Nagy. Turnhout: Brepols, 2018, 21–38.

Madox Brown, Ford. *Chaucer at the Court of Edward III*, 1847–1851, oil on canvas, 372 × 296 cm, *Art Gallery of New South Wales*, Sydney. http://www.artgallery.nsw.gov.au/collection/works/703.

Manly, J.M. "Chaucer and the Rhetoricians: Warton Lecture on English Poetry, no. 17, read before the British Academy June 2nd, 1926." In *Proceedings of the British Academy* 12. London: Humphrey Milford, 1926, 95–113.

Mann, Jill. *Chaucer and Medieval Estates Satire*. Cambridge: Cambridge University Press, 1973.

Masefield, John. *Chaucer*. Cambridge: Cambridge University Press, 1931.

McAlpine, Monica. "The Pardoner's Homosexuality and How It Matters." *Publications of the Modern Language Association* 95, no. 1 (1980), 8–22.

McCormack, Frances. "Chaucer and Lollardy." In *Chaucer and Religion*, ed. Helen Phillips. Woodbridge: Boydell and Brewer, 2010, 35–40.

McDonald, Nicola. "Introduction." In *Medieval Obscenities*, ed. Nicola McDonald. Woodbridge: York Medieval Texts, 2014, 1–16.

Mieszkowski, Gretchen. "Chaucer's Much Loved Criseyde." *Chaucer Review* 26, no. 2 (1991), 109–32.

Milman, Henry Hart. *History of Latin Christianity; Including that of the Popes to the Pontificate of Nicolas V*. 3rd edn. 9 vols. London: John Murray, [1855] 1872.

Minnis, Alastair. "From *coilles* to *bel chose*: Discourses of Obscenity in Jean de Meun and Chaucer." In *Medieval Obscenities*, ed. Nicola McDonald. Woodbridge: York Medieval Texts, 2014, 156–78.

Mooney, Linne R. "Chaucer's Scribe." *Speculum* 81 (2006), 97–138.

Musson, Anthony. "The Sergeant of Law." In *Historians on Chaucer: The 'General Prologue' to the* Canterbury Tales, ed. Stephen H. Rigby. Oxford: Oxford University Press, 2015, 206–26.

O'Connor, Garry. *Chaucer's Triumph*. Lancaster: Petrak Press, 2007.

Owen, Charles A. "What the Manuscripts Tell Us About the *Parson's Tale*." *Medium Aevum* 63 (1994), 239–49.

Palomo, Dolores. "The Fate of the Wife of Bath's 'Bad Husbands.'" *Chaucer Review* 9 (1975), 303–19.

Patterson, Lee. *Chaucer and the Subject of History*. Madison, WI: University of Wisconsin Press, 1991.

Patterson, Lee. *Negotiating the Past: The Historical Understanding of Medieval Literature*. Madison, WI: University of Wisconsin Press, 1987.

Patterson, Lee. "'What Man Artow?' Authorial Self-Definition in the *Tale of Sir Thopas* and the *Tale of Melibee*." *Studies in the Age of Chaucer* 11 (1989), 117–75.

Pearsall, Derek. "Chaucer's Tomb: The Politics of Reburial." *Medium Aevum* 64 (1995), 51–73.

Pearsall, Derek. "Editing Medieval Texts: Some Developments and Some Problems." In *Textual Criticism and Literary Interpretation*, ed. Jerome J. McGann. Chicago, IL: University of Chicago Press, 1985, 92–106.

Pearsall, Derek. *John Lydgate*. Charlottesville, VA: University of Virginia Press, 1970.

Pearsall, Derek. *The Life of Geoffrey Chaucer: A Critical Biography*. Oxford: Blackwell, 1992.

Phillips, Helen. "Auchinleck and Chaucer." In *The Auchinleck Manuscript: New Perspectives*, ed. Susanna Fein. York: York Medieval Press, 2016, 139–55.

Phillips, Susan E. *Transforming Talk: The Problem with Gossip in Late Medieval England*. University Park, PA: Pennsylvania State University Press, 2007.

Pigg, Daniel. "With Hym Ther Was a Plowman, Was His Brother." In *Chaucer's Pilgrims: An Historical Guide to the Pilgrims in* The Canterbury Tales, eds. Laura C. Lambdin and Robert T. Lambdin. Westport, CT: Greenwood Press, 1996, 263–70.

Prendergast, Thomas A. *Chaucer's Dead Body: From Corpse to Corpus*. New York: Routledge, 2004.

Prendergast, Thomas A. *Poetical Dust: Poets' Corner and the Making of Britain.* Philadelphia, PA: University of Pennsylvania Press, 2015.

Prendergast, Thomas A. "Politics, Prodigality, and the Reception of Chaucer's 'Purse'." In *Reinventing the Middle Ages and the Renaissance: Constructions of the Medieval and Early Modern Periods*, ed. William Gentrup. Turnhout: Brepols, 1998, 63–76.

Prendergast, Thomas A. and Stephanie Trigg. *Affective Medievalism: Love, Abjection and Discontent.* Manchester: Manchester University Press, 2018.

Puhvel, Martin. "The Death of Alys of Bath's 'Revelour' Husband." *Neuphilologische Mitteilungen* 103, no. 3 (2002), 329–40.

Richmond, Velma Bourgeois. *Geoffrey Chaucer.* New York: Continuum, 1992.

Rigby, Stephen H. "The Knight." In *Historians on Chaucer: The "General Prologue" to the* Canterbury Tales, ed. Stephen H. Rigby. Oxford: Oxford University Press, 2014, 42–62.

Robertson, D.W., Jr. *A Preface to Chaucer: Studies in Medieval Perspective.* Princeton, NJ: Princeton University Press, 1962.

Robinson, F.N. "On Two Manuscripts of Lydgate's Guy of Warwick." In *Studies and Notes in Philology and Literature 5.* Boston, MA: Published under the direction of the Modern Language Depts. of Harvard University by Ginn & Co., 1896, 177–220.

Rowland, Beryl. "On the Timely Death of the Wife of Bath's Fourth Husband." *Archiv für das Studium der neueren Sprachen und Literaturen* 209 (1972), 273–82.

Ruud, Martin B. *Thomas Chaucer.* Minneapolis, MN: University of Minnesota Press, 1926.

Sands, Donald B. "The Non-Comic, Non-Tragic Wife: Chaucer's Dame Alys as Sociopath." *Chaucer Review* 12 (1978), 171–82.

Sayers, Dorothy L. *Unpopular Opinions.* London: Victor Gollancz, 1946.

Scattergood, V.J. "Chaucer and the French War: *Sir Thopas* and *Melibee*." In *Court and Poet: Selected Proceedings of the Third Congress of the International Courtly Literature Society*, ed. Glyn S. Burgess. Liverpool: Francis Cairns, 1981, 287–96.

Schoeck, R.J. "Chaucer's Prioress: Mercy and Tender Heart." In *Chaucer Criticism*, eds. R.J. Schoeck and Jerome Taylor. Notre Dame, IN: University of Notre Dame Press, 1960, 245–58.

Seton, Anya. *Katherine.* 1954. London: Hodder and Stoughton, 2006.

Shoaf, R. Allen. *Chaucer's Body: The Anxiety of Circulation in the* Canterbury Tales. Gainesville, FL: University of Florida Press, 2001.

Shuffleton, George. "Chaucerian Obscenity in the Court of Public Opinion." *Chaucer Review* 47, no. 1 (2012), 1–24.

Sidhu, Nicole Nolan. *Indecent Exposure: Gender, Politics, and Obscene Comedy in Middle English Literature.* Philadelphia, PA: University of Pennsylvania Press, 2016.

Sidnam, Jonathan. *A Paraphrase upon the three first Bookes of Chaucers Troilus and Cressida* (MS 1630). In *Geoffrey Chaucer: The Critical Heritage, Vol. 1, 1385–1837*, ed. Derek Brewer. London: Routledge, 1978, 149–51.

Simpson, James. *Reform and Cultural Reformation*. Oxford English Literary History Series, vol. 2. 1350–1547. Oxford: Oxford University Press, 2002.

Sobecki, Sebastian. "A Southwark Tale: Gower, the 1381 Poll Tax and Chaucer's *Canterbury Tales*." *Speculum* 92 (2017), 630–60.

Sobecki, Sebastian. "Wards and Widows: *Troilus and Criseyde* and New Documents on Chaucer's Life." *English Literary History* 86, no. 2 (2019), 413–40.

Sova, Dawn B. *Banned Books: Literature Suppressed on Social Grounds*. New York: Facts on File, 2006.

Spearing, A.C. *Medieval to Renaissance in English Poetry*. Cambridge: Cambridge University Press, 1985.

Speght, Thomas. "Arguments to euery Tale and Booke." In *The Workes of our Antient and Learned English Poet, Geffrey Chaucer, newly printed*, ed. Thomas Speght. London, 1598, sig. c iii–c vi *b*.

Spurgeon, Caroline. *Five Hundred Years of Chaucer Criticism and Allusion 1357–1900*. 3 vols. Cambridge: Cambridge University Press, 1925.

Strohm, Paul. *Chaucer's Tale: 1386 and the Road to Canterbury*. New York: Viking, 2014.

Strohm, Paul. *Hochon's Arrow*. Princeton, NJ: Princeton University Press, 1992.

Strohm, Paul. "Politics and Poetics: Usk and Chaucer in the 1380s." In *Literary Practice and Social Change in Britain: 1380–1530*, ed. Lee Patterson. Berkeley, CA: University of California Press, 1990, 83–112.

Strohm, Paul. "Saving the Appearances: Chaucer's 'Purse' and the Fabrication of the Lancastrian Claim." In *Hochon's Arrow: The Social Imagination of Fourteenth-Century Texts*. Princeton, NJ: Princeton University Press, 1992, 75–94.

Strohm, Paul. *Social Chaucer*. Cambridge, MA: Harvard University Press, 1989.

Strohm, Paul. *Theory and the Premodern Text*. Minneapolis, MN: University of Minnesota Press, 2000.

Strype, John. *The History of the Life and Acts of the most reverend father in God, Edmund Grindal*. Oxford: Clarendon Press, 1821.

Trigg, Stephanie. *Congenial Souls: Reading Chaucer from Medieval to Postmodern*. Minneapolis, MN: University of Minnesota Press, 2002.

Trigg, Stephanie. *Shame and Honor: A Vulgar History of the Order of the Garter*. Philadelphia, PA: University of Pennsylvania Press, 2012.

Tupper, Frederick. "Chaucer's Lady of the Daisies." *Journal of English and Germanic Philology* 21, no. 2 (1922), 293–317.

Turner, Marion. *Chaucer: A European Life*. Princeton, NJ: Princeton University Press, 2019.

Turner, Marion. *Chaucerian Conflict: Languages of Antagonism in Late Fourteenth-Century London*. Oxford: Clarendon Press, 2007.

Vance, Eugene. *Mervelous Signals: Poetics and Sign Theory in the Middle Ages*. Lincoln, NE: University of Nebraska Press, 1990.

Vaughan, Míceál F. "Creating Comfortable Boundaries: Scribes, Editors, and the Invention of the *Parson's Tale*." In *Rewriting Chaucer: Culture, Authority, and the Idea of the Authentic Text, 1400–1602*, eds. Thomas A. Prendergast and Barbara Kline. Columbus, OH: Ohio State University Press, 1999, 45–90.

Vaughan, Míceál F. "Personal Politics and Thomas Gascoigne's Account of Chaucer's Death." *Medium Aevum* 75, no. 1 (2006), 103–22.

Wagner, Bernard. "Chaucer's Scrivener." *Times Literary Supplement* (13 June 1929), 474.

Wakelin, Daniel. *Scribal Correction and Literary Craft: English Manuscripts 1375–1500*. Cambridge: Cambridge University Press, 2014.

Wallace, David, ed. *The Cambridge History of Medieval English Literature*. Cambridge: Cambridge University Press, 1999.

Wallace, David. *Chaucerian Polity: Absolutist Lineages and Associational Forms in England and Italy*. Stanford, CA: Stanford University Press, 1997.

Waller, Edmund. *Poems ... upon several Occasions ... The third Edition with several Additions ....* London: Printed for Henry Herringman, 1668.

Warner, Lawrence. *Chaucer's Scribes: London Textual Production, 1384–1432*. Cambridge: Cambridge University Press, 2018.

Warton, Thomas. *The History of English Poetry from the Close of the Eleventh to the Commencement of the Eighteenth Century, to which are prefixed two Dissertations I: On the Origin of Romantic Fiction in Europe; II: On the Introduction of Learning into England*. 3 vols. London: Printed for and sold by J. Dodsley, J. Walter, T. Becket et al., 1774–81.

Weir, Alison. *Mistress of the Monarchy: The Life of Katherine Swynford, Duchess of Lancaster*. New York: Ballantine Books, 2009.

West, Richard. *Chaucer 1340–1400: The Life and Times of the First English Poet*. London: Little, Brown, 2019.

Whitney, Elspeth. "What's Wrong with the Pardoner? Complexion Theory, the Phlegmatic Man, and Effeminacy." *Chaucer Review* 45, no. 4 (2011), 357–89.

Williams, George. *A New View of Chaucer*. Durham, NC: Duke University Press, 1965.

Wimsatt, James. *Chaucer and the Poems of "Ch"*. Kalamazoo, MI: Medieval Institute Publications, 2009.

Wurtele, D.J. "Chaucer's Wife of Bath and the Problem of the Fifth Husband." *Chaucer Review* 23, no. 2 (1988), 117–28.

Wurtele, D.J. "The Penitence of Geoffrey Chaucer." *Viator* 11 (1980), 335–59.

Yeager, R.F. "Chaucer Translates the Matter of Spain." In *England and Iberia in the Middle Ages*, ed. María Bullón-Fernández. New York: Palgrave, 2007, 189–214.

Yeager, R.F. "Chaucer's 'To His Purse': Begging, or Begging Off?" *Viator* 36 (2005), 373–414.

Young, Karl. "Chaucer's 'Troilus and Criseyde' as Romance." *Publications of the Modern Language Association* 53, no. 1 (1938), 38–63.

Zitter, Emily Stark. "Anti-semitism in Chaucer's *Prioress's Tale*." *Chaucer Review* 25, no. 4 (1991), 277–84.

Zunshine, Lisa. *Why We Read Fiction: Theory of Mind and the Novel*. Columbus, OH: Ohio State University Press, 2006.

INDEX

Note: Page numbers followed by "n" indicate notes.

30 Great Myths About Chaucer, First Edition. Thomas A. Prendergast and Stephanie Trigg.
© 2020 John Wiley & Sons, Inc. Published 2020 by John Wiley & Sons, Inc.